Watching Sport

Do we watch sport for pure dumb entertainment? While some people might do so, Stephen Mumford argues that it can be watched in other ways. Sport can be both a subject of high aesthetic values and a valid source for our moral education. The philosophy of sport has tended to focus on participation, but this book instead examines the philosophical issues around watching sport. Far from being a passive experience, we can all shape the way that we see sport.

Delving into parallels with art and theatre, this book outlines the aesthetic qualities of sport from the incidental beauty of a well-executed football pass to the enshrined artistic interpretation in performed sports such as ice-skating and gymnastics. It is argued that the purist literally sees sport in a different way from the partisan, thus the aesthetic perception of the purist can be validated. The book moves on to examine the moral lessons that are to be learned from watching sport, depicting it as a contest of virtues. The morality of sport is demonstrated to be continuous with, rather than separate from, the morality in wider life, so each can inform the other. Watching sport is then recognised as a focus of profound emotional experiences. Collective emotion is particularly considered alongside the nature of allegiance. Finally, Mumford considers why we care about sport at all.

Addressing universal themes, this book will appeal to a broad audience across philosophical disciplines and sports studies.

Stephen Mumford is Professor of Metaphysics at the University of Nottingham and Professor II at the Norwegian University of Life Science (UMB). His previous books include *Dispositions* (1998), *Russell on Metaphysics* (2003), *Laws in Nature* (2004), *David Armstrong* (2007) and *Getting Causes from Powers* (2011, with Rani Lill Anjum).

Ethics and Sport

Series editors
Mike McNamee
University of Wales Swansea
Jim Parry
University of Leeds
Heather Reid
Morningside College

The Ethics and Sport series aims to encourage critical reflection on the practice of sport, and to stimulate professional evaluation and development. Each volume explores new work relating to philosophical ethics and the social and cultural study of ethical issues. Each is different in scope, appeal, focus and treatment but a balance is sought between local and international focus, perennial and contemporary issues, level of audience, teaching and research application, and variety of practical concerns.

Also available in this series:

Watching Sport
Aesthetics, ethics and emotion

Stephen Mumford

Routledge
Taylor & Francis Group

LONDON AND NEW YORK

First published 2012
by Routledge
2 Park Square, Milton Park, Abingdon, Oxon OX14 4RN

Simultaneously published in the USA and Canada
by Routledge
711 Third Avenue, New York, NY 10017

Routledge is an imprint of the Taylor & Francis Group, an informa business

British Library Cataloguing in Publication Data
A catalogue record for this book is available from the British Library

Library of Congress Cataloging in Publication Data
Mumford, Stephen.
Watching sport : aesthetics, ethics and emotion / Stephen Mumford.
p. cm. -- (Ethics and sport)
1. Sports--Philosophy. 2. Sports spectators. 3. Sports--Moral and ethical aspects. I. Title.
GV706.M85 2011
796.01--dc22
2011015294

ISBN: 978-0-415-37790-4 (hbk)
ISBN: 978-0-203-80711-8 (ebk)

Typeset in Goudy
by GreenGate Publishing Services, Tonbridge, Kent

Printed and bound in Great Britain by
CPI Antony Rowe, Chippenham, Wiltshire

Contents

Preface

In November of 2007, I drove through the night from Valencia to Madrid. The aim of my journey was Estadio Santiago Bernabéu, the home of Club de Futbol Real Madrid. After hanging around for most of the day, including watching a third division game at Rayo Vallecano, I took my seat high in the stands. I chose a ticket near the very back, behind the goal, so that I could see the whole stadium and the entire crowd in front of me. Real were top of La Liga and their visitors, Mallorca, were healthily placed in seventh. They turned out to be very good and, although Madrid took an early lead, Mallorca equalised almost straight away with a fine finish into the goal behind which I was sitting. Madrid scored again, within a few minutes, but before the interval Mallorca levelled once more with an outstanding 30-yard shot. I had to get my breath back at half time. The football was amazing. Sometimes, at ice hockey games, the puck moves too fast for the eye to keep up. The players were passing the ball so quickly that it was having the same effect. It was all one-touch and move. I didn't believe the second half could be quite so good. But five minutes after the restart, Mallorca took a shock lead with another superb effort from outside the penalty area. Madrid upped their game again, finding an extra gear I didn't realise they could have. Raul scored and it was 3–3. At that point I realised two things. One was that it was inevitable that Madrid would win this game. The other realisation was that of all the football matches I had attended – nearly 1,400 at that time – this was the best. It had it all. The play was superb, the stadium setting was fantastic and the 80,000 crowd provided a spectacular back-drop. On top of all that, breathtaking goals were flying in and adding high drama to the proceedings. As it dawned on me that this was the best game of my life so far, I felt some tears welling up. Perhaps it was the sleep deprivation from the journey but at the time it felt like I had found football utopia. Even I, one of the biggest fans of the game, had not realised that football could be this good. It seemed a moment wherein I had glimpsed the sublime. This had transcended mere sport, and the contingencies of human existence generally. The game seemed to have become something else: something that made a profound comment on the human condition. Was sport of this level art? Was it something more? Inevitably, Real Madrid did score a fourth and winning goal, Ruud van Nistelrooy popping one in off the post. All too soon, the game was over. The 90 minutes had felt like nine. I left breathless and deep in thought.

I was stunned and couldn't quite figure out what had happened. I had to drive back to Granada that night – another four-hour journey – and was not at my hotel until 1.30 am. But still I could not sleep. I had experienced a moment of revelation. I had spent years enjoying the game as a partisan: supporting a single team through thick and thin. This had its ups and downs but, as every fan will testify, it's worth taking the rough with the smooth because of the sheer intensity of the emotional experiences. Yet I had just watched a game with no interest in who won and who lost and it was nevertheless the deepest emotional moment I had experienced in sport. And with this, I had become a true purist. I had to write about it.

This book is in the well-established tradition of the philosophy of sport. There are many philosophical issues to be found here. Most of the current work being produced, however, centres on the participants in sport. Issues such as fairness in competition, use of performance-enhancing drugs, what constitutes winning, what constitutes participation, health and well-being, how dangerous we should allow sports to be and how sport is distinguished from games and play are all worthy areas for philosophical investigation. But many people's experience of sport is not as a participant. There are, nevertheless, philosophical issues around the watching of sport that I think require further examination. Is there less interest in those issues because watching sport is somehow seen as inferior to playing it? If we think of Homer Simpson, for instance, watching the Superbowl in front of the TV, with a beer in one hand and a huge bag of potato chips, is he getting anything out of watching sport? Is it just pure, dumb entertainment for him? Are there any philosophical issues around what he is doing? I argue that there are. There are many such, and in that respect this book is only a start. Are there different ways of watching sport? Do two similarly placed viewers of the same event see the same thing? Why is it more exciting to watch the event 'live', as it happens, than to watch an unedited recording of it? Why is it more exciting to watch with others than alone? Can the watching of sport be morally improving or is it all about selfish competitive people trying to establish dominance? And is there a connection between the ethics of sport and its aesthetics? These are some of the questions to be addressed in this book, but I do not see them as exhausting the limits of the topic. My hope, therefore, is that more philosophical work on the philosophy of watching sport will follow.

I have had a lot of fun writing this book. At times it has felt like the book I have wanted to write for the past 20 years. I have always watched sport but I have been a professional philosopher for only two decades. During most of that time I have practised metaphysics and, with specialisation being the order of the day, I have had little time to stray into other areas of interest. But I have nevertheless been thinking of this book for much of that time and, when I came to write it, I found I was bringing to bear thoughts that had been lurking in the dark corners of my mind for a long time. It was a surprise to me when they appeared in this book; but I am pleased that they did. Anyone who has also read my work in metaphysics is going to find lots of surprises in store here. They might doubt it is the same author: but I can assure them it is. I have aimed for the account to be a general one that applies to the cases of many different sports. A lot of the examples used are from association football or soccer, however. I don't think this needs an apology as it is, after all, the most popular spectator sport in the world. But I have been happy to use examples from other sports where it has been appropriate. There are issues that are specific to some sports and not others, so we have to recognise that diversity.

I have been a part of the sports philosophy community for only eight years and I realise this still makes me something of a novice. But it is a most welcoming, eclectic and open-minded bunch that has right from the start paid an interest in my project and offered me every assistance and encouragement. I am grateful to all who have supported me through discussing the ideas, both in response to talks and also informally. Regular annual conferences of the International Association for the Philosophy of Sport (IAPS) and the British Philosophy of Sport Association (BPSA) have provided a perfect environment to try out new ideas and various parts of this book have been explored there. I also thank Verner Møller for arranging for me to be a visiting scholar at their seminar at the University of Aarhus and Itir Erhart for organising such a well-publicised event at Bilgi University in Istanbul. Gabriela Tymowski and Charlene Weaving arranged a wonderfully rewarding visit to eastern Canada, which I enjoyed greatly. I was also a very fortunate visitor to the University of Sport in Porto, arranged by Teresa Oliveira Lacerda, who put on a special event for me. Douglas McLaughlin invited me to Cal State University in Northridge and it was while there in LA that I finished the book. I have presented philosophy of sport talks also at Hertfordshire, Lund and Nottingham and am grateful for the opportunity and the feedback. I must also thank the regular gang with whom I have passed such lovely, fun and stimulating days at philosophy of sport conferences (sorry if I've accidentally left anyone out): John Michael Atherton, Andrew Bloodworth, Ask Vest Christiansen, Leon Culbertson, Cathy Devine, Nick Dixon, Andrew Edgar, Lisa Edwards, Itir Erhart, Peter Hager, Alun Hardman, Leslie Howe, Stephen Howell, Jesús Ilundáin-Agurruza, Ivo Jirásek, Carwyn Jones, Kevin Krein, Teresa Oliveira Lacerda, Sigmund Loland, Douglas McLaughlin, Mike McNamee, Bill Morgan, Arno Müller, Verner Møller, Jim Parry, Heather Reid, John Russell, Emily Ryall, Barış Sentuna, Heather Sheridan, Sarah Teetzel, Cesar Torres, Gabriela Tymowski and Charlene Weaving. And how could I forget Jeffrey Fry (no one can forget Jeffrey Fry!)? Thank you all for such a wonderful time. A special mention must go, however, to Leon Culbertson, who has been with me every step of the way. You're a special guy, Lee. I also owe a huge thanks to Elvio Baccarini. Elvio read the whole book as it was being written and not only spent hours discussing it with me but also participated in a wonderful symposium on the book at the University of Rijeka in Croatia. Thanks to all who participated in that, especially Milica Czerny Urban, and my thanks to Luca Malatesti and Predrag Šustar for organising it. The stories at the start of Chapter 7 come from my art historian colleague Mark Rawlinson. I am grateful to Alaska Williams for encouragement and support and similarly to all my fellow philosophers at the University of Nottingham. I know I am not always the perfect colleague. Many of my followers on Twitter have given me both moral support and helpful suggestions. Twitter is so useful in philosophy: I am @SDMumford, if anyone wants to follow. My family has, as usual, been a great support and I am sorry for all the additional absences that the writing of this book involved. The final personal thanks goes to Vince Taylor, to whom I owe various debts, intellectual and probably financial as well. Vince is an unsung hero in the world of sports writing.

Chapter 13 is based on my article 'Allegiance and Identity', which was published in the *Journal of the Philosophy of Sport* in 2004. I am grateful to the editor, John Russell, for permission to use this material, which has undergone redrafting in several places.

1 The starting line

Our subject of investigation is watching sport, and the investigation will be a philosophical one. Before we can embark on that in any great detail there are two basic questions we must answer. First, what do we mean by watching and, second, what do we mean by sport?

Although the concern of this book is watching sport, we do not mean only *watching* sport, as opposed to listening to it or perceiving it in other ways. 'Watching' is intended as a general term that encapsulates any such sport spectatorship. We do not, for instance, want to exclude the blind from enjoying the experience of an observing sports fan. Many blind people like to attend sports events, sometimes listening to a specially detailed commentary. There is much excitement to be gained in doing so, which is borne out by the fact that sighted people also like to listen to sport on the radio. Sometimes it can seem an even more exciting experience over the radio as the commentary paints a picture verbally and builds the suspense. Any such person still counts as a sports-watcher in this book.

Apart from the special case of radio commentary, however, the experience of watching sport clearly is enhanced by the presence of sound. Sounds can be just as important as sights in forming an exciting and memorable sporting experience. Sometimes it is the noise of the crowd that intensifies one's experience, as will be discussed later (Chapter 12). It is through hearing that one comes to know of the excitement of others watching the same spectacle. The crowd also add their own atmosphere, through applause, firecrackers, chants and songs. Sometimes it is the playing of sport itself that one hears. One may hear the players calling to each other; hear their feet pounding the turf or track; or sometimes hear even their gasps for breath as they stretch the capacity of their lungs. Some sports are noisier than others, as I found when I attended my first speedway meet. The roar of the motorcycle engines was the most memorable feature of the night. Horse racing provides a special experience of sound, with the rumble of horses' hooves on grass getting closer and closer, and then passing with a Doppler effect. Setting aside commentary, therefore, there is every reason to appreciate the sounds produced in sport.

More than sight and sound should be included in our investigation, however. Non-participants can enjoy sport using any kind of sensation. Smell and touch can also play a role. The smell of the grass, freshly cut and watered, is one of the delights of a new football season. Many athletes use muscle rub with a strong 'smell of sport' that reaches the spectators. And touch is also part of the aesthetic of sport, ranging from the cold air on one's face to the grip one holds on the crush barrier in front. Taste seems one of the least utilised of the senses in watching sport. Certainly there are tastes that we associate with sport – the beer, popcorn and hot dogs sold at the stadium – but these are not intrinsic to sport. They are rather more to do with the consumer experience that has grown around sport and they can be experienced just as much at the cinema. One is not tasting the sport, whereas one may see it, hear it and, if one is physically located in a sporting venue, smell it and feel it. Nevertheless, those who enjoy watching sport may do so at least partly because of the accompanying tastes of the catering provision.

Watching should be understood broadly to mean observation through any sense faculty, therefore, but we also need to say something about the mode of watching, for there are different ways that we can choose to watch sport. Some prefer to attend the sporting event live and in person while others may be content with watching the TV transmission. Radio has already been mentioned as an option. Others may have a more casual engagement. An edited highlights package may provide a shorter and condensed version of sport that could satisfy the less seriously engaged if not the purist. One might even follow at a greater distance, through newspaper or internet reports. These different modes of watching can no doubt be further subdivided. Among those who attend games at the venue, there is more variety. Some fans stand behind the goal, squashed together with other like-minded supporters. They may enjoy the experience of being part of a crowd, speaking with one voice, as much as being there to study the game. Some fans drink alcohol before or during these games and might not remember too much about them. By way of contrast, there are others who prefer to study the game from a side view, deep in concentration and not wanting to miss a minute of play. Still, others gather in corporate hospitality facilities, perhaps again with alcohol on offer, and watch from indoors, behind plate glass. Watching sport may be part of work-related networking where the conversation is the key thing, sport merely forming a common interest around which people of business gather. All such enjoyment of sport should be within the scope of this study, from the fanatic to the casual viewer.

There is, however, a less obvious sense in which there are different ways of watching sport. The expert sees a different game from the novice, and the aesthete sees a different game from the partisan. There may be a thought that these are mere clichés that should not be taken literally. For the expert, novice, aesthete and partisan may all be watching the same TV transmission and, one would think, it is obviously correct to say that they saw the same game. But one of the arguments of this book is that watching means more than just having light hit one's retina, hearing means more than air vibrations moving one's ear drum, and so on. There's more to seeing than meets the eye, as Norwood Russell Hanson argued (1958: ch. 1). Watching is something one does: the mind is active in it, I will claim, and there are thus different ways in which two people can look at the same thing. Two viewers with the same retinal image may not see the same.

One taking an aesthetic attitude to sport may 'see a different game' to the committed fan, for instance, even though they observe the same event. These will be philosophical and theoretical claims, but the example of watching sport provides an exemplary illustration of them.

Another aspect to this same issue, also relevant to sport, is the idea that one learns how to watch. The first time I attended an ice hockey game, I couldn't see where the puck was. It seemed too small and moved too fast. As soon as I thought I saw it, it had shot off elsewhere and my eyes had to search afresh. I saw a lot of the players in that game (and heard a lot of organ music) but I saw little of the small black contested object. I nevertheless watched a few more games and gradually found it easier and easier to see where it was. I spoke to a more experienced fan (a Canadian, and Canadians really know their hockey) who explained how one learns to see the puck. One anticipates where it will go. I was too slow, playing catch up, but the experienced fan stays one step ahead. While I was searching for it, it had already left the place I was getting to. The experienced fan, on the other hand, is looking at the place where the puck will be before it even gets there. The players' movements act as a first indicator for them. But they also understand the trajectory of the puck and the way it can sweep around the boards behind the goals. They are able to anticipate and get it wrong less frequently than I did. They have a degree of experience and expertise that I had not yet acquired. Similarly with other sports, one can learn how to see. In football, it is easy to follow the ball, but the experienced football fan has already moved beyond that. Instead, they see how the play develops, watching the movements of players and reading their intentions. The novice knows little of the tactics. They may only follow the ball. The expert, however, understands that all the really interesting action is occurring away from the ball, in the formations and movements of the players. That is where the game is really won and lost, for control of the territory of the pitch brings control of the ball and that is what produces goals.

The more experienced one is at watching sport, it thus seems, the more one sees in the sport. Our novice and expert attend the same event, let us assume, and perhaps sit side-by-side with virtually the same view on play. But one sees so much more than the other and this is not, of course, a comment on the state of their eyesight.

Much more will be said about watching as we proceed but, in similar fashion, we also need an initial grasp of what is meant by sport. This book will be more about watching than about sport. An account will be given, for instance, that allows us to distinguish aesthetic from partisan ways of watching. But no detailed theory will be offered of what sport itself consists in. Something should nevertheless be said, albeit only briefly, on what sport is assumed to be. We are aided in this by the account of games given by Suits (2005). Sport is not the same thing as playing a game, though all sports are also games. Not all games are sports, however, as backgammon and tiddlywinks clearly demonstrate; and chess probably also, though more contentiously. If we understand what a game is, then we will have gone some way, though not all the way, to understanding what a sport is.

Suits takes up Wittgenstein's (1953: §66) challenge to find a definition of game. Wittgenstein asked us to look rather than assume that there is something in common to everything called a game (other than, of course, merely that every such thing is called a game). There is nothing in common, concludes Wittgenstein, and proceeds from there to offer an anti-essentialist, family resemblance account of games. An inference seems often to be then drawn that nothing has an essence and many or all of our concepts are family resemblance concepts. But we will not go into the question here of just how many concepts are family resemblance concepts. Instead, Suits takes up Wittgenstein's challenge afresh to find some commonality among all the many different things called games. Running races, golf and backgammon, among others, are considered and Suits does succeed in finding something in common. What he then offers us is a definition of what it is to play a game, which is that it is

> to engage in an activity directed towards bringing about a specific state of affairs, using only means permitted by the rules, where the rules prohibit more efficient in favour of less efficient means, and where such rules are accepted just because they make possible such activity.
>
> (Suits 2005: 48–9)

There is a simpler and more casual way of summing this up: 'playing a game is the voluntary attempt to overcome unnecessary obstacles' (Suits 2005: 55).

Suits's account can stand a little further explanation. The state of affairs one aims to bring about in sport is what he calls its prelusory goal. The aim in golf – its prelusory goal – is to get one's ball in the hole and in running races it is to cross the finishing line first. It is possible to achieve such a prelusory goal without playing the game (prelusory means pre-game). One could simply lift, carry and place the ball in the hole, or one could cut across the infield to be first at the finishing tape. But to achieve the prelusory goal in this way is to not play the game, quite literally. To make the activity of playing a game possible, one must adopt a lusory attitude towards the prelusory goal. The lusory attitude is a game-playing attitude, though Suits does not define it that way (for that would lead to his definition of game being circular). Rather, the lusory attitude is to accept rules without which there could be no such activity (of game playing). Instead, therefore, of carrying the ball to the hole, the golfer accepts the rule that they have to hit the ball towards the hole with a stick – at least a golf club – which is a relatively inefficient means of achieving the prelusory goal. Similarly, the race runner accepts a rule that they cannot cut across the infield. These rules are not accepted because they assist in the achievement of the prelusory goals: they are actually obstacles to such achievement. But without the lusory means towards the goals, there could not be activities such as golf, race running and backgammon. The rules are constitutive of the game, for one cannot be playing the game unless one accepts them. One might do something similar to a game, as when a policeman runs to catch a robber, but he is not playing a game as he is not adopting a lusory attitude in his running.

There are many possible objections to the definition of game offered by Suits, and in his book he tries to answer them, but as our own aim is not Suits's scholarship, we need not detail every twist and turn. It suffices to say that the definition of game that Suits provides will be provisionally accepted. But where does that get us with respect to sport, a subject about which Suits says surprisingly little? It seems that we need some further account, on top of the definition of game, that explains why some games are sport and some are not. Association football (soccer, for Americans) is clearly a sport while tiddlywinks is not. What's the difference?

The difference between games that are sport and 'mere' games is not, I suggest, a philosophical one. It is not that there is a philosophically interesting, objective property that belongs to one and not the other. The difference is, on my account, explicable more sociologically than philosophically. This explains why the definition of sport does not get any greater treatment in this book, for it is not primarily a philosophical issue. As Reid has said, 'sport is a human construction. Play may be natural, even common to humans and animals, but sport only has existed and only will exist as long as we choose to make it so' (Reid 2010: 115). Sports tend to be more obviously physical than games, requiring strength, fitness and agility, but not always so. Darts is usually classed as a sport even though some of its players are not enormously fit, while skipping is 'only' a game even though to do it well one needs to be fit and agile. Instead of seeking such a distinguishing feature, I favour an institutional theory of sport: one that matches the institutional theory of art that will be developed later in the book (Chapter 4). According to an institutional theory of sport, sport is a status that is bestowed by various social institutions upon certain forms of practice. Those institutions grew up around those practices – running, jumping, ball playing and so on – first organising them and then taking authority over them. There are individual governing bodies for each sport but also some overarching bodies such as the International Olympic Committee (IOC). The relevant institutions consist in more than just governing bodies, however. The media, athletes and their agents, political bodies and so on all have a role to play in determining which forms of practice deserve the status of sport. The IOC is an especially powerful body, however, in that they are able to grant the status of Olympic sport on certain games. Athletics is thus a core part of the Olympics and thus of sport, as are swimming and gymnastics. But BMX biking, for instance, began as fun: a pastime, leisure. Only once a game was made out of it – racing over a course – did it become a possible sport, and its practitioners, no doubt, thought of it as a sport from the outset. Eventually, others were persuaded to take it seriously. The IOC gave it the ultimate stamp of approval when it was made an Olympic sport for 2008 in Beijing. By contrast, tiddlywinks has never been close to approval as a sport. It has much in common with some of the things that are sports. Like darts and pistol shooting, it involves aiming projectiles at targets. Some of the participants may see it as sport but it has not been given the IOC approval. The rules of tiddlywinks are yet to receive a universal codification, though it's more serious than you might think: there are two rival associations with their own codes. But many people play it without any knowledge of either of these. A common code is not, however, suggested as either a necessary or sufficient condition for recognition as a sport: rugby has two different codes. But codification is a sign of having a governing body, which is the sort of thing more likely to lead to recognition as a sport.

There need be no key difference, therefore, between a sport and mere games. It is more that the former are endorsed by certain central institutions. Sport is thus an institutional notion, to be understood sociologically. There is a useful distinction in Danish, Norwegian and Swedish that recognises this. Sport is reserved for organised, professional and elite games. Practised in a less organised and amateur way, similar activities would be called idræt/idrett/idrott, which might be translated into English as recreation. Hence, when I jog in the park, or play an informal game of football with friends – without a referee or timekeeper – I could be thought of as participating merely in recreation, under the jurisdiction of no governing body. When my game is officially recognised and controlled by the relevant institutions, I am doing sport. In English, however, sport clearly has a much broader sense than it does in Danish. The jog or the football kick-about would most likely still be classed as sport, despite the lack of official jurisdiction. How so? On the institutional theory, the answer is that one is participating in a type of practice – running and footballing – that has had the status of sport bestowed upon it. One is participating in a type of activity that counts as sport, even if that particular token of the type – the individual park game – has not had the status bestowed upon it directly.

As already mentioned, it will be argued later that we should have an institutional theory of art. If we have both an institutional theory of sport and an institutional theory of art, what distinguishes them? Might an essentialist about both sport and art rejoin that there must be some intrinsic differences between the two forms of practice, for the institutions that surround those practices are structurally isomorphic (or at least they could be in principle) and thus there is no principled difference between them? Such an argument does not prove that either sport or art has an essence. Instead it might be the case that the difference between the institutions of art and sport is to be explained historically. The institutions of art were those that grew around certain forms of practice, such as painting and sculpture. The institutions of sport were those that grew around other forms of practice: running, jumping, swimming and shooting. There may have been factors that united these groups of practice. Painting and sculpture could be used for representation, for instance, or for creativity, while running and jumping involved physical strength and prowess. But the development of those institutions has led to practices classified as art and as sport that have little in common with the original exemplars out of which the institutions grew. Much art is now non-representational, and some sports do not now require what might be thought of as physical fitness.

These preliminaries established, or at least stated, we can now introduce the argument of the rest of the book. The focus will be on three main reasons for watching sport. They are aesthetic, ethically educative and emotional. But, it will be argued, there are different ways in which sport can be watched and people may watch sport for different reasons. Purists are distinguished from partisans, where the former watch sport for more aesthetic and intellectual reasons while the motivation of the partisan is more emotional and victory-seeking. The aesthetics of sport will be examined and it will be argued that there are many legitimate sporting aesthetic categories. This raises the question of how sport relates to art, and how the watching of sport for aesthetic reasons compares to art appreciation. It will be argued that sport is not art but that this is not because they have incompatible essences. Rather, institutional theories of both art and sport will be favoured. Art and sport are both made by our social practices, with the two domains having differing historical ancestries. Some disanalogies between art and sport have been alleged, however. While there is an aesthetic of sport, it is alleged that it is never its principal aim. And while sport contains drama, it is said never to be the same as the artistic drama of the stage and screen. But both of these disanalogies will be dismissed and thus the aesthetics of art and sport brought closer together.

A major claim of the book will then be made in Chapter 7. Different people can see the same sporting event in different ways. A purist and a partisan, for instance, or even two opposed partisans, can look at the same game but see it differently. This is more than a matter of simply holding different beliefs about what one sees. Perception is something that occurs with the mediation of thought, not separate from it. The idea that there is a distinctive aesthetic way of seeing, for instance, is defended, whereas the partisan will have what we can call a competitive way of seeing the same sporting event.

The emphasis will then shift from aesthetics to ethics but not without first noting the close connection between these two families of value. Ethical values can to a degree determine aesthetic values such that if a work of art contains a moral flaw then that can also be an aesthetic flaw of it. Although such a claim is well established in the philosophy of art, it will be argued that sport gives a perfect exemplification of it. Sporting aesthetics can be either lessened by ethical flaws, such as cheating, or enhanced by ethical virtues.

This leads us to consider the ethical questions of sport more directly. The watching of sport, it is claimed, can provide us with knowledge of the virtues and vices in operation. To lay the groundwork for this, we first must establish that the morality of sport is continuous with the morality of wider life, rather than distinct from it. This done, we can then move on to consider more specifically how sport provides its viewers with these moral insights. Support is given to the so-called moral laboratory thesis. Sport can be understood as providing contests of virtue, where the various virtues and vices clash in a genuine competition. Fiction also provides examples of such clashes but its results are contrived. Those of sport are real. The understanding of virtue and vice is defended as a means of moral improvement, but they should be grasped in the abstract. It will be argued that, although sport can improve us, it would be a mistake to take athletes as moral role models. This concretises virtue too much and places unfair expectations on our sports stars.

We move on to the philosophy of emotion, for emotional involvement is an oft-cited reason for watching sport, especially though not exclusively for the partisan. Three topics will be considered in detail. First, it will be claimed that there is an especial intensification of emotion when watching sport in groups, and the bigger the group the greater the intensity. Our emotions, both positive and negative, compose with those of others in a non-linear fashion. Second, there will be consideration of the objects of our emotions, in particular our love and allegiance for sports teams and clubs. Clubs are complex social entities. Our attachments to them require belief in their persistence through time, which is not a simple matter to explain. It will be argued that the fans and their allegiance are parts of these complex entities and the persistence of such clubs through time is partly conspiratorial in nature. Finally, there will be consideration of why we care about sport. The theory will be supported in which our care is determined by choice, rather than discovery of some 'careworthy' essence of sport. But there will be an account of what it is about sport that is particularly apt for our care as an aesthetic pastime. The outcomes of sport are largely fabricated. Its victories and defeats are inconsequential and this makes it particularly suitable for the kind of care we have chosen to take in it. It is appropriate to take aesthetic pleasure in sport in a way that would not be appropriate if, for instance, the outcomes were a matter of life and death. There may also be something that sport displays that cannot be found so readily elsewhere: that we are embodied rational creatures, able to exercise our physical capabilities as free agents. Thus, while the watching of sport is not to everyone's taste, it is nevertheless a perfectly legitimate activity for those who enjoy it. They will tend to do so for some mixture or variety of aesthetic, morally educative and emotional reasons, which can play a role in enhancing their lives. We should now proceed to consider the first of those.

2   Partisans and purists

I have been at different times both a partisan and a purist. These look to be two kinds of sports fan. They are, but they are so much more than that. They involve completely different ways of watching sport. It will be argued that the partisan and purist see a different game, even when they are present at the same event. But what do we mean by a partisan and a purist?

A partisan is a fan of one particular sports team: and it usually is a team. Partisanship is rarer in the case of individual sports and I will shortly offer a reason why it is mainly team sports that attract partisans. Such fandom can take many forms, some of them more extreme than others. Mild partisanship may consist in identifying with a team and following their progress in the media, watching an occasional game that gets televised. Some merchandise can be bought and a team shirt worn with a degree of pride and self-identification. The more enthusiastic fan is likely to attend the sports events in person, cheering for their team and chanting with others. There are cases of extreme partisanship with supporters who follow their team home and away, never missing a fixture, adorning their home with memorabilia, thinking and talking of nothing but their team, writing about them and keeping detailed records. As Crawford (2004) notes, such extreme partisanship is rare, although the media reports of fandom tend to concentrate on this unrepresentative case. The vast majority of partisans are likely to be of the first kind: the mild partisan who identifies with a team but attends a game only rarely or not at all. Clearly there are degrees of partisanship on a spectrum.

I have first-hand experience of partisanship, ranging from merely enthusiastic to extreme. Between 1980 and 1998, I followed the fortunes of an obscure and unsuccessful football club in the north of England. At times, this verged on obsessive support. England being a small country, it is possible to follow your team to all their away matches as well as having a season ticket for the home schedule. During the football season, which lasts about eight or nine months, there is at least one match a week and often two. Hence there would be gaps of only a few days between fixtures, so as soon as one was over there was another to look forward to. These games had a huge impact on me as a partisan. If the team won, everything was alright. But if they lost, which was a frequent occurrence, a depressed mood would hang over me. Such a way of life was abandoned in 1998, at which point I tended towards purism.

The purist is a fan of a sport, and may love deeply the sport concerned, but has no allegiance to any particular team. They may attend games and enjoy them despite having no preference for either team to win. I contend that Dixon (2001) gets the purist wrong in this respect, identifying them as someone whose allegiance shifts according to which currently is the best team. That just makes them a different (fickle) kind of partisan. But instead, the purist enjoys the game in a different way from a partisan. They may enjoy working out the tactics of the two teams and seeing how the play develops, how the tactics are adapted to fit new circumstances, and how the game has key moments of drama. They may also enjoy seeing individual skilful players, perhaps competing against each other, and will want both sides to play well, to their full potential. A partisan, in contrast, may be very happy if the opposition team underperforms. An eventful game will be more pleasing than an uneventful one to a purist, who will certainly want to see a 'good' game. But what makes a good game is not necessarily dependent on the result, given that they have little preference for either of the teams. The purist, I will argue, has not been correctly understood, and in this chapter I will be defending the purist against various claims made by those who think that partisanship is the right way to watch sport. In response, I will be advocating a more aesthetic mode of sports watching.

How could partisanship be defended? I will concentrate on two kinds of argument: one psychological and the other ethical. While I will not support the psychological argument, I will accept a part of it, which is that the partisan sees the game in a particular way that the purist does not. The partisan has a competitive perception whereas the purist's perception of the game is an aesthetic one. The ethical argument is that it is in a broad sense ethically more commendable to support one particular team insofar as the lack of an allegiance is symptomatic of a character flaw.

The psychological argument points to alleged benefits that the individual gains by supporting a team. Some of these are related to the experience of watching a sporting event, but there are also wider benefits. Wann *et al.* (2001: 164), for instance, think that being a fan brings psychological benefits as a buffer against depression. My own experience as a fan of a losing team seemed to indicate the contrary. Perhaps, however, it did tend against a more serious, clinical depression, from which I never suffered. Having broader interests in one's life, away from narrow personal concerns, does seem to be psychologically beneficial (an explanation of this will be offered in Chapter 14). One's sphere of concern can be broadened in supporting a team. One cares for something else: a sporting club, which is also a social institution. One cares for the club, its players and, perhaps more importantly, the friends one makes among the supporters of the same team. Hence, while I endured almost weekly defeats, I did it with a circle of friends, and the shared suffering helped us to bond just as much as the shared joy of following a successful team might have. In addition, Wann *et al.* mention the benefits of increased self-esteem and group esteem (pride in the group to which one belongs), although this may also come more from a winning than a losing team. But even fans of losing teams can feel a sense of pride in supporting their team, especially when it is their local team. A small town that supports a team of high status is often a source of great civic pride, even if the team is not successful at that level. The supporters of small-town clubs tend to come from the area and see the club's achievements, such as they are, as reflecting on them and their community. Bigger and more successful clubs can attract supporters from all over the world, including fans who have never visited the club's home region, let alone the stadium. There may be a degree of what Wann *et al.* call BIRG-ing: basking in reflected glory, which again may improve a fan's sense of self-esteem. Dixon also argues that there are benefits to be gained from supporting a team. The fan feels 'enlarged' through their support, especially when the team is successful (Dixon 2001: 150). I won't venture into what it means to be enlarged but clearly Dixon does not mean it literally.

This gives us a possible explanation of why partisanship seems to be more common in team sports than individual sports. Teams represent nations, cities, towns and villages, and sometimes an ideology, sector of society or political stance. In supporting them, a fan is siding with what the team represents. The fan wants to be a part of such a grouping and they indeed are, according to one account of what constitutes a sports club (more detail is provided in Mumford 2004 and Chapter 13, below). By contrast, the players of individual sports are perceived more as representing themselves. Of course, in an Olympic Games track and field event, individuals do race in their nation's colours but others may also be representing the same country. As a result, it is harder for the fans to unite behind one individual. And issues such as the personality of the individual come into it, whereas in a team sport the individual personalities have to be subsumed into the whole. The team comes first. One may decide to not support an individual tennis player, for instance, if one thinks they are not a nice person; but in team sports one is far more able to abstract away from such considerations.

The benefits of being a partisan that have been mentioned so far have been indirect consequences of watching sport, and those same benefits may be gained elsewhere. But it has also been claimed that there is a more direct benefit, essential to the activity, which is that one sees a better game if one has a partisan interest in the outcome. The purist, it can be argued, in having no interest in who wins, misses some of the crucial elements of a sporting contest. Elliott developed this line of argument:

> the ordinary spectator ... does not fully enjoy a football match unless he has an interest in the victory of one side or the other. We have no right to tell him that he ought to adopt a detached aesthetic attitude unless we can assure him that by doing so he will gain more than he loses. In fact, he will gain very little and lose a great deal.
>
> (Elliott 1974: 110)

Elliott argues that the purist misses all the appeal of watching sport that accrues from its competitive nature. They can see that a move is likely to succeed but they cannot feel the menace the partisan would feel if it's 'their' goal that is under threat, nor the excitement if 'their' team is attacking (1974: 110). The purist, Elliott alleges, would see a blunder, such as a player tripping over, or a contingency, such as a freak bounce of the ball, as flaws in the game. But for the fan it adds to the excitement (1974: 110). Hence, the purist sees only an impoverished version of the game, stripped of its competitive aspect: 'Under the circumstances, there seems to be no good reason why a spectator at a sporting event should adopt a special detached aesthetic attitude' (1974: 112).

There does seem to be something psychologically plausible about this account. Sports fans often do find a game more exciting if they want one of the teams to win. When the ball nears the goal, they feel excitement of either a good kind, when it is the goal they attack, or a dread when it is the goal they defend. The emotions feel so much more intense than that of the purist who, at most, will feel a relatively tranquil pleasure. The scoring of a goal brings such an intense thrill for the diehard fan that the purist could never hope to attain a detached aesthetic pleasure that comes anywhere near it. Such is the addition to the experience that sports enthusiasts, watching a game that does not involve their own team, will often take sides on relatively little pretext. An extreme example is to be found in a story involving the late American philosopher David Lewis, who was a frequent visitor to Australia. The story goes that he was at his first Australian Rules football match and thought it would be much more exciting if he supported one of the teams. He could see no reason to side with one rather than the other, however, so he decided it on the toss of a coin. The coin told him to support Essendon and he did so ever after. This is a good story, though, unfortunately, it's not true (as I confirmed in conversation with his wife Stephanie). Even though Lewis didn't go through this, no doubt others have, or have favoured teams on some basis not quite so random but almost as arbitrary, such as the colour of the shirt or whether the team's name is evocative (A. J. Ayer supported Tottenham Hotspur because the name Hotspur was so dashing).

What such a fan seeks is the adoption of a competitive perception of the game. By this, I mean that, in favouring one team and wanting them to win, the fan perceives the game in a certain way, different from the purely aesthetic perception of the purist or a neutral. All of the game's incidents will be perceived through this lens of competitive interest. A shot on goal is seen as more than just that but also as an opportunity to win the game and attain glory. A player injured can be seen as a tragedy and relegation can seem like a disaster.

I became persuaded that there was a competitive perception when I attended, as a neutral, a football match between Heart of Midlothian and Celtic in Scotland in 1996. Football in Scotland has a sectarian dimension as well as rivalry between cities. Although matters are not quite so clear cut, this match paired what is perceived to be the Protestant team of Edinburgh against the Catholic team of Glasgow. The fans around me were fiercely passionate and highly vocal in this game. They appealed to the referee for every decision to be given in their favour: not just corners and free kicks but even throw-ins. There were many occasions where, with no interest in the outcome other than it being an entertaining match, I could see clearly that the throw-in should go Celtic's way. But when the referee made such an award the Hearts fans around me were outraged and gave strong vent to it. As they saw it, it was a clear Hearts throw-in. The ball had touched a Celtic man last. But such was the passion and conviction of the supporters' appeals, I could conclude nothing but that they saw it as being a Hearts throw. In their perception, the ball really did seem to have come off a Celtic player last before leaving the field. I was sat next to one fan, with a virtually identical perspective on the incident, and a very good view of it, yet I saw it one way and they saw it the other. Were they being disingenuous? Or could this really be two different and honest perceptions? I decided it could be.

There is, in philosophy of science, a thesis known as the theory dependence of observation. This idea is old but it has been defended in modern times by, for instance, Kuhn (1962). The thesis is that what you see is to a degree theory-laden. This means that one's beliefs and desires can determine what one sees. It is not that one sees something and then forms a belief about it, based on one's theory of the world. Rather, one's theory of the world can determine what one actually sees.

I have some reservations about the theory dependence of observation because, in its most radical form, it is anti-realist and relativistic. It also leaves us trapped within our belief system with no obvious empirical checks or constraints on theory. But there could be more moderate versions of the thesis in which not all our perceptions can be affected by our beliefs to an unlimited degree. My preference would also be for a more sophisticated account of how belief can affect perception, such as the multiple drafts model developed by Dennett (1991). But the competitive perception does seem a good candidate for perception that is theory dependent. In that case, my neighbour at the football match, with an almost identical view of the same incident, could indeed have seen it differently. By this, I do not say that we had the same kind of perception and he just had a different opinion about it; rather we saw different things and both had honest beliefs about what we saw. His belief that Hearts were the more deserving team, and his strong desire that they be awarded every decision, could have interfered with what he saw. But the case illustrates why there should be some limitations. The contested incidents at least involved opposing players going for the same ball. Had a Hearts player volleyed the ball into touch with no player near him, nor the ball's flight, it would be very hard even for a partisan to see it as their ball. But where the play was contested, it became a possibility that we saw different things. The account might also be able to resist the relativistic conclusion that one person's perception is as good as any other's. As a neutral, I think my impartial perception was far more trustworthy than that of a partisan, which is, of course, why referees should always be neutrals.

These are some of the psychological arguments in favour of partisanship. They allege that the purist is missing something valuable and vital by supporting neither competing team. I turn now to the ethical argument. This has been offered by Dixon (2001). Dixon defends partisanship in a different way. It is more virtuous, or a better way to be, though it is only moderate rather than extreme partisanship that he recommends. First, though, we should look at how Dixon defines a partisan and a purist. He does so as follows:

A *partisan* 'is a loyal supporter of a team to which she may have a personal connection or which she may have grown to support by dint of mere familiarity'.

A *purist* 'supports the team that he thinks exemplifies the highest virtues of the game, but his allegiance is flexible'.

(Dixon 2001: 149)

But Dixon has got the purist wrong here, as I suggested earlier. The purist is depicted as someone who makes a choice of which team to support based on their style of play. As the purist understands the correct virtues of the sport, their team plays the game right. And their allegiance is flexible in that, if their team stopped playing the game right, the purist would stop supporting them and move on to another team that plays better. However, the true purist instead, as I understand purism, should be depicted as supporting no team at all. It is not that their allegiance merely shifts more regularly than the partisan's; rather, they have no allegiance. Any interest that the purist has is for the sport itself. They want to see it for all its beauty and drama. They do not go into the game wanting any one particular team to win in that they would much rather see a beautiful game irrespective of the winner. They may want to see the highest virtues of the sport succeed and be rewarded but have no interest in which of the sides exemplifies those virtues. They support the virtues in the abstract, not the particular team that at that moment displays them. A true supporter of the virtues of the sport could have no team allegiance because, in any game or passage of play, which team plays virtuously could alternate rapidly. Not only can the same team play to a different level from game to game, but even within a single game there is ebb and flow. One team or individual can make a good move, and then the other team might also impress. The purist is excited by such excellence whatever its source: indeed their ideal would be that both sides play to an excellent standard. Dixon's notion of there being a flexible allegiance does not do justice to this kind of purist. Dixon is aware of this kind of concern but his response to it is to concede that the purist may not count as a fan at all (2001: 153). Is this right? The purist can be a fan of the sport, and love it as much as the partisan loves their team. They simply don't see the need or the point in confining their sphere of care to one single club that may, after all, play the game in an ugly way quite often.

The purist that I will be defending will not, therefore, be a fan with a flexible allegiance. They will be someone who is unallied but nevertheless a lover of the sport concerned. They could watch many games and have a deep knowledge of and understanding of them. They may have a far superior tactical grasp of the game than the partisan whose chief concern is with the result. The partisan, for example, may consume alcohol before a game and go to the stadium to have a good sing-song with their friends, and to cheer the goals, but without following the tactics closely (I have even seen partisans so drunk that they have slept during the game). Their concern is with a good day out. The purist, however, would tend to shy away from alcohol before a game as it could deaden their understanding of what they see and, ultimately, inhibit their aesthetic experience.

There is one concern of partisanship that used to worry me, but Dixon has done a good job of answering it. The partisan can often adopt their team through some random circumstance. Perhaps they choose their team because of their colours or name. Perhaps they meet someone at school or work who invites them along and their interest takes off from there. These seem like pretty chancy reasons to support a team. They are not rationally based. And even if one supports the team of one's local town, assuming it has no more nor less than one team, then even that is an accident of one's birthplace. It seems, therefore, that the partisan has no good reason for selecting one team to follow rather than another, other than some accident of circumstance. And maybe that reason alone is enough to recommend purism. Supporting a team is not rationally based if I know that, had I been born in the next town instead of my own, I would not have supported my team but the team of the next town. This argument is no recommendation of purism, however. It can be accepted that one's initial adoption of a team rests on chance, either of circumstance or place of birth, but that makes the allegiance, bond and attachment no lesser. Analogously, a person meets their spouse by a comparable matter of chance, and they may then go and start a family with them. Their bond to their spouse and children will be no lesser just because it started with a chance encounter. One may, for instance, meet someone from the same town and think that, had they been born in a different town or country, you would not have met. This could be true, but the bond between the couple and with their children is in no way diminished by this fact of chance. The partisan may, therefore, have no truly rational basis for supporting the team that they adopted, but this does not mean that their love for their team is any less real. And by extension, it does not mean that they cannot still enjoy the supposed psychological benefits of supporting a team and nor would it make them any less ethical a partisan, if partisanship is indeed the ethical option.

Let us then look at this argument that partisanship is more ethical than purism. Dixon's argument is that the purist exhibits some kind of character flaw. They are unable to form bonds with the sporting community and empathise with others who have an interest in the success of a particular team. It is worth citing Dixon's argument in full:

> A fan who regularly watches a local team but never identifies with its fortunes fails to exhibit the perfectly natural, healthy tendency to form a bond with those with whom we are familiar. While this is innocuous enough in the case of a sporting team to which no one owes any allegiance, it may betoken an inability to develop empathy for other people. A person who lacks this ability may have difficulty forming friendships and lasting romantic attachments. Granted, no one has a moral obligation to form such close personal relationships in the first place, but being unable to do so seems to be a character flaw that would be condemned from a standpoint of virtue ethics.
> (Dixon 2001: 155)

How is one to defend the purist against such accusations? Are they really less virtuous than the partisan? One might point out that there are partisans who behave in an anything but virtuous way. Taken to its extreme, partisanship can lead to unhealthy obsession, antisocial behaviour and even violence. But Dixon does not defend this kind of partisan. His defence is of moderate partisanship, which contains some of the positive elements of purism. Moderate partisanship, he says, is 'a prima facie good' (Dixon 2001: 157). It combines 'the tenacious loyalty of the partisan, tempered by the purist's realization that teams that violate the rules or spirit of the game do not deserve our support' (Dixon 2001: 153). The moderate partisan will not tolerate absolutely anything. If their team plays in a vicious manner, or the club abuses and exploits its own supporters, the moderate partisan may cease their support. This kind of partisan does, therefore, accept that there are virtues to be exemplified in sport and without which support is not deserved. The moderate partisan will also condemn supporter violence and avoid any self-destructive obsession with their team.

The moderate partisan does sound reasonable and I am not arguing here that they should be eradicated. But nor do I accept that purism exhibits a character flaw consisting in inadequate empathy or inability to form relationships and I do not accept that the purist is in any significant way inferior to the partisan. The purist is one who values the sport itself and wants to see it played in the best way possible. Lacking an allegiance to a single club does not seem automatically to indicate a vice. I could point out that I am a purist and that I'm honestly a nice, regular guy (just ask my imaginary friend) but that would be *ad hominem*.

Dixon draws an analogy between supporting a team and forming personal relationships. But there are ways in which the analogy fails. Sport is a competitive business in which the aim, within the sport itself, is victory and the defeat of one's opponents. The purist stands back from this concern with victory and defeat. In one's personal relationships, one does not, however, have to choose between rivals whose aim is the other's defeat. When I have a friend, for instance, the friendship is not premised on me forsaking all other friendships or wanting to see my friend triumph over everyone else. The purist is more in the position of a parent with a number of children or someone who has a large circle of friends. The parent wants to see all their children do well in life and realise their full potential. They do not choose a favourite among their children and hope for them to do better than their siblings. Similarly, if one has a number of genuine friends, one does not see them as being in competition. Wanting all to flourish as much as possible does not seem an especially vicious stance. There is, of course, one personal relationship that does have an exclusive character, which is that of a monogamous marriage. Here it is assumed that there is a special loyalty to one person. But marriage is not for everyone. The purist is in the position of someone who treats a group of friends equally, without picking out one who deserves any special treatment above what they give to the others. Such a lifestyle may be preferable if it allows one to see the good in many different people and wish them all well. Similarly, the sporting purist wants to see the best possible sporting interactions, which will be ones in which both sides perform to a high level.

Just as it would be condemned if a parent favoured one child over another, the impartiality and neutrality of the purist can seem entirely appropriate.

There is a further kind of criticism that Dixon raises. He goes on to say: 'The purist shows a commendable appreciation for the fine points of the game but seems to lack the passion and commitment that is the lifeblood of competitive sport' (Dixon 2001: 155). But why is this so? Can't you be totally passionate about the sport itself, and so much so that you have risen beyond the limitations of having a singular allegiance? Some purists can be far more passionate about the game than the partisan. They may see more games, for instance, and the partisan's interest may be limited only to the games of their own team. The purist could research the players, the teams and the tactics in far more depth. Although they wear no replica team shirt, the purist may devote more time and energy to the sport than does their partisan counterpart. The difference is that the purist's passion may be less conspicuous than that of the partisan. They enjoy an aesthetic rather than competitive perception of the game and this gives them a gentler, less frenetic enjoyment. But philosophers have recognised that this can be passion and pleasure nevertheless. Hume spoke of both calm and violent passions (Hume 1739–40: 417–18). The purist's passion for their sport is a calmer one which, as Hume notes, can sometimes be mistaken for no more than reason. But it is a passion nonetheless. It is an interest and a care that reason alone could not dictate. And it is a source of pleasure but, again, a gentler one. It was suggested earlier that the purist could never gain the intense pleasure felt by a partisan when their team scores. The purist could, however, invoke Mill's distinction of higher and lower pleasures (Mill 1861: 211). Although they don't experience the intense excitement of the partisan when a goal is scored, the purist nevertheless takes a deeper and more satisfying pleasure in the game. They are pleased by the finer things. They appreciate the game for its aesthetic qualities and will find some such in every game. Their pleasure is not determined primarily or solely by the result, so they may concentrate on other matters: the style of play, the tactics, the movement of the ball, rapidity, grace, economy, incisiveness and so on. A concern with the mere result looks a crude measure of the worth of a game, by comparison.

We may answer the point of psychology similarly. It was alleged that, without the competitive perception, our purist would miss out. It was agreed that it was a different experience when one was not competitively engaged in the contest, including the possibility of having different perceptions of an event from that of a partisan spectator. But in exchange, the aesthetic perception offers liberation from the narrow concerns of partisanship. Without victory being the primary or sole concern, one is free to take pleasure in all the other aspects of the game. And this includes taking pleasure in the good play of both the competing sides, not just one's own. One can appreciate the competition as a competition and not just as an opportunity for victory or risk of defeat. And then, being governed by calm passions and seeking the higher pleasures, there is no reason why watching sport cannot bring the psychological benefits that were alleged to accompany partisanship. Even the group esteem that is mentioned by Wann *et al.* is possible, though it would be the esteem of belonging to a much wider group of fellow purists who all appreciate the finer points of the game. In having a far broader circle of interests, the purist has just as much protection from depression as does the partisan, if not even more so.

There seems to be no really compelling argument in favour of being a partisan, therefore. In that case, I recommend the more purist stance, while allowing that there are degrees of partisanship and purism on a spectrum. One can forgo the highs and lows of victory and defeat for a more smooth and gentle ride in which the pleasure may be less intense but more satisfying. And there will be no more relegation seasons or closing day disappointments but a life instead enjoying sport for its purely positive and aesthetic aspects.

But there has been a simplification in all of this. It is not quite as if every sports watcher divides clearly into the purist camp or the partisan camp. Won't there be lots of people who are in between? I agree that there will be. Just as Dixon distinguished moderate and extreme versions, we should acknowledge that the purist and partisan tendencies can come in degrees and mixtures. A single individual may have both tendencies to some extent, with varying amounts from person to person. We can have a sliding scale of purism and partisanship. Or it may be that for some games someone is a partisan while for others they watch as a purist. Why the simplification, then? There can be a good reason for it. I am keen to isolate the traits of purism and partisanship in the abstract even if they appear in mixtures in concrete cases. We need to know what it is that we say can appear to a degree in a person. There are also interesting questions to be explored about what such tendencies involve, as I hope to demonstrate in coming chapters. By looking at these in the abstract, therefore, it is expected that our understanding will be enhanced, even of those sports fans who have a mixture of both tendencies within them.

But now, in having defended the trait of purism, we are left with a task of justifying the aesthetics of sport. Unless there are, after all, ample aesthetic pleasures to be had in watching sport, our purist's aim of seeing a game aesthetically is an empty one. In the next chapter, therefore, we will look more closely at the aesthetics of sport.

3 Aesthetics in sport

The purist we saw is a fan of sports whose interest is mainly in the aesthetic experiences it can provide. The partisan is a fan whose interest mainly is in winning. One purpose of this book is to defend the purist against the charge that they are in some way missing out on a full sporting experience by taking no serious interest in the winners and losers. It is argued, however, that they gain in other ways. But one thing the argument against the purist should not be allowed to ignore is that victory and defeat can themselves be part of the aesthetic experience of sport. One may be able to enjoy a last-minute winning goal in football, for instance, or a long-distance runner winning the race from behind in the last ten metres. The purist can appreciate the drama that such sporting contests are able to produce, but their difference from the partisan is that they don't mind which of the sides achieves the late victory or which of the athletes it is that is able to come from behind and win dramatically. The partisan prefers a dull victory to an exciting defeat. The purist appreciates excitement and other aesthetic experiences that sport provides.

We need now, however, to say something more about the aesthetics of sport. It is, after all, primarily in works of art that we are encouraged to take our aesthetic experiences, so might it be simply a confusion to talk of aesthetic values in sport? What are those values? Are they to be found in every sport? And are they the same values in each sport or do different sports embody different values? It will be argued in this chapter that sport should indeed be seen as a legitimate aesthetic source. Sport is as good a place as any for us to seek our aesthetic pleasure. A pluralistic notion of sporting aesthetics will be supported in which different sports provide different kinds of experience. Indeed, different incidents within the same sport can provide very different aesthetic encounters. Something will also be said on what the nature of aesthetic experience is taken to be. This is not intended to be a fully worked-out theory of aesthetics, which would be inappropriate in a book of this nature. Rather, it is intended to provide the background against which the discussion of sporting aesthetics is developed in this book.

At one time, Ziff (1974) discouraged work into the aesthetics of sport and alleged it was vacuous. Ziff had assumed a dubious principle that only something that individuated an activity could be an aspect of it. Given that sport needn't always have aesthetic value, then he said aesthetics wasn't one of its aspects.

There are, after all, plenty of unattractive athletes and bad games. But aesthetic value could still be an aspect of most instances of sporting activity, if not them all, so it seems unduly restrictive to rule out the consideration of sports aesthetics on Ziff's criterion. As Cooper (1978: 52) showed, this would mean nutrition was not an aspect of eating and reproduction not an aspect of sex. We should not worry, therefore, if not all sport aesthetically pleases us. It may still be aesthetic experiences that the purist is seeking, even if they occur infrequently. One wouldn't deny that a birdwatcher wants to see a certain bird just on the grounds that most of their time is spent looking at an empty tree. The sports enthusiast takes a risk over what will be available to their experience, but the aesthetic experience, when it comes, may justify the wait.

What kind of aesthetic experiences are we talking about in the case of sport? There are some obvious parallels with the art of dance and any aesthetic enjoyment that can be found in the body, its form and motion. This can be gained by concentrating on the movement of just a single athlete while performing their sport. In the pole vault, for instance, the movement of the human body over the top of the bar is something that captivates us and warrants slow-motion television replays. Here we can take pleasure in a finely honed human form, beautifully toned and athletic, and gracefully tracing a movement through the air. A particular shape to the body, direction over the bar and ease of style are among the aesthetic attractions we seek. These are intimately connected with the aim of the sport. It is not just that the athlete aims to shape their body so, which they might just as well do in dance or in diving into a swimming pool. What enthrals us is also the fact that this is done as a way of achieving the prelusory goal. The performance is to some purpose; yet aesthetic values can be realised in achieving that purpose. Indeed, those beautiful bodily movements are required in order to get over the bar. The sport sets up a situation in which competing to win nevertheless creates the possibility of beautiful bodily motion.

In many other sports, similar possibilities are fostered. In football, for instance, it is not mandatory to play with grace, elegance and fluidity. Some players look clumsy and ungainly but are nevertheless effective. But the physical challenges of the sport require for success that the players be fit, healthy and toned, and that they sometimes stretch their limbs to their full extent, making various shapes with their bodies. Speed of movement is a competitive asset, so we naturally see players running in full flow with an efficient style. Speed, swiftness and lightness of footfall all qualify as aesthetic categories. They are among the things that we appreciate for their own sake. And different sports will see the realisation of different aesthetic values by the athletes according to which athletic excellences the sport requires. Speed may be an asset in football, for instance, but not so much in weight lifting. And the strength, size and sheer muscle power required in weight lifting would be a disadvantage in gymnastics where some of the best competitors are toned but petite. In human movement, all sorts of aesthetic categories come into play. As well as speed, strength and grace we also find pleasure in more specific aspects such as fluidity instead of jerkiness of motion, coordination, poise, balance, precision, symmetry, rhythm and so on. There are also aesthetic features of the surroundings of the athlete, from the colour of their sports strip to the greenness of the grass on which they play, or the blue of the pool in which they swim, to the architecture of the stadium in which they compete and the colour and sound provided by the crowd watching them. There is clearly much detail that could be provided further on this.

Aesthetic values are not just realised in the bodily movements of the individual competitors, however. There is a less immediate and more abstract kind of experience to be gained from sport that is important nevertheless, particularly for the purist. As well as appreciating the way individual players might move, there are also sports in which a pattern of play can be experienced. This is most obvious in team sports, such as football and rugby, where tactics and formations are often the key to success. Because of this, the movement of the players on the pitch can fall into patterns, with key general areas of pressure, or coordinated movements that are done as a team. The purist can enjoy these both aesthetically and intellectually. They may spend time figuring out what the respective formations and tactics are of the two teams and they can think of the relative successes of the two approaches and the possible changes that the coach ought to make. There is an intellectual delight to be found in such discoveries. It is the same kind of delight that is to be found in learning and acquiring a new understanding that one previously lacked. It is a pleasure in the satisfaction of wonder, curiosity and desire to understand. Such pleasure could be understood as an aesthetic experience, perhaps corresponding to one of J. S. Mill's (1861) higher pleasures. It is not just in team sports that one can experience this kind of pleasure in the abstract tactical aspects of sport. There are of course patterns of play and tactical aspects to individual sports. In the track cycling races of the velodrome, for instance, the race typically starts slowly. It's a game of cat and mouse as no one wants to take the lead too early. There is a big advantage to be found in slip-streaming and timing one's sprint finish so that one leads the race only in its last few moments. We find this also in tour cycling and motor racing. Tactics are less to the fore in other sports, however. In the long jump there is usually only one tactic: to jump as far as you can. And in the 100 metres the only tactic is to run as fast as you can until the finishing line. No doubt the athletes of these sports will know all the nuances, though. Perhaps they break the 100 metres down into ten-metre segments and have a plan for each. But the intricacy and impact of such tactics is far slighter than in sports such as football.

Given that we have noted different aesthetic categories in play, and have allowed that different aesthetic categories can be more important for certain sports rather than others, then it seems we have established some kind of aesthetic pluralism for sport. There is not one clear and simple aesthetic value to be found in sport and we should thus be cautious about oversimplifying the nature of the aesthetic experience sport gives us. Diversity has to be acknowledged. Unlike painting or sculpture, there are relatively few overall rules for the practice of sport, formal or informal. To appreciate sculpture, one must inspect a three-dimensional object: its shape, colour and texture. To appreciate painting, one must look at the colour, shapes and images depicted, usually in two dimensions on a canvas, board or a wall. But sport is a higher-level category than painting or sculpture. It is a determinable category, having various determinate sports under it. It may be likened to the notion of art in general, which may be considered as a determinable relative to painting, sculpture, drama, poetry and so on that are some of its determinate forms. A single account of the aesthetics of sport would thus need to be as abstract as would be a single account of the aesthetics of art.

It might, nevertheless, be useful if there were some broad classification of types of sport onto which we could map different aesthetic possibilities. This has indeed been attempted. Kupfer (1983) distinguishes the following different kinds of sport:

> *Quantitative/linear*: e.g. long jump, running races. One sees how far one can travel, or how quickly one can travel a set distance. These sports depend essentially on measurement.

> *Qualitative/formal*: e.g. diving, figure skating, ice dance. Everyone dives the same distance or skates the same rink so the competition becomes about style and form. Aesthetic considerations are to the fore.

> *Competitive sports*: e.g. football, rugby, fencing. One competes directly against others: not just doing your best, but also stopping others from doing their best. The key is the overcoming of opposition.

It is not the task here to comment on how accurate, inclusive and exhaustive Kupfer's division is. Perhaps one may think of a sport that does not fit easily into any of the categories. But even from this three-fold distinction one can see how aesthetic distinctions can be created by their differences. In competitive sports, for instance, the possibility for sporting drama is optimised. There are two or more teams or protagonists, each striving for a limited resource: victory or first place. A win for one means a loss for the rest. And as the participants compete, there are many incidents along the way in which hopes can rise and fall, like the plot twists of a novel. As Kupfer (1983: 463) puts it, human opposition brings the opportunity for social drama: competitors must react and readjust in response to each other. Improvisation becomes necessary (Kupfer 1983: 465). A similar type of drama could be created in the quantitative and qualitative sports but it would not be nearly so apparent and common. The ice dance pair might try to create a sense of drama in their routine, for instance, or there may be a moment of drama when the long-jump competition is won with the very last attempt. But this tends to be less regular and is not what the nature of these sports is all about.

In the qualitative sports, however, there are other aesthetic values that are clearly to the fore. The aesthetic values exemplified in the performance can be a key determinant of victory. This is not to say that these are purely aesthetic competitions. There are still techniques to be mastered in the qualitative sports. One needs to be able to skate on the ice, in figure skating, and perform certain elements such as the triple axel or salchow. This can be appreciated in itself.

But one may also distinguish technique and style, where the style is seen as something that enriches the technique (Hohler 1974: 51). A triple axel could be executed perfectly efficiently but still without style. Hence, marks can be given for artistic interpretation of the routine. This makes qualitative sports the most obviously aesthetic. The division between technique and style should not be exaggerated, however. In diving, for instance, attempts at codification of the aesthetic values of the sport mean that to display the required aesthetic qualities, such as entering the water entirely perpendicular to it, one must master a high degree of technique.

That leaves the purely quantitative sports, of travelling fastest or furthest. Here, one might think that there is the least scope for aesthetic appreciation of the sport. The interest of one who watches, it might seem, is only to see who crosses the finishing line first or who jumps the highest bar. But there is more to it. These are some of the sports in which appreciation of the human form, stretched to the limit of its capacity, is most clearly to the fore. Swiftness being something that we tend to appreciate, the winner of the 100-metre sprint in a high-level competition is always a cause of marvel. We may be able to see the fastest man or woman on the planet explode into action in a short but thrilling burst: proving in competition that for those ten seconds or so they were the finest physical specimen alive, judged on the basis of the athletic excellences of that event. Similarly with high jump, pole vault or shot put, we get to appreciate the best at those excellences.

There are different ways in which we could divide up the sports, however, and it is worth commenting on one further division that also has an aesthetic significance. Kretchmar (2005) believes that some sports are flawed, both as games and as spectacles. Some games are time limited: what he calls T games. Others are not time limited but instead require a fixed, minimum or finite number of skilful events or encounters: the E games. Are T games aesthetically inferior to E games? Kretchmar argues that time limitation is a game flaw because it encourages those in a winning position to delay and stall, thus spoiling the contest as a game and detracting from it as a spectacle. E games require a set number of skilful interchanges to occur irrespective of the time it takes, for example 18 holes of golf, nine innings of baseball and so on, so stalling has no point. You cannot run down the clock instead of playing. Not every E game would require a fixed number of such skilful exchanges, however. Match-play golf, such as in the Ryder Cup, is still event regulated but can end as soon as one player or pair has an unassailable lead, for instance by being four holes up with only three to play, in which case the contest ends with only 15 holes played.

Setting aside the question of whether time limitation within sport is a game flaw, we can consider specifically whether it is an aesthetic flaw or not. An obvious problem with such an argument, though it cannot be decisive on its own, is that football is time limited and yet it is the most popular spectator sport in the world. And it is not just among partisans that it is popular, whose only interest might be in winning. One can also argue that it is the most popular from a purist's point of view too. FIFA claimed a TV audience of 700 million for the 2010

World Cup Final, played between two relatively small countries population-wise. The vast majority watching were clearly not committed partisans but, rather, 'neutrals' viewing the game aesthetically or they had chosen one of the teams to support on some tenuous pretext.

Davis (2006) took Kretchmar to task for his claim, and argued that he had exaggerated the degree to which stalling would occur (see also Kretchmar's 2008 response). But there is another way to tackle the issue. Let us grant that stalling can, and often does, occur, as seems plausible, even if it may be relatively infrequent (for one form of stalling, see Mumford 2010). Every football fan has seen it and yet they still love the game and think it the greatest sport in the world to watch. How can this be if time limitation is an aesthetic flaw of games? The answer is that it isn't an aesthetic flaw. There is a way in which the very time limitation of a sport can appeal to us. The time structuredness of sports has its own appeal to us as time-limited creatures, as any Heideggerian is likely to point out (Heidegger 1927). It mirrors the structure of our lives, with a feeling that we must do what we need to do within a finite period: we cannot simply take as long as we want. And time limitation also enhances the dynamic of the sport: teams that trail have to play with more urgency and be more adventurous and risk taking. This creates the danger of conceding a goal from a rapid breakaway, which is one of the most exciting things to see in football. There is also a tactical battle to impose your desired pace on the game as the winning team seek to slow it down and the trailing team seek to speed it up. Such a contest can make for high drama as each goal in a game can change the dynamic, teams going from being content with their game situation, and seeking to hold it, to a position where they require a change in the game situation. Contrary to Kretchmar's (2008: 329–31) claim, therefore, it does not seem that all stalling in a sport should be corrected. Some of it may contribute to the spectacle and chime with our time-limited view of the world.

Kretchmar also defends E games because they permit enough skilful interchanges for the best team to be very sure of winning. If you limit the number of skilful interchanges then the weaker team increases its chance of winning. But, again, the popularity of football suggests that we don't necessarily see it as a flaw of a game that it gives a weaker team more of a chance. After all, would sport really be exciting to watch if the better team always won? In some sports, such as golf, we even introduce handicaps to correct imbalances and make it a more even game and put the result in doubt. Unless the weaker team or player can win the contest, it seems that it has relatively little interest to us. One of the most pleasing events in sport is when a weaker team or individual player is able to beat all the odds against them and spring a surprise on their opponents and those of us watching.

There is a prominent aesthetic value to which we should turn that many profess to find in sport and which therefore deserves our attention. This is the notion of grace, which has been mentioned already in passing. What is meant by this in the case of sport? In considering it, however, we also have another motive. We have talked of various aesthetic values and experiences to be gained from watching sport but we still haven't yet said much on what we take these aesthetic features to be. By looking at grace as a case study, it will bring some of these issues into focus and allow us to tackle the big question of aesthetics. Should we see the issue in terms of there being aesthetic properties of objects or events, and aesthetic values realised in those events, or should we see the aesthetic as a way of looking at things in the world? Grace will provide a good case study in respect of these questions as well as having its intrinsic interest for the philosophy of sport.

The question of graceful movement in sport has been a subject of debate. It is a term that is often mentioned when we talk about the aesthetics of sport but without serious analysis. When we admire an athlete's body in motion, for instance, we prefer to see one that is graceful than one that is graceless. But is there any theory we can give of what grace consists in? Is it a simple and superficial feature of bodily movement or can we analyse it down into simpler conceptual components? One theory is that grace consists in functionality, by which is meant efficiency and economy of style. There could be successful athletes that lack grace, and graceful athletes that lack success, so the notion of grace is independent from that of winning in sport. Best defends this functionality account and shows how the lack of economy in style is considered an aesthetic flaw:

> We may admire the remarkable stamina and consistent success of an athlete such as Zapotek, but he was not an aesthetically attractive runner because so much of his movement seemed irrelevant to the ideal of most direct accomplishment of the task. His style was regarded as ungainly because there were extraneous waggles, rolls or jerks which seemed wasteful in that they were not concisely aimed at achieving the most efficient use of his energy.
>
> (Best 1974: 204)

Some time later, Cordner argued against Best that functionality is not the explanation of grace. Cordner points out that there can be examples of grace in sport without economy or efficiency and, likewise, cases of economy and efficiency without grace. For example, we could have a bowling machine in cricket that delivers balls with perfect economy and precision, with no redundant action whatsoever. But this would lack grace (Cordner 1984: 305). Perhaps this is a bit of a cheap shot on Cordner's part because the subject matter of the debate thus far was grace of human movement and introducing the notion of a non-human bowling machine is rather changing the terms of the discussion. The pertinent question would be to ask whether we could have a perfectly efficient and economical human bowler who was nevertheless graceless. Cordner thinks such examples could be produced, however. Martina Navratilova was the dominant woman tennis player of her era, for instance, but according to Cordner (1984: 305), despite her efficient style, she didn't have grace.

As well as criticising an earlier account, Cordner advances one of his own. Cordner's positive account is that grace consists in the 'unity of being in the performance' or, to be slightly more specific, it 'displays a harmony or accord in all its elements. In a graceful display, everything comes together in a harmonious whole' (1984: 308). And, speaking later of his account:

The central concept in the sketch was that of unity of being. In graceful movement all elements of the movement are harmonized. What I called unity of being is then, I argued, manifest in grace of movement, and this is the source of its attraction for us.

(Cordner 2003: 132)

Such harmony manifests itself in effortlessness and easiness, but this is only the perceptual criterion of grace. This is how we recognise it visually: 'those elements, if present, are absorbed into a total harmony of being, the perceptual criteria of which are the effortlessness and easiness of the display' (Cordner 1984: 311–12). This perceptual criterion accompanies the philosophical account of the essence of grace consisting in unity of being. And there is a third element to Cordner's account. Grace is a property of persons, not actions. Cordner says: 'grace qualifies not just the stroke, but the whole being of the player of it' (1984: 310). Thus, when we see a player play a graceful shot in tennis, that whole player is transformed in our view. They become a graceful player. If Navratilova really was a graceless player, therefore, Cordner's theory rather suggests that she never played a graceful shot in public in her life, which is somewhat implausible.

In contrast to both Best and Cordner, Davis (2001) offers us a minimalist account of grace and aesthetics generally. Beauty is simply what pleases us and it is a mistake to probe for something deeper, lying behind it. Plato had this misconception, for instance, suggesting that beauty was meaningful for us because it allowed us some access to the Forms. For Davis, then, grace in sport is simply an appearance that pleases us, and we can say little more than that. In particular, we cannot analyse it down into more fundamental components. This is the mistake of both Cordner and Best:

My suspicion is that no theoretical account of graceful movement will suffice, and that we should therefore abandon – or at least suspend – the Platonic inclination to desuperficialize it. We are hung-up on appearances, unwilling to accept that a pleasing appearance might be intrinsically just that: a pleasing appearance.

(Davis 2001: 94)

Davis duly offers counter-examples to Cordner's own theory. There can be cases of grace without 'unity of being in the performance'. An expert tennis player, for instance, may play a graceful stroke against an amateur even while they are thinking of what to cook for dinner that evening. They seem to lack the requisite unity of being. It is not clear that this is a genuine counter-example to Cordner's theory, however, mainly because of the vagueness of the central idea of unity of being. What is it supposed to mean? In a reply, Cordner (2003) protests that he was not adopting a psychological criterion of unity of being – so a player might indeed have their mind on other things while being graceful – but then what does the notion mean? The following might help a little, though again suffers from vagueness:

Grace is the appearance of an easy presence. And such presence involves a harmonious relatedness to one's context. Sometimes this will show in the way a person achieves a goal, but that is not the root description of the source of grace, because sometimes no achievement of a goal is involved. The root description is the apparent easiness of the person's presence or, as I shall sometimes describe it, her 'at-home-ness' in her situation.

(Cordner 2003: 138)

Despite Cordner's reply, Davis still has one very strong argument in his arsenal. Surely the only really essential requirement for something to be gracious is that it looks gracious to us. There is no such thing as 'fool's grace': something that looks like grace but is not (2001: 92), comparable to fool's gold (iron pyrite) that looks like gold but is not. If it looks gracious to us, then it is gracious; and if it doesn't, it isn't. We ought, therefore, to accept grace as a superficial and unanalysable feature of certain movements and not others.

This doesn't end the matter, however. In the first place, if Davis is right, then grace is not so much a quality of bodily movement as a response that we observers have to it. And is it right to suggest that grace really is superficial and simple? Is there no reason why we think that some movements are graceful and others are not? And isn't there some difference between us finding some 'pleasing appearances' to be appearances of grace and other pleasing appearances to be of speed or power? In other words, there are a number of pleasing appearances that we are able to see but only some of them would we describe as graceful appearances. Others we would not. Is there some reason for this or is it simply a primitive brute fact? To answer these questions we need to probe a bit deeper into the more general question of aesthetics.

A realist position might take it that there are objective aesthetic properties or values residing in the things themselves, awaiting our apprehension of them but able to exist without us. It is hard to see how this view could be defended, however, for our responses play no part in the account. Instead the approach recommended here would take Hume's view as its starting point:

Beauty is no quality in things themselves: it exists merely in the mind which contemplates them; and each mind perceives a different beauty. One person may even perceive deformity, where another is sensible of beauty; and every individual ought to acquiesce in his own sentiment, without pretending to regulate those of others. To see the real beauty, or real deformity, is as fruitless an inquiry, as to pretend to ascertain the real sweet or real bitter. According to the disposition of the organs, the same object may be both sweet and bitter; and the proverb has justly determined it to be fruitless to dispute concerning tastes. It is very natural, and even quite necessary, to extend this axiom to mental, as well as bodily taste; and thus common sense, which is so often at variance with philosophy, especially with the sceptical kind, is found, in one instance at least, to agree in pronouncing the same decision.

(Hume 1741–2: 230)

There is something that is right in Hume's statement and something that is wrong. There are no aesthetic properties as such, in the kind of objective, mind-independent sense mentioned above. The universe cares not for one property more than any other. Davis is right, therefore, to concentrate on the pleasant appearance to us. And Hume also seems right to say that beauty can be found wherever we think we find it. One person may see mess or waste where another sees beauty, in the autumn leaves that clutter the ground, for instance. What we might want to say, therefore, is that we shouldn't concentrate on aesthetic properties as being in the things themselves but, rather, there being an aesthetic way of seeing something. Best (1974) correctly says that we should think of the aesthetic as a way of looking: one can regard the aesthetic 'as a way of perceiving an object or activity' (1974: 197). And anything can be looked at in such a way, regardless of its objective properties: 'one can look at any object or activity from the aesthetic point of view' (1974: 197). How one looks at something from the aesthetic point of view is a question to which we will return in Chapter 7.

Nevertheless, there is some degree of agreement among people as to what is beautiful and what is not. This agreement is not total and we love to discuss and dispute opinions about such matters. But in the case of grace, for instance, we may find that there is a rough consensus as to which athletes are graceful and which are not, even though this consensus is not total. In the quoted passage from Hume, he seems to be suggesting there is something subjective, almost arbitrary, about aesthetic judgements, such that further discussion between those who disagree is pointless. But if that were the case, we could never have meaningful disagreement over our aesthetic judgements. To call something beautiful would just mean that it pleases the speaker: and no one is in a position to deny such a subjective report. Given that we do argue over questions of taste, we must have some other theory of aesthetic judgement in mind: something that is in between pure objectivism and pure subjectivism.

The answer ventured is to be found in another Humean theme. His chief work was called *A Treatise of Human Nature* (Hume 1739–40). Many of the judgements we make have no purely rational basis, such as causal and inductive inferences, but are in part determined by the customs and habits of human nature. We could say the same of aesthetic judgements. There needs to be something in the world about which we make such judgements, however. In the current case, the judgements are about the properties we find instanced in sport. But the judgement of taste is also partly determined by human nature. We have dispositions to react to certain properties of the world as pleasurable. There can be differences in aesthetic judgement among people looking at the same object, but this is because different people are differently disposed. Human nature is not entirely uniform. But nor is it completely arbitrary. Just as most of us would tend to make the same kinds of inductive inferences in the same kinds of circumstance, so most of us will tend to make the same aesthetic judgements about the same kinds of object. The picture this gives us is that the aesthetic appearance is a mutual manifestation (see Martin 2008) created by the properties of things and our dispositions towards aesthetic judgement working together. Thus, while we find it hard to accept that there are aesthetic properties existing mind-independently in the world, we would also not want to accept that the aesthetic judgement is merely a subjective report. One is not after all pleased by one's aesthetic judgement: rather, one is pleased by the thing in the world about which one is judging. The meaningful disagreement, therefore, is over which properties in the world are disposed, along with our natural inclinations, to result in aesthetic pleasure. And if another person does not feel the same as us, we seek to persuade them that there is something wrong, unrefined or non-standard about their natural aesthetic sensibilities. We can even persuade someone to cultivate and refine their taste.

Returning to the issue of grace, we can see that some of the questions we asked of Davis's theory can now be answered. There is good reason why we tend to judge similar athletes or physical movements as graceful and tend to judge others as not. There is some explanation of why some aesthetic judgements concern grace specifically, rather than some other aesthetic category. We can say that there are specific properties that tend to solicit these aesthetic judgements within us. And, once we allow that, the possibility is open of explaining further what we mean by grace. Although the appearance is the key, and Davis is right that there is no such thing as 'fool's grace', we can also say a bit more on what it is about the features that makes it specifically a graceful appearance. We could analyse further and find, for instance, that graceful movements should be fluid rather than jerky, or that a graceful pose must exhibit balance, equilibrium, poise and effortlessness. Such features – and this is a far from complete list – allow us to distinguish grace from the other athletic aesthetic categories such as speed, power, vibrancy and so on.

We can now sum up some of our findings on aesthetics in sport. Sport is, I conclude, a legitimate arena in which to find aesthetic values. Although competition and winning are the goals, the manner of achieving the goal often encourages athletic virtues that require physical excellence of technique or fitness. In displaying such excellences, the human body is often pushed to extremes that manifest aesthetic values of various categories. We noted that different sports will promote different excellences and we thus allowed for a position that could be called aesthetic pluralism. We noted that some aesthetic values are to be found simply in the concrete bodily movements of the competitors while others were to be found at abstract, higher levels. We considered an even more abstract aesthetic notion: whether time limitation was an aesthetic flaw or strength. We then looked closely at the notion of grace, which is an aesthetic category particularly prominent in the aesthetics of sport. We saw that there are at least three competing theories of grace: that it consists in efficiency and economy, that it consists in unity of being in the performance, and that it is a mere appearance that cannot be analysed any further. This led us into the general question of what our aesthetic stance should be. There is an aesthetic way of seeing, which will be considered in a later chapter. But once we look in an aesthetic way, we note that there tends to be some agreement on matters of aesthetic judgement and this suggests there must be some further explanation of the consensus. The explanation was offered, which is an attempt to reconcile the subjective and objective components: we have natural dispositions to respond to types of properties or features of the world with particular types of aesthetic judgement. There are properties within human movement or within a still human form that tend to solicit judgements of grace within us. This same type of account, it is ventured, could be extended to the aesthetic judgements of other categories.

We may indeed watch sport, therefore, for the aesthetic pleasure it affords. In this respect, the reasons we watch sport may just as well serve as reasons we consume art. Sport and art are thus brought closer together. The comparison and contrast should not end there, however. We will see that there are a number of complex ways in which sport and art relate, and we will start to consider these in the next chapter.

4 What is art?

We have found that sport is a worthy area for aesthetic enjoyment. The question naturally arises of how sport relates to art, another area of aesthetic experience. We can only consider this issue seriously if we have an understanding of what art is. We examine the question here, and it will lead us to a conclusion that sport is not art. Such will be the similarities, however, that it is still a reasonable claim that sport could have been art, and it will be explained how in due course. The account of art may be more detailed here than is expected of a book in philosophy of sport, but it is hard to see how one could consider the credentials of sport as art unless one has a theory or definition of art with which to work.

I will be defending an institutional theory of art. If the institutional theory is correct then it becomes very clear to us that sport is not art because sport has not been deemed art by the institutions of the artworld. We need not, then, argue the details of whether the aesthetic content of sport is equal to that of the arts, or whether it has adequate expressive power to match the arts. While such factors can carry aesthetic significance, they are not, in the institutional theory, relevant to whether something is an art. If they were, our decision over whether sport is art would be much more difficult than it is. The truth of the institutional theory in that respect makes our job much easier.

One motivation for an institutional theory of art is taken from Danto's so-called paradox. Danto uses Warhol's Brillo box example to motivate the intuition that two artefacts A and B could be indistinguishable though one of them is art, or a work of art, and the other is not (Danto 1964: 581; see also Wieand 1994). Warhol's work consisted of a stack of boxes, made of wood and printed on the outside, that were superficially indistinguishable from the 'real' Brillo boxes that were to be found in any grocery store at the time. Of course, on closer inspection, Warhol's Brillo boxes were indeed distinguishable from the cardboard, mass manufactured originals. They were made of wood, they were heavier and bigger than the originals, and so on. But these are relatively minor considerations, as Danto's case could clearly in principle be satisfied. Consider Carl Andre's *Equivalent VIII* piece, which was bought by the Tate Gallery in London in 1972. This sculpture is more popularly known as *The Bricks* because it is a pile of 120 regular bricks, arranged in two layers in a rectangular shape. This raises the possibility that, at the same time, outside the Tate, a builder could have left an indistinguishable pile of bricks. *Equivalent VIII* is a work of art, but the builder's indistinguishable pile is nevertheless not. How can we explain this? What theory of art could allow what Danto's so-called paradox claims, and does so apparently truly?

There are, of course, two ways of denying Danto's intuition. One would be to claim that the builder's pile of bricks is just as much art as Andre's pile. This seems highly implausible unless one is willing to accept that the concept of art is an extremely broad one that almost reaches the point of vacuity. People do sometimes speak of things being works of art in a broad sense – a wall that a builder builds, for example – but it seems this should not always be taken too seriously as it would effectively exclude nothing from the realm of art. The other option is to deny that Andre's exhibit is a work of art. Eaton (2004: 70–1) insists, for instance, that purely conceptual art is not art at all but something else, such as philosophy or politics. If *Equivalent VIII* is a purely conceptual piece, then perhaps neither it nor the builder's bricks are art. Eaton sees artistic objects as a sub-class of aesthetic objects, however, and this aesthetic theory is an account we will, in due course, reject. With the two options rejected – that A and B are both art, and that neither are art – it seems we have to explain how an object can be a work of art while one that is indistinguishable is not. The most plausible general explanation, it seems, must accept what Danto said: 'To see something as art requires something the eye cannot descry – an atmosphere of artistic theory, a knowledge of history of art: an artworld' (Danto 1964: 580). Or, as Dickie (1974: 37) puts it, the status of a work as art must depend on some 'nonexhibited characteristic'. Effectively, this means that we should opt for a relational theory. Objects A and B may be intrinsically indistinguishable but they may differ relationally. One may bear an appropriate relation to the art-world that the other does not. The context in which the two objects are situated could make all the difference.

The institutional theory provides this but it also does another job. It explains how there can be any unity to the concept of art, given its modern development in which it seems that almost anything goes. The innovations in modern and con-temporary art can leave one with a strong attraction towards anti-essentialism in which there is no one thing in common to all works of art: there are no necessary and sufficient conditions for the concept. Weitz (1956) developed this view and opted for a Wittgensteinian family resemblance account of art. This emphasised the wide variety in the things that count as art: novels, tragedy, painting, drama, dance, music, found objects, performance, poetry, happenings, Dadaism and so on. One need only make a cursory inspection of the Tate Modern to see how wide this variety is.

The problem with the notion of family resemblance, however, is that resem-blance cannot explain the unity of a concept (Pompa 1967; and in specific response to Weitz, see Davies 2005: 229). Resemblance is far too weak given that some resemblance can be found between any two objects. A raven and a writing desk, for instance, both have legs. Throwing a ball against a wall and catching it (which is not a sport but, rather, play) resembles fielding in cricket (which is a sport) more than cricket resembles Formula 1 motor racing (which is also a sport). Hence we can have two sports that resemble each other less than a sport resembles a non-sport. Something more is needed, therefore: an account of what makes a group of resembling things be of the same family. Wittgenstein's (1953: §67) bare statement of the idea of family resemblance cannot tell us this. The institutional theory can accept that there is a wide variety of things that count as art but also tells us what unifies all these things under the single concept.

Let us then look directly at the institutional theory. Following on from Danto's paradox, Dickie was the main proponent of the theory and offered various, progressively more sophisticated versions of it (Dickie 1969, 1974, 1984). The theory is not now as popular as it was but, as Yanal (1998) states, the theory has never been refuted and it has more recent adherents, such as Davies (1991).

The basic idea of an institutional theory of art is that art is a status bestowed on certain kinds of practice or artefact by a group of social institutions. These institutions will be the main players in the so-called artworld and will consist of various groupings: the galleries, the agents, the critics, the artists themselves, the collectors, those who attend galleries to enjoy the exhibits, the media and so on. These institutions can be more or less formally constituted. The artists themselves may be only an informal institution, for instance, in a degree of competition and rarely speaking with one voice. Even if there is an artists' guild, they may not all belong to it or agree with it. At the other end of the spectrum, there could be an arts funding council that is strongly formal in its constitution as it may be an organ of the state. Another factor that can be more or less formal is the bestowal itself of the status of art. If a powerful gallery exhibits a piece then it is a strong endorsement of its status as art. But it may yet be contested. The status of *Equivalent VIII* as art was contested in the media, for example. Similarly, gaining funding from a government arts funding council would also be a strong endorsement of artistic status. The institutional theory leaves open the possibility of contested cases, however, and this seems a virtue of the theory. The artistic status of at least some works clearly is contested and a theory of art ought to be able to explain how and why that is so. The institutional theory allows that there are competing institutions with a degree of autonomous function that may make different judgements and thus the status of an individual work may be disputed. Such status becomes a social and sometimes political matter. It thus makes it difficult for one person acting alone to confer the status of art upon one of their works, contrary to one of Dickie's (1974: 38) claims about the theory. Even if an established artist throws some litter in the high street and claims that it is art, their action does not automatically have that status unless endorsed by enough of the other institutions. Art is thus an irreducibly social phenomenon and, just as one person cannot have their own private language (Wittgenstein 1953: §269ff.), one person acting alone cannot bestow, nor prevent the bestowal of, the status of art.

There remain a number of further details to be explained but we have now seen enough to understand Dickie's second version of the institutional theory – the first to be set out in detail – which offers us the following definition:

> A work of art in the classificatory sense is (1) an artefact (2) a set of the aspects of which has had conferred upon it the status of candidate for appreciation by some person or persons acting on behalf of a certain social institution (the artworld).
>
> (Dickie 1974: 34)

Returning to *Equivalent VIII*, we can now see in the light of this theory why it is a work of art. The status is bestowed on it by the facts that it has been exhibited in an influential gallery, it was made by a member of the artworld (an artist), it was sold by an agent to the gallery for exhibition, it was discussed by the critics, and so on. The indistinguishable pile of bricks outside the Tate has had none of this history. Those bricks were bought by a builder who needed to construct a wall, let us assume.

Dickie's artefactuality condition (Dickie 1974: 27) raises some issues. It seems intended initially to exclude from the realm of art certain natural objects, such as a leaf of a tree, which can be a beautiful object but not art. A work of art has, instead, to be created by a human being. (On the institutional theory, it is at least logically possible that a chimpanzee could create art but it would have to do so self-consciously, intentionally participating in a practice.) There is a threat to this from the genre of art that consists in found objects, however. An artist may find various leaves on the ground and assemble them in a certain way. But there is still human agency involved in selecting and arranging these natural objects, offering them to a gallery and so on. The bigger issue from a philosophy of sport perspective, however, is what counts as an artefact. Is it just a physical object, such as a painting or a sculpture? This would seem to exclude sport immediately from the realm of art because sport produces no artefact in this sense. But it is clear that Dickie has a much broader notion of artefact because one of the core arts he discusses frequently is theatre (Dickie 1974: ch. 8, for instance). Here, the work of art is the play, but this cannot be an object in the same way a painting is. The painted object is a single, unique, particular thing. The play is a sequence of words to be spoken by actors, sometimes together with stage directions. A printed version of it seems the only object that is a physical manifestation of the play, but it is certainly not a unique object, as the painting is, because there will usually be multiple copies of the play. And could this anyway really purport *to be* the play rather than just a printed token of it? A play need not even be constituted by a performance of it. It seems possible, for instance, that there be a play that has never yet been performed. If a play is an artefact, it seems a relatively ethereal one for which one must have a very inclusive sense of artefact. It is an artefact in the sense that it is a deliberate creation even though it is not a physical object. With such an inclusive sense, there seems no especial reason why a particular game of baseball, for instance, should be excluded from the classification. The game is an event or series of events, but it is staged deliberately so that a competition can ensue for the enjoyment of spectators. The artefacts in sporting cases are thus events rather than objects.

Dickie's second condition is the institutional one and clearly the more complex of the two. It explains the relational element of the theory. To be art, the artefact must bear the right sort of relation to the artworld. I have tried to spell out this notion of an artworld in institutional terms. The way Dickie does so differs slightly from my formulation above (Dickie 1974: 31). A third attempt to spell out the institutional theory is also made by Dickie (1984), offering more detail. This time, he has a five-fold account. The social character of art is exhibited in Dickie's later theory like so (summarised in Davies 2005: 230):

1   An artist is a person who participates with understanding in the making of a work of art.
2   A work of art is an artefact of a kind created to be presented to the artworld public.
3   A public is a set of persons, members of which are prepared to understand an object that is presented to them.
4   An artworld is the totality of all artworld systems.
5   An artworld system is a framework for the presentation of a work of art by an artist to an artworld public.

It is explicitly acknowledged that there is circularity in this account, which is a matter to which we will return below. What it is to be an artist cannot be understood apart from the notion of an artworld, but an artworld also cannot be understood independently of the notion of the artist. We have a circle of interdependent concepts, as Dickie advertises in calling his book *The Art Circle*.

I have offered no direct argument in favour of an institutional theory. What counts for it is that it is able to explain the data of what we know about art better than the alternatives. There are many other theories of art available (see Davies 1991) but all face counter-examples: ruling out cases that should count as art or including cases that shouldn't.

One of the first theories was the *imitation* or *representation theory*, attributed to Plato in the *Republic*. This is the idea that in art we are merely trying to represent some object or scene where the more accurate the representation then the better the work of art. But, as Dickie (1974: 19) points out, this has been an inadequate conception since at least the mid-nineteenth century and the rise of modern art. Some art still has a mimetic function but clearly not all does. It is worth noting, however, that the imitation theory would, like the institutional theory, be a relational account. It would not be the intrinsic properties of a piece that determined whether it was art but the relations it bears to another thing: the object or scene to be represented. Representation is a relational notion.

A modern response is to say that art is not about representation but about *expression*. Tolstoy (1896) told us that art was about transmission of feelings and Croce (1920) that it was about intuitive expression. To this, we might want to add that it could be an idea or concept that is expressed, rather than just an emotion. This would also be a relational theory but an implausible one. It would mean that a piece was not art unless it expressed or transmitted such a feeling or idea. This could exclude much representational art, which might be attempting to do no such thing, but also there can be modern, non-representational art in which there is no intention of expression. An abstract artist may instead be playing with shapes and colours, seeking just a pleasing image.

The production of aesthetic pleasure is closely connected with the consumption of art, which raises the prospect of *aesthetic theories* of art. An aesthetic theory would have at its core the idea that that something is art only if it exhibits the correct aesthetic properties. There are a number of objections that can be brought against aesthetic theories, however. One is the question of whether they would automatically rule that there is no bad art. Presumably, bad art would be art that didn't exhibit the right aesthetic properties. But as the correct properties are part of this definition of art, such works would not count as art as all (Dickie 1974: 40). We do not, however, think of the notion of bad art as self-contradictory. Indeed we all too often judge works to be bad art. A theory of art needs more than just to state why something is art but also what makes something good or bad art. A second objection is that there are forms of modern and conceptual art in which appropriate aesthetic properties are not instantiated. The aim of such works is not to exemplify beauty but, perhaps, to make a statement. In answer to this, Eaton (2004: 71) defends the view that the artistic must be a sub-class of the aesthetic. Her brave step has already been noted of insisting that purely conceptual art is not art at all (2004: 70–1). It is not clear that many would want to follow this judgement. A third objection to an aesthetic theory is that it would rule objects to be of the same aesthetic value if they were indistinguishable observationally. That may seem like no bad thing, but we will see in a later chapter that there are plausible cases in which the morality behind a work of art can affect its aesthetic value. Further discussion of this point will be deferred until Chapter 8.

Two other theories might be classified as aesthetic. In *functionalism* (Beardsley 1958, 1982; Zangwill 1995) art is designed to serve a purpose: for example to provide a pleasurable aesthetic experience. Kant's version of the aesthetic theory was *formalism* (Kant 1790; see also Bell 1914), in which it is *forms* that produce aesthetic pleasure. But Kant also saw a separation of aesthetics and art, noting that much that gives us aesthetic pleasure is not art: none of a sunset, a birdsong or a honeycomb, for instance, are art (Kant 1790: §43). This shows us at the very least that something more is needed than aesthetic properties for something to be art. But it also raises the prospect that we may go beyond Kant and Eaton and seek an even bigger divorce of art from the aesthetic. Some contemporary art may not look to realise any aesthetic properties or positive aesthetic values at all. The production of beauty is no longer seen as the only function of art. Commentary on a political situation or philosophical idea may be seen as a legitimate role for art whether or not it does so beautifully. The aesthetic could be incidental to art, as we will see in Chapter 5.

Susceptibility to counter-example is one motivation of the *open concept theory*, one version of which is the family resemblance view of Weitz (1956). We saw that the institutional theory was in part a response to this: acknowledging that there is no single property in common to all works of art, and thus anti-essentialist in that respect, but instead offering a relational account. However, there is an alternative theory of what this relation stands in, to be found in Danto's (1973) *historical theory* of art. The historical theory claims that what makes something art is how it is related to a certain historical evolution, especially its forebears. The pile of bricks that is *Equivalent VIII* is art because it follows a historical line involving other modern art sculptures. Had Rembrandt suddenly produced it in 1660, it would not have been art because the work would have been discontinuous with the prior history of art. Carroll (1988) has a variant on the historical theory, saying that what counts is that a narrative story can be told of how one got to the present work from the previous antecedent works. And there is no reason then why past art works could not be brought into the narrative: that is, the reason object F could be a work of art is because it was an antecedent to work G, which clearly is art, even though F preceded G.

I think that a defensible institutional theory of art needs to be supplemented with a historical dimension, so I do not have major objections to lodge against the historical theory. It does, however, have the consequence that there could not have been a first work of art because it would have had no historical forebears to which it could hold the correct relation (Davies 2005: 232). And what this shows is that it does not really provide a definition of art, even if it is a theory of art. If we said that a number was something that followed in an ordered sequence from a prior number then we would have a similar problem. How does one first get a grasp on what is a number? And this is the job I claim, in the case of art, that is provided by the institutional theory.

Many objections have been raised against the institutional theory, however. Some of them are more serious than others. I will take them in turn and indicate how I think an upholder of the institutional theory should answer.

Beardsley (1976) questioned whether we can base the artistic status of an artefact on institutions whose practices and limits are so little understood. We have a good idea of whether something is art, for instance, though we have relatively little idea of the institutions that supposedly awarded that status, and how or when they did so. Dickie's (1984) later work was partly an attempt to spell out more clearly what the mechanisms of the artworld were. But even so, this kind of criticism has only limited strength. There are many things I can know with some certainty even though I have limited knowledge of the mechanisms that generated them. I can know that something is a law of the country, for instance, with greater certainty than I know the constitutional procedures and bodies that generated it. There seems no reason, then, why the institutions of art could not have (eventually) deemed Duchamp's *Fountain* art, and I know that it is art, even though I do not know all the institutional bodies and processes that made it so.

There are two related objections that concern 'lonely' artists. The objections are similar in that they both purport to show that there can be art without there being institutions of art. The first objection is based on a Robinson Crusoe case. This is a man who is washed up on an uninhabited desert island (or perhaps he is left there as an abandoned and yet to be educated infant). He nevertheless passes his time painting and sculpting. It seems that he is creating art even though, on his island, there are no institutions that can deem his work to have the status of art. The second case concerns ancient cave paintings such as those found at Chauvet-Pont-d'Arc, which are thought to be in the region of 25,000–30,000 years old. Weren't cave paintings works of art? Yet how could they be so prior to the establishment of art institutions?

The institutional theory should rule that our Robinson Crusoe is producing art. He is deliberately engaging in an activity – producing painted images and sculpted objects – that has had the status of art bestowed upon it by the institutions of art. The key move for the institutional theory is to allow that the status of art is bestowed directly onto types of object and practice rather than each individual token of that type. It need not be, and it is implausible to suppose, that the institutions bestow the status of art on each individual piece. An amateur painter could not be producing art, if that were the case, if they merely hung their paintings in their own garden shed. But if the institutions endorse certain types of practice, such as painting in general, then that status automatically transfers to each token of the type, irrespective of whether that individual piece has been seen by anyone other than the creator. This follows from the theory of universals in which something that is true of the type must also be true of all its tokens because there is a strict identity that runs through every instance of a type (Armstrong 1989). At times, Dickie seems to suggest that it is individual works upon which the status of art is bestowed, such as in his first definition quoted above (Dickie 1974: 34). The Robinson Crusoe case shows why this would be a mistake.

In relation to cave art, the institutional theorist need not deny that people have always engaged in certain forms of activity, such as painting, regardless of whether it had the status of art bestowed upon it. The status of art was bestowed much later. Shiner (2001) claims, for instance, that there was no concept of art before the eighteenth century in Europe. Once the concept of art was available, and was being bestowed, there is no reason why we cannot apply that status retrospectively. So, yes, the cavemen or cavewomen of Chauvet were producing art even though they did not understand their practices in those terms.

How can there be bad art according to the institutional theory? Doesn't 'anything go' as long as it is deemed art by the institutions? We saw above that there was reason to criticise an aesthetic theory of art if it seemed to make the notion of bad art self-contradictory. But an institutional theory, properly developed, need not contain this defect. Unfortunately, this requires again that we dissent once again from Dickie's version of the theory. What makes something an x need not be the same as what makes something *a good* x. What makes something a telephone, for instance, is that it is a device that can receive and send sounds such that a conversation is possible over distance. But what makes something a good phone can be other factors: design, weight, mobility, the number and variety of its other functions and applications, memory size, cost of purchase and so on. And it may be a balance between various such factors that is the key. Likewise, what makes something a work of art can be that it is of a kind that has had such a status bestowed upon it by the institutions. But what makes it a good work of art is not how well the institutions bestowed such a status, which would be absurd, but whether it has aesthetic value, whether it expresses an interesting idea or emotion, whether it imitates successfully, and so on, or some such combination of the above (Young 2001 has an account of such evaluations made within the framework of an institutional theory). This kind of response would be shunned by Dickie, however, who goes to lengths to deny the significance of aesthetic properties and aesthetic appreciation in the theory of art (Dickie 1974: chs 4–8). There seems no reason to do so, however, given the Kantian separation of art and aesthetics. There could be aesthetic properties of art, and aesthetic ways of seeing art, as will argued in Chapter 7, without that being constitutive of what makes something art. In that case, despite Dickie's protests, we can defend the claim that there is an aesthetic way of seeing because that in no way threatens an institutional theory of art.

Wollheim (1987) gives us a more serious objection, which he presents in the form of a dilemma. When the status of art is bestowed by the institutions on a piece, then there is either a reason for the institutions doing so or there is not. If there is not, then the institutions and art itself are left in irrationality. But if there is a reason for bestowal, doesn't that suggest some prior essence of art, other than institutional, that the institutions are using as their guide? This is a serious problem because it suggests that having an institutional basis is insufficient for defining something as art because there must be some prior notion of art upon which the artworld rests. Dickie's admission of circularity in the notion of art seems to concede this. Another way of looking at the problem is to consider how the institutions of art differ, for instance, from the institutions of sport. They could be structurally isomorphic, for all we know. And that would then suggest that the difference can only reside in the fact that one set of institutions deals with the world of art and the other with the world of sport. But then doesn't that tell us that there must be a prior notion of art (and of sport) onto which the institutions latch?

The best way for the institutional theorist to answer this is to appeal to the historical aspects of the relevant practices. I do not see that this compromises the institutional theory as I see no reason why it is only the present institutions that are to be considered. Such institutions have themselves been subject to a historical evolution. The institutions of art are those that developed around certain forms of practice, such as painting and sculpture. These would then be treated as the core or paradigm cases from which the contemporary notion of art developed. But then there would be new types of practice, sometimes performed by existing artists, which would be candidates for the status of art. If the institutions accepted those practices, then they expanded their sphere. And their decisions whether to bestow the status of art on a practice could well have rested on such pragmatic matters as how closely the candidate resembles the practices in the existing sphere of art, around which the institutions are built. What makes the institutions of art different from the institutions of sport is, then, that one set grew around practices such as painting and sculpture, and expanded from there, and another set of institutions grew from practices such as running, jumping, swimming and playing with a ball. To say this is not to concede any essence of art other than the social one provided by the institutional theory of art.

For a book on the philosophy of sport, this excursion into the theory of art is now long enough. One major reason for watching sport is the aesthetic experience it provides. That is bound to raise the question of how sport relates to art, an area that can also provide us with aesthetic experience. Is sport then art? I said at the outset of this chapter that the answer to that question depended on what we took art to be, so the subsequent artistic theorising has been unavoidable.

Given that the institutional theory of art has proved the most attractive, then we are presented with an answer to our question. It is very clear that the status of art has not been bestowed upon the practice of sport. But for a philosopher, the matter will not rest there. Might the status of art be bestowed upon sport at some future date? It seems that there is no reason in principle why it could not be. Given the institutional theory's anti-essentialist view of art, then logically anything at some future point could fall within its sphere. But before we judge the matter too hastily, it is necessary that we look further into the relationship between sport and art, for there are alleged to be some significant differences.

5 The principal aim

One reason to watch sport is because it gives us aesthetic pleasure. There is a release to be found in the contemplation of aesthetic value. We will now simplify, somewhat, and refer to this positive aesthetic value as beauty for short. Aesthetic value contains a host of other categories, but it will be easier if we call positive aesthetic value beauty and negative aesthetic value ugliness. The release that aesthetic completion gives us is similar to that which we gain when we contemplate art, as Schopenhauer (1818, 1851) claimed. Sport and art can serve very similar functions, therefore. But does that mean that they are more or less the same? What, if anything, is the division between them? Is it only that they have evolved distinct institutions? We have already seen an argument that beauty alone is not enough to make something art. Sunsets, animals and mountains can all be beautiful without being art. The evident aesthetic value of watching sport does not, therefore, mean automatically that sport is art, nor even the weaker claim that sport is art-like.

The case has been made, however, that there is a decisive difference between art and sport in respect of its relation to aesthetic value (Elliott 1974; Best 1978). While beauty is certainly to be found in sport, can we not see that it is merely incidental? It is a kind of by-product of good sport, but it is not the goal for which it aims. In sport, the aim is to win; it is not to be beautiful. Similarly, the sports fan wants to see a win, at least the partisan does, not to see beauty. It is alleged that there is a contrast with the arts here. The primary aim in art is to produce beauty, by which I mean something with positive aesthetic value. This is intrinsic to the practice of art. The intrinsic aim or goal of sport is winning.

To illustrate this, we can consider how it is for the spectator and the player alike. The player creates beauty as they play and they may be conscious of the fact that they are doing so. But their direct aim is not to create such beauty. Their aim is to win, even if they know that winning could happen to be beautiful. It is of course possible to create beauty without that being one's aim. One may have a baby because of a biological urge or because one wants to have a carer in later life. But in so doing one creates something beautiful in the form of a newborn baby. One has deliberately created something that is beautiful but one did not create it because it was beautiful. This is the position of the sports player, one might contend. Even if they produce beauty in their contests, they do not do so for the reason that it will be beautiful.

To see why it can be claimed that beauty is not the athlete's aim, we need only consider what would be more important to the competitor. The athlete would, in virtually every case, prefer to win ugly than to lose pretty. In some sports, there are effective negative strategies that can stifle a game. Consider a snooker player who can play good safety shots or a football team that packs the midfield to outweigh a more inventive team's creativity. These strategies can sometimes be the key to victory but it does not tend towards a beautiful victory. A more exciting game of snooker could involve a player going for his pots and taking risks, building a carefree flowing break. But a stifling safety game can be the winner. Another example is the defensive style of football associated with the Italian national team, for example, which has brought them notable World Cup success. By defending deep and absorbing pressure, the Italians left lots of free space in the opposition half which set up the possibility of the swift and lethal counter-attack. But the spectator had to endure prolonged spells of negative defensive work before the rare moment of excitement.

Just as the players prefer an ugly win to a beautiful defeat, so do the fans watching. The partisan supporter would far prefer to see a poor game that ends in a 1–0 win than a dramatic end-to-end, to-and-fro game that their side loses 3–4. These two games, let us imagine, cost the same to watch and are alike in all the surrounding factors, yet the supporter is likely to feel far less satisfied with the 3–4 defeat than the 1–0 win. They may concede that their winning goal was an ugly one. Let us suppose it was a clumsy own goal from the opposition. That would also matter little to the fan. They may prefer a pretty goal to a clumsy one but each goal counts exactly the same, namely one. Any beauty there is to be found is purely optional. Three ugly goals always beat two pretty ones. We granted in Chapter 3 that victory itself could enhance the aesthetic experience, but should we allow that it always outweighs every other aesthetic factor? Fortunately, we do not need to answer this question here as the line of argument developed so far is eventually to be rejected.

There is a further and allegedly stronger argument for the separation of beauty from the goal of sport. As Aspin (1974: 128–9) argues, to perceive aesthetically is to perceive something for its own sake. It cannot be 'for' anything. So it cannot be that being beautiful is useful to sport. It shouldn't have a use at all. So it is, therefore, quite right that a beautiful goal shouldn't count any more than an ugly one. We have some preliminary reasons to affirm such a consideration. To consider something aesthetically is to see it for its own intrinsic value rather than its value for something else. One has to enjoy something simply for what it is. But does this really disprove that we want to see goals and wins because they are beautiful? Does it really show that the principal aim of sport is not beauty?

We will eventually offer some arguments against this way of distinguishing art and sport, but first let us state the position we will be rejecting. The aforementioned considerations prompt the thought that in watching sport we are not in the same position as art appreciators. We are not watching sport for the aesthetic qualities of the event; we are looking for the win. Elliott defends this line. Aesthetics is not the primary concern. Indeed, if a player were to take aesthetics as his or her primary concern, it would be thought that he or she was ceasing to play sport and instead perhaps engaging in the activity of art. As Elliott puts it: 'If a cricketer is seen to be concerned about the elegance of his strokes he is thought to be behaving inappropriately' (Elliott 1974: 111). Suppose, then, that a ski jumper at the top of a hill decides that he is not going to aim for distance in the jump but, while he is flying through the air, to instead trace out a number of forms with his body such that he is, as it were, dancing through the air. He aims to look appealing and please the crowd aesthetically without any regard of his distance or winning the competition. He has then effectively opted out of the sport. He should still be regarded as having opted out even if by some perverse fluke he ends up recording the greatest distance of the competition. Hence Elliott claims:

> The goddess of sport is not Beauty but Victory, a jealous goddess who demands an absolute homage. Every act performed by the player or athlete must be for the sake of victory, without so much as a side-glance in the direction of beauty.
>
> (Elliott 1974: 111)

Best (1974 and 1978: ch. 7) is in agreement with this line. The aesthetic is incidental in sport, never the main purpose. There is an obvious contention, however. Best acknowledges, as one surely must, that at least some sports do seem to have the attainment of aesthetic values as their chief goal. There are certain aesthetic sports – Kupfer's (1983) qualitative sports – for instance, such as diving, gymnastics and ice dance, in which marks are awarded on the basis of an explicitly aesthetic assessment. But, even here, Best is keen to emphasise that there is still a further aim that must be achieved, such as leaping into the pool, clearing the vault in gymnastics, and performing a number of required and optional elements in ice dance. One must achieve these technical goals first, even though one then receives a mark for how well one did so. It is not as if there is a sport in which one just aims 'to be beautiful', without any further limitations or requirements. Even in ice dance, there are certain obstacles put in one's way and rules to be obeyed. One, of course, has to move around specifically on ice, wearing skates, and perform a number of recognised manoeuvres. The aesthetic sports can certainly be distinguished from the merely purposive ones, such as high jump where one wins simply by clearing the highest bar irrespective of grace and beauty, but even the aesthetic sports have a prior non-aesthetic aim.

The view of Elliott and Best is, therefore, that in sport the aim is scoring or winning, with any aesthetic value an additional and secondary element. And even for the aesthetically minded spectator, the aim for victory will always be foremost in the mind. A personal experience brought this home to me. I once attended the first leg of a European football tie between Paris St Germain and Ujpest TE. On the Paris side was the Brazilian player Ronaldinho, still relatively early in his career. With the game still alive, and a second leg to come, he spurned a number of chances to play a dangerous pass and instead preferred to juggle the ball and perform a number of other tricks. This was very frustrating to watch even though in another context, outside of a game, it would have been a delight. It seemed as if Ronaldinho's primary goal was not for his team to score and to that extent he had stopped playing football. One immediately suspected some further motive on his part: trying to impress and stand out individually, looking for a big-money transfer out of Paris or, to interpret it more generously, trying to be more artistic than sporting.

The argument thus far looks a strong one. Sport never could be art because, while it may involve beauty, such beauty is always incidental or a by-product. Similarly, watching sport cannot be likened to viewing art because the spectators' interests are always in winning rather than beauty. Even the purist, who wants to see beauty, wants to see it in the context of competition and winning being the principal aim. Nevertheless, I am now going to argue that this is not an entirely conclusive argument and that the positions of the sports fan and the consumer of art are not so different after all. I will argue that, just as one may liken beauty in sport to a by-product, so one could in the case of art. Furthermore, if we stand back and look at sports in more general terms (and the same with the arts), one could indeed make a case for saying that they do ultimately answer to our aesthetic sensibilities. We can square these two criticisms, which seemingly pull in opposite directions, if we make play of what Roberts (1986) calls *the Best equivocation*.

First, let us consider how works of art relate to beauty, understood in our sense of any positive aesthetic value. Just as one looks at individual players in specific sports, and says that their principal aim is to score or win, shouldn't one look at individual artists making specific works of art? And, when we do so, wouldn't we also say that their aim is not principally to create beauty? A sculptor, for instance, is aiming to make a clay statue resembling a horse or to chisel a stone statue representing the god Neptune. A painter may be aiming to paint a picture of a certain mountain in dawn light. Another painter may be aiming to experiment in contrasting colours and opposing shapes in a largely abstract piece. A poet may aim to convey the loneliness of human existence and a novelist may be trying to create a fictionalised story based on the life of Bertrand Russell. At this specific, fine-grained level of description, none of our sample artists are aiming either directly or principally at the attainment of beauty. They are aiming to represent some very specific thing, for example, or convey some story or emotion, or to express themselves (see Keller 1974: 90). Beauty may emerge from these endeavours, or be found in them by an observer who adopts an aesthetic stance, but it emerges in a way that is arguably analogous to the emergence of beauty in sports. The sports player aims to score an ace in tennis, to swim the 100-metre front crawl as quickly as they can, or to bowl as accurate a delivery as possible in cricket. The sports fan can adopt an aesthetic attitude to any of these actions, regardless of the fact that beauty was not the player's principal aim. In both cases, and not just in sports, the beauty can be understood as a by-product of the activity (Gaskin and Masterson 1974: 149). It is hard to see how the artist could just aim to produce beauty itself without first producing some specific piece. They may be interested in something like perspective, colour, form, human anatomy and so on, and beauty is sometimes a by-product of working on these interests. We do not ask the athlete to be beautiful: we ask them to achieve some specific purpose and might be pleased if they do so beautifully. And, similarly, the artist aims for some specific achievement and might please us if they do it beautifully. Sport and art are thus in the same boat in relation to aesthetic aims.

But might it yet be objected that this analogy remains always limited because in art, even if beauty is not the primary aim, it is always *an* aim? Some sports happen to produce beauty but not all do, and there are some cases, as we have seen, where winning ugly is the target. In these cases beauty is not even a secondary aim of sport. Certainly some players can be ugly by accident and lack of grace, just as some artists might accidentally produce unattractive works, but at least the artist always aims at beauty, even if they cannot achieve it, whereas in some sports a player or team might not even aim at beauty. But this objection also fails in its intention to draw a sharp line between the arts and sport. There is no reason in principle why an artist must aim to produce beauty and, in some cases, they might even aim at its opposite. In certain forms of contemporary and conceptual art, beauty need not come into the equation. An artist may be attempting to express something or to make a statement: perhaps even a statement about art itself. Such statements may have zero aesthetic value and this may have been the intention. But there is also the possibility that intentionally a work of art has negative aesthetic value. Many films and novels are intended to be disturbing, for example. The aim may be to shock, scare or provoke thoughts rather than produce something aesthetically pleasing. An artist may be playing with and exploring our sensibilities and may aim deliberately to produce works that are repulsive or disgusting to us. The Lakeside art gallery in Nottingham once had such an exhibition full of repulsive images and titled *Ugly*. There seemed little doubt that such exhibits were indeed works of art, though this of course rests ultimately on what we take to be constitutive of art: a topic of the previous chapter. Being ugly, and being ugly intentionally, does not therefore seem automatically to exclude something from being a work of art. And if that is the case, then just as we can say that there are some examples of sport where beauty is not any kind of aim, so can we say the same of some works of art.

Neither beauty, nor any positive aesthetic value, need be an aim in art – let alone its principal aim – when we look at its particular instances. But suppose we look at both sport and art generally and in the abstract. Can their relationship to aesthetic values be differentiated at that level? Again, we think that the positions of sport and art look the same.

Art in general seems to have a primary association with aesthetics even if not each of its instances seeks to attain beauty. Maybe the idea of art has beauty at its core even if there are activities at its fringes that do not. But the problem with this is that we may say the same of sport if we are in the business of considering it generally. Kupfer has laid much groundwork for this view. Best had insisted that the aim of sport is scoring a goal, jumping highest, swimming fastest and, in

general, winning. It is easy to be seduced by such a thought. But Kupfer's interpretation casts a different light on this:

> Scoring is not the *raison d'être* of competitive sport. It was not that in virtue
> of which the sport came to exist or is engaged in. 'The play's the thing' and
> it includes scoring and winning. Since neither scoring nor winning is the
> reason or basis for competitive sport, it cannot be its purpose.
>
> (Kupfer 1983: 460)

Kupfer contrasts sporting goals with goal-directed activities such as roof building.
We build roofs because of some pre-existing need: to keep our homes dry and
warm. We can think of more or less efficient ways of satisfying that need and we
may have no particular attachment to one method or another as long as it works
effectively. But sports are very different in this regard. As Kupfer argues, it is not
as if we had some pre-existing need – of scoring goals, for instance – and had to
invent football, hockey and water polo to satisfy that need. Outside the contexts
of those sports, such goals have no significance. We would not continue scoring
the goals if those sports came to an end. The purpose of sport cannot, therefore,
be the scoring of goals, taking of wickets, jumping of hurdles and so on. In a
sense, the goal of sport is not even winning. Again, it is not obvious that we
had a winning instinct and invented sport as a way of satisfying it (maybe some
anthropologist has ventured such a theory). If we did, it will have been a pretty
poor invention, given that in sport there are at least as many losers as winners
and usually more (Skillen 1998).

In reply to Best's contention that the aim of sport is to score and win, Kupfer
tells us: 'People confuse two ways in which purposes relate to activities: as the
goal of and as a goal within an activity' (Kupfer 1983: 461). The point of sport –
why it was invented – is not scoring, even if that is the aim within some sports.
Elliott's goddess of victory reigns only within the sports. The primary goal of sport
would be some other thing. If we think of why we have sport we could come up
with a list such as exercise, entertainment, celebration of embodiment and so on.
These are the things that we should consider the principal aim of sport even if
the aim within the sport is to score goals and so on. And when we consider the
issue of spectator entertainment, we can see that the aesthetic element will come
to the fore. One need only consider how many rule changes are designed specifically with the spectators in mind: to make it a better game to watch. In football,
for instance, the game used to become slow and stale when a defensive team
repeatedly passed the ball back to their own goalkeeper. A side that held a lead
could use this tactic to slow the game down and limit the scoring opportunities of
the opposition. In response, the game's authorities amended the rules so that the
goalkeeper couldn't pick up such a back pass, which made it riskier to pass back
and also meant that the goalkeeper couldn't slow the game by holding the ball
in his arms for a period of time. Sports like this have gradually evolved through
various rule changes over time. Such rule changes have not been intended to
make the game easier, nor are they always to correct some injustice or flaw in

the existing rules. Often they will be made so that the game becomes a better spectacle – becomes more aesthetically pleasing – with the aim of it being a more popular sport to watch. Sports can thus exhibit a phenomenon called response-dependency. If a rule change gets an approving response from those who watch, it is more likely to stay. If a rule change meets with disapproval, it is less likely to stay. Again, in football, there was an idea of having tied cup games decided by a 'golden goal', which meant that the next team to score would be the immediate winner, with no restart to the game. In theory, this would make it a more exciting and dramatic spectacle that the fans would love. In practice, however, it had the opposite effect. Such was the ultimate cost of conceding a goal that the teams tended to become more defensive than attacking when a golden goal was in the offing. No one dare risk committing defenders forward. And even when a golden goal was scored, there seemed something too abrupt about the game ending at the point. It was like a piece of music lacking a coda. The other team ought to have some opportunity to reply and the clock ought to count down to the referee's final whistle. After a few years, therefore, the golden goal experiment was revoked and one can argue that this was ultimately on aesthetic grounds. Of course, not all sports are primarily aesthetic sports. Squash, for instance, was traditionally played in an enclosed space with very little room for spectators. The primary reason we have squash is not for the entertainment of viewers but for recreation, exercise, socialising and competition, and it is these needs to which the sport will respond as it evolves. The chief response-dependency for the mass spectator sports, however, will be to the aesthetic reactions of those who watch. We have a case, therefore, where the watching of sport is crucial to, because it is partly constitutive of, the sports in question. It makes and shapes the sport. Had football not become the spectator sport it is, it might not have evolved in the way it did. Yet one can also argue that football became the most popular spectator sport in the world precisely because we rate it the highest in all-round aesthetic value.

Kupfer's division between the goal of sport (exercise, entertainment, fulfilment and so on) and the goal within sport (scoring, jumping highest, running fastest) has been given a more nuanced presentation by Suits. The goal within the sport can be divided along the lines of his lusory and prelusory distinction. The prelusory goal of a sport, it will be recalled, is the specific achievable state of affairs to which one aims (Suits 2005: 50), for example crossing the finishing line first, getting the football across the line between the posts and under the crossbar, getting a golf ball in the hole. But the lusory goal is to do these things within the rules that are constitutive of the game (Suits 2005: 49). The simplest way of achieving the prelusory goal would be cutting across the infield, shooting down opponents with a machine gun or just picking up the ball and dropping it in the hole. But to achieve the prelusory goals in these ways would mean that one was no longer running the 200 metres or playing football or golf. The lusory goal is to achieve these prelusory goals within the relevant sports, which will mean obeying their rules and thus achieving the goals within the sport's confines. Only if one achieves the lusory goals of the sport can one be a winner. The purpose within the sport is, then, the attainment of its lusory goals. The purpose of the sport in general is something bigger and probably deeper. Human beings love to play sport: it says something fundamental about human existence. Play could be an end in itself, as Suits argues, even though some people are involved in sports for reasons such as earning a livelihood. These larger concerns are candidates for the true purpose of sport, not some simple prelusory act.

The divide that has been enforced between sport and art is not, therefore, something that can be established by looking at the principal aims of the two spheres. On closer inspection, sport and art look to be in the same position in the ways in which their aims relate to the aesthetic values. We have seen that there was an initially seductive idea that, while art aims first and foremost at the aesthetic, sport aims first and foremost at victory. Any beauty in sport was said to be a by-product. But we then saw that a similar argument could be made in the case of individual artistic endeavours. The artists do not seem to be aiming primarily to create beauty but to achieve more specific and targeted goals. When we look at a particular and detailed level, therefore, sport and art seem to be in the same position. We then looked in more general terms and found that, if we consider what sport itself is for, then a good answer in the case of spectator sports was that it was for the satisfaction and entertainment of the spectators. Aesthetic values can play a big role in such satisfaction, which again lessens the divide between the characteristics of sport and art. This is not to say that there is no distinction at all between sport and art. But it is to say that the distinction is not found here.

6   Real and imagined drama

In the 2010 World Cup in South Africa, Ghana had the chance of becoming the first ever African team to reach the semi-finals. As the five other representatives had been knocked out, the whole continent put their support behind the Black Stars of Ghana. Their quarter-final was against Uruguay and the teams were evenly matched. Support for Uruguay was limited to their nationals. Almost every other football fan in the whole world thought that Africa deserved its day of glory. The game was as close as expected and the two sides were inseparable at full time: one goal apiece. Another 30 minutes of extra time was required, after which we would need a penalty shoot-out competition to decide it. In the final minute of extra time, Ghana made one last assault on the Uruguayan goal. There was a final chance. The keeper was beaten. A defender cleared a shot off the line. But the ball sat up for a free attacking header. It was on target and above the head of the last defender on the line, Luis Suarez. Instinctively, Suarez lifted his arm and beat the ball away with his hand. The referee saw it, awarded a penalty to Ghana and red-carded Suarez. But was that enough? Suarez had stopped a certain goal. Ghana would have been through to the semis. And as there was no more time to play, what kind of disadvantage to Uruguay was it to be reduced to ten men? What kind of advantage was it to Ghana? In return, they had their penalty kick but it seemed a poor trade for a certain goal, illegally stopped on the goal line. Everyone in the stadium watched as Asamoah Gyan ran up to take the penalty kick. The whole of Africa was hoping, and those who believed in God prayed. The vast television audience around the world all saw that there was only one just outcome and, but for a small audience in Montevideo, it was an outcome they thought the continent of Africa deserved. Gyan ran up and blasted the ball. It hit the crossbar and ballooned into the sky.

Gyan was personally distraught. His tears were matched all over the continent and in many other parts of the world. The referee blew the full-time whistle immediately. It would be a penalty shoot-out. But such was the blow to the Ghanaians, having missed the best chance an African side ever had of reaching a World Cup semi-final, and such was the boost to the Uruguayans, having 'got out of jail', it already seemed that the penalty shoot-out was a foregone conclusion. That duly came to pass. Uruguay won the penalty competition with ease. It was one of the most dramatic-ever finishes to a football match. There had been intense emotional highs and lows, with hopes at their highest just moments before they were utterly dashed. Could one expect to find such drama in any other setting?

Sport contains what looks for all the world like drama. It has a great potential for the twists and turns that play with the emotions of the fans. Their team can achieve victory against all the odds. But they can also have victory taken from them at the last minute. Triumph and defeat are often separated by so little that they can be faced within seconds of each other. The result of a whole season's worth of play can come down to one kick, ball or shot, at the end of which one team faces joy and the other tears. Rather like a theatre play, however, there can be many plots, sub-plots and surprises along the way before we get to the end point. If a play is art, shouldn't sport also be considered so for containing an equal measure of such drama? And it might be supposed that the drama is all the more intense because it is unscripted and real. If we knew the events in a sport had been pre-arranged, as many have believed to be the case in some forms of wrestling, then this would actually detract from the drama of sport. The drama would not be real but only contrived, and would not engage us nearly as much as when we believe in its veracity.

Here we come to a major distinction, however, which might be a ground for separating art and sport. Best (1974), as we have already seen, has pointed to some of the distinguishing characteristics of art and sport that show why sport can never be art. Drama may provide a further case in which art and sport differ.

First, however, we have to concede that, as in the case of all aesthetic properties, even if sport does contain drama, that would not be sufficient to make it art. Politics also contains drama, as does war, and any ordinary person's life will contain many dramatic elements. We do have expressions such as 'the art of politics' and 'the theatre of war' but these seem to be arts in only a derived sense. Few would class war and politics alongside painting, sculpture and dance as proper art disciplines. There can be skilled politicians and tacticians of war but we cannot say immediately that every skill is an art. Setting aside the issue of skill and artistry, dramatic moments in our own lives, such as rushing into the delivery suite of a maternity hospital, show pretty clearly that drama is not sufficient for art. Drama seems to suggest some kind of story with interesting and perhaps surprising twists. It is clear that there are many contexts in which there is such a story, but they are not art and they are not performed in a real, non-metaphorical theatre.

What, then, is the alleged difference between drama in the full artistic sense and drama in the derived sense, which Best thinks is all that can be found in the case of sport? The following distinction is offered by Best. The objects of art are imagined. In the theatre, for instance, tragedy happens to the characters in the play; it does not happen to real people. One character may die on the stage, but the actor does not die (except in the metaphorical sense of going down badly with the audience). In sport, however, we are not dealing with imagined objects: 'It is the character of the athlete which is shown in sport, whereas in drama it is the character not of the actor but of the person he or she is portraying' (Best 1985: 536). When a boxer recovers from a knock-down and comes back to win, it is their own strength and determination that wins the day. They are not playing an imagined character who exhibits that degree of strength and determination.

A comparison might be developed, however, between a script and the rules of a sport. There are certain script-like elements in the rules. They tell us how, in abstract terms, a sporting event begins and how it ends and a good deal about the sorts of things that could happen in between. Instead of the old cliché of sports being unscripted theatre, we can take the rules to an extent to be scripted. We can now develop this idea further. The objects in a play are imagined, says Best. In sport, they are real. But the idea of sport as the acting out of a script allows us to understand its players like actors who, in a quite reasonable sense, are playing their allotted roles and characters.

I argue that there is indeed a sense in which, in playing a sport, one adopts a certain role. Consider the difference between team sports played at club level and at international level. Club teammates are sometimes opponents when playing for their national sides. Hence, teammates could be on the same side on a Saturday and in opposition the following Tuesday. When they take to the field, each adopts the relevant role. An adversarial role can be adopted when in opposition even if these individuals are friends off the field or members of the same club side. Once the adversarial role is adopted, hard tackles may be made, in rugby and football for instance, or any contact sport. Personal friendships need not be harmed by hard tackling. The competitors understand that the tackle is within the script, and necessary for them to play their allotted role properly, even in cases where it might push the boundaries of that script. In the adversarial roles, it will be accepted that one's opponent will tackle as hard as they can get away with, on the assumption that it is advantageous in that particular sport to tackle hard. Risk of inflicting an injury on one's friends will even be tolerated. It is known in football that legs can be broken with firm-but-fair tackles and this is an accepted risk that follows when playing the game properly at a serious level. Once the game ends, however, the players step out of their adversarial roles and can become personal friends or professional associates once more. The role is dropped and the relationship is unaltered. There are even cases where a serious injury is sustained but nevertheless a friendship, or at least a professional respect for the other party involved, can remain unaffected.

We can compare this with a theatre play in which there are non-sporting adversaries (though, for this discussion, it wouldn't matter if the play was on the subject of sport). The play is about a conflict, and the script, we imagine, requires that one actor slaps another across the face. The two actors who play the antagonists may well be friends off stage, or at least have a professional working relationship. The theatre audience will see, let us suppose, if the slap is pulled or faked, so actor B must inflict an actual strike on the face of actor A and make it look convincing. In film, such things often happen as, with the camera so close to the action, faking a strike is not easy. The actors, like the sportspersons, accept that the strike and any subsequent injury or pain are administered to the character playing the adversarial role. Injuries are not administered to the opponent *qua* friend, colleague or human being. If one slapped the friend *as* a friend, the friendship would most likely end. But actors A and B understand that the slap is administered by one character to the other character and it is thus not taken personally. Indeed, one skill of acting is acting out of character, so the fact that a fellow actor slaps you in the play should allow you to infer nothing about how they would treat you outside of their work. Actor B has adopted a role in which they must do something they would not do ordinarily. Both A and B understand this when playing their roles.

An analogy is there to be drawn between the stage and the sports field. A player may have to adopt a role for the game. At the simplest level, but most obviously, players adopt adversarial roles against their opponents and, if it is a team sport, cooperative roles with their teammates. One may dislike a team-mate personally yet cooperate with them during the game, just as one might be a personal friend of an opponent. To look deeper, however, we see that there are also different roles to be played within a team. Some are clearly distinct, such as the goalkeeper in hockey or football. But knowledge of the game will usually show that there are many different roles needed in the team: goalscorer, stopper, winger, midfield ball-winner, midfield distributor and so on. In American foot-ball, the roles are very specialised. In cricket, the roles are rotated, though with some specialisation. It is possible for a cricketer to bat, bowl and field all within the same hour. These roles can be likened to all the different characters needed to complete a cast. All of them are required to successfully compete in a game. Yet even within one's sporting role in the team, there are various ways in which they can be realised. There are sub-roles that could be chosen within each of the positional roles. A goalscorer may be good in the air, big and strong, or lightning fast. They may hang back deep and arrive in the danger area late. Or they may lead from the front, winning the long ball and holding up play while they wait for support. In midfield, there are all sorts of roles to be played and the good team will have the right balance of them all. The coach may ask a player to adopt one of the roles for the day, and tell them how they want them to play it. The hard-tackling midfielder, playing the chief aggressor and 'enforcer' of the side, may be a lovely man who is kind to children and animals off the field. They nevertheless see it as a part of the sport that they play a tough character within it.

This is not to deny that a player may well be bringing something of themselves to the role: they may have gained some aggression from their life experiences that they then channel into their performance on the pitch, hopefully in a controlled and positive way. So the sportsperson plays a role that need not be entirely true to their non-sporting persona but may also manifest at least some of that indi-vidual's character traits. A player who is generally determined in everything they do in life, for instance, may be able to channel that into the sporting context and find it to be a major asset (this theme is discussed in Chapter 9). But the fact that we see something of the real person, manifest in the role they play in sport, also does not distinguish it sharply from stage acting. A director might encourage an actor to look inside themselves for life experiences they can bring to their stage or screen role. A moment of screen sadness, for instance, might appear more effective if the actor can draw on some tragic personal experience and discover real sadness inside. The idea of 'method' acting is to almost become the type of character one is playing so that one can play the role more convincingly. Similarly, a sportsperson may search inside for some extra motivation when they are exhausted and tempted to give up.

This discussion shows that the division in characteristics between art and sport is not as wide as is claimed. Best argues that tragedies on the stage occur only to the characters, not to the actors. But actor A's face is indeed smarting as they leave the stage. Perhaps Best has in mind the way in which a team or individual can be genuinely disappointed by their defeat or individual performance. But exactly the same thing can happen in the theatre. One night may go badly, with many lines fluffed, poor performances and negative audience reactions. An actor can indeed be very disappointed with their own individual performance and an entourage with their collective performance. On the other hand, injuries and tragedies that occur in sport can also be understood as occurring to the characters and not just to the individuals who played the role. When a tackle results in serious injury, there is an understanding that it was inflicted by an opponent in their adversarial role. It was not inflicted on an opponent as a person, friend or colleague. It is rare that personal grudges are held in sport from injuries that are acquired in the ordinary run of the game. Very occasionally, however, there is a truly terrible incident such as a permanently disabling injury or even death that occurs on the sports field. The Celtic goalkeeper John Thomson, for instance, was accidentally killed in a football match with Rangers in 1931. Is this the kind of tragedy that Best has in mind? It is claimed in the theatre that only the characters rather than the actors die on the stage. But such sporting injuries or deaths are indeed pure accidents that are not in any way integral to the sport. It would be just as much the sport it is even if no such accident had ever occurred. And it can be noted that exactly the same can happen in drama, or any other form of art. Breaking a leg (literally) on the stage can happen by accident. There was even a case of an actor dying during a live TV play in Britain (Gareth Jones on *Armchair Theatre* of 30 November 1958), forcing the remaining cast to improvise around his sudden absence in order to continue the transmission. The disanalogy between the imagined objects of art and the real objects of sport, therefore, can be undermined.

Is the idea that there really are winners and losers, or victories and defeats, in sport, whereas in the theatre any such victory is imagined? The tragedy of defeat is thus also an imagined one, whereas in sport it is real. The job of the script is to create an illusion of reality, yet we all know that we can step back from that illusion and see it for the contrivance that it is. But in sport, one team or individual really does win and the rest really do lose. Again, however, this difference of characteristic can be challenged. The boundary between the two domains is not so sharply drawn. Certainly there are winners and losers in sport, and there is no doubt some genuine joy and sorrow. But this again can be to a degree a question of pretence. The individuals and teams try to do their best, as any actor does. Some days it goes well and some days it goes badly. An actor may be elated after a good performance and despondent after a bad one. Clearly there is something at stake on each evening that the actor takes to the stage (contrary to the claim of Elliott 1974: 110). Why else would they get nervous? There is a question of being professional and dedicated and wanting to put all one's years of training to good use and perform well. But even in defeat there is always the prospect of the next performance. After a bad night, the sportsperson can look forward to the next game and the losing team can look forward to the next season. The sportsperson's role is to do their best to win, and many of them are available for hire if they are effective at performing that role. A good player in a losing team may yet be able to look forward to the prospect of being bought by a better team and employed on a higher salary to take on a similar role elsewhere. And this is similar to a fine actor being wanted by different producers to display their talents in a new venture. The division does not withstand scrutiny, therefore. Accidental tragedies can be found in both sport and the theatre. And something that counts as success and failure can also be found in stage drama as much as the sporting arena.

Seeing that one adopts a certain role when playing sport also explains another difficult question concerning the limits of fair play. There are cases of 'sledging' in cricket where the wicket keeper and surrounding fielders continuously talk to the batter in order to undermine their confidence. In other sports but even in cricket, this sometimes spills over into personal abuse, involving insults, swearing and, in the most extreme cases, racial slurs. In a most notorious case, Marco Materazzi 'sledged' Zinedine Zidane in a football World Cup Final, soliciting a headbutt from Zidane who was then dismissed from the game. Should we just accept this in sport? Is it 'all part of the game' that the players try to wind each other up in an attempt to put them off? Does 'anything go' in sport if it gains a competitive advantage? The preceding analysis of this chapter suggests not. The key question would be whether one is attacking the other player *qua* opponent or *qua* individual human being. One's race, for instance, is something that belongs to the person and only derivatively to the player. The sportsperson cannot discard their race when they leave the sports field. The judgement to be made, therefore, is whether the provocation was directed at the opponent in their adversarial character, and thus something that does not pertain to them as soon as they are out of that character, or is it directed to that player as an individual human being and something that they will still have once they leave the field of play. In the Zidane case, the allegation was that the slur was a deeply personal one (the details varied in different accounts) and FIFA, the governing body, seemed to agree as Materazzi, the headbutted player, also received a two-match ban following the incident. Similarly, there have been cases of players spitting at each other, punches being thrown, kicks dished out when the ball was nowhere near, and the biting of ears in boxing and rugby. Again this is no part of the sport and can be considered a personal slight rather than a tackle on one's opponent *qua* opponent. Such actions are not integral to the sport and can have an impact beyond the sporting context. The boxer does not grow back his ear, for example, when he leaves the ring. He has to live with its loss after the event. These are the sorts of actions that do make personal enmities and end friendships. If two teammates in a club side were on some day opposed in different national sides and one racially provoked another, for instance, then there are firm grounds for saying that it is unacceptable and should not be tolerated in the sport. It is a slur delivered to the person, not their character of adversary.

To see that there is a line to be drawn in the case of sledging, we can compare it again with our play in which there is a slap in the face. Actor B is obliged by the script to slap A's face. Actor A accepts it as a necessary part of successfully performing the play. But then suppose that B sees it as an opportunity to seek revenge on A for a personal grudge, or perhaps B merely has violent tendencies that he cannot control, and B conceals a knuckleduster in his pocket. When the time for the slap comes, he puts his hand in his pocket and into the knuckleduster and almost fractures the cheekbone of A. Actor A has every right to take this personally. Such a hard strike was not demanded by the script and nor by the role that B was employed to play. The use of an implement was not required by the director, and if it had been B would have been equipped with a fake rubber one. B has overstepped the role and, for a short while, come out of character. It was B personally who struck A, not the character played by B. This compares with 'going over the top of the ball' in football. This is a tackle in which one player deliberately misses the ball and instead stamps on the shin of their opponent. This 'tackle' is known to be one of the most dangerous as it often produces a broken leg for the recipient. It is despised in the game precisely because it is understood as a personal slight, directed towards the individual rather than the 'character' of one's sporting opponent.

If we are talking about sports and acting, we cannot ignore the issue of so-called 'play acting'. By this we mean a case where one player feigns something, usually a foul or an injury, but you can also feign to pass so as to deceive an opponent. Such feigning is usually seen as a problem as it can be used in various ways to cheat. Injuries can be faked so as to delay a game (Mumford 2010) or get an opponent in trouble. And fouls can be feigned so as to gain some penalty. There is a role that is being played here. Sometimes it might be thought to have some legitimacy. In the penalty area, for instance, it is common for a player who might score to be tugged back or tripped. The defender will be attempting to hinder the striker, though not to so high a degree that they will concede a penalty kick. In such a game, where the referee is making evaluative judgements, there can be a fine line between what is legitimate and what is not. Yet the fine line is likely to translate into a huge difference in outcome: the attack breaking down, on one hand; or bringing a penalty goal on the other. There is a thought that, if a striker really is being hindered in such a way that will prevent them from scoring, they are 'entitled to go down', which basically means that they can simulate a more serious hindrance so as to make it clearer to the referee that a foul has been committed. Professional sports are full of such acting and it is a practice largely encouraged. A player who persists through an illegal hindrance that prevents them from scoring will often be questioned: 'Why didn't you go down?'

We have already considered the comparison between sport and theatre. Best criticised the cliché of sport as unscripted theatre, but in response we argued that it could indeed be considered as scripted theatre. We have advanced the topic in this chapter by considering sportspersons as actors, playing out an assigned role. An objection has been levelled that the drama found in sport is real while the drama of theatre is imaginary only. We have shown that such a sharp division is not to be found. In a perfectly reasonable sense, sport sees an interplay of characters acting out roles. Certainly some injury or defeat can be sustained by the persons playing those roles; but a similar case can be made for actors, who might sustain accidental injury and find something akin to defeat in a bad performance. It will be a character in a play that falls in love with the leading lady, and not necessarily the actor playing that character, but likewise one can argue that it is the sportsperson in their character that wins or loses the match. Outside of the sport, there may be other criteria by which they judge their successes or failures. We are left, therefore, with some closer parallels between art and sport which explains why many people say it is right to think of sport as art. The question is not settled by this alone, however. We remarked that drama is to be found in many other areas of life, outside the arts. Even if the drama of sport were to be indistinguishable in nature from drama in the arts, this would not make sport art.

7 Purism and the aesthetic perception

I heard a story from an art historian colleague that may be apocryphal but nevertheless illustrates the main point of this chapter. A tourist in an art gallery was found by a security guard looking at one of the fire extinguishers hanging on the wall. It was a regular, fully functioning fire extinguisher hanging there in case of fire. With such valuable art on show, it would be essential to put out any fire as quickly as possible. The tourist was spending a long time pondering the object. They stood back with their hand resting on their chin. They tilted their head and looked at it from various angles. They seemed to be deep in thought. The security guard realised that there had been some mistake. He told the tourist that the object really was a fire extinguisher and not an art exhibit after all. The tourist was quite embarrassed, laughed, shook their head and moved on. There is a complement to the story that works in the opposite direction and may be equally apocryphal. An art exhibit, possibly in the same gallery, included a black plastic bin liner as part of the piece. One night a cleaner saw it and didn't realise it was art. They picked up the bin liner, used it to collect rubbish from the bins and then threw it away.

These two stories are amusing for a variety of reasons but they illustrate a serious philosophical issue that will be addressed here. It has been alleged that there is a distinctly aesthetic mode of perception of which we are capable and we deploy when we look at art. We can deploy this aesthetic perceptual mode when observing other things as well as art. The beautiful sunset is an instance, as is the newborn puppy, the fire extinguisher and so on; and of course sport. The purist is someone who has this aesthetic mode switched on most of the time, looking at the sporting contest aesthetically. The partisan rarely has it switched on. But there are many possibilities between the fanatic partisan and the out-and-out purist. Many who watch sport will have some combination of partisan and purist tendencies and will switch their aesthetic mode on and off as the occasion takes them. In order to substantiate this claim, however, we need first to justify the theory that humans indeed have this aesthetic way of perceiving, because it has been alleged by a number of aestheticians that it is dubious.

Our two stories provide some credibility to the initial assumption. The tourist switches on their aesthetic mode of perception in the mistaken belief that the fire extinguisher is a work of art. Such a mode concerns not just the narrow question of the visual properties of the object. The tourist may well contemplate those but they may also think about what the work means or what statement it would make about the nature of art. What is funny is that they are using their aesthetic mode of perception in an inappropriate situation. The cleaner removing the bin liner, on the other hand, is failing to view something aesthetically when it was meant to be viewed that way. This raises the prospect that, when there are two observers look-ing at the same thing, one may be viewing it aesthetically and the other not. The tourist and the security guard may be looking at the same object but one is looking aesthetically and the other non-aesthetically, it seems. We can call non-aesthetic perception *purposive* because the guard sees the extinguisher as something that can be used in the case of fire for the purpose of putting it out. But does that mean that they literally see different things? Or is it rather that they see the same thing but think different thoughts about what they see? The tourist thinks aesthetic thoughts about what they see; the security guard thinks only purposive thoughts. In the case of sport, we can ask the same question. Does the partisan sitting next to me literally see something different from me if I am a purist? I have already indicated my answer (Chapter 2), but now it needs a more serious justification.

The key problem we need to address is that of what occurs when we perceive aesthetically. The first thing to make clear is that we are dealing with a broad conception of aesthetic perception. As we have already stated, aesthetic quality is no longer restricted just to beauty (though for ease of reference we sometimes refer to the range of positive aesthetic values as beauty). New works of art, such as Duchamp's *Fountain*, challenged the narrow conception. As well as beauty, we now use aesthetic concepts such as a work being interesting, dramatic, challeng-ing, moving, evocative and so on (Eaton 2004: 73). Eaton thinks the concept of the aesthetic should be broadened to encompass such additional notions, and I follow her in this.

There's also the issue of whether the aesthetic properties of a thing are restricted to its intrinsic perceptible properties. That would mean that two indis-tinguishable objects – let us call them intrinsic duplicates – should be alike in their aesthetic properties. But then a portrait and its forgery must be aestheti-cally equal. This is disputable (Eaton 2004: 75). The forgery gives us far less pleasure just because it was not an original creation. Originality – being the first such exemplar – may be a distinct aesthetic feature (Lacerda and Mumford 2010) but it seems to be a relational one. In Chapter 8, we will consider another case in which intrinsic duplicates can differ aesthetically, where they have different ethical value. Aesthetic qualities do not, therefore, have to be intrinsic, though perhaps many of them are.

But what are these aesthetic properties? This was a question we considered in Chapter 3. On the one hand there is a subjectivist view that aesthetics is entirely in the mind of the perceiver rather than in the objects themselves. Hume articu-lated this kind of view in a passage already quoted:

Beauty is no quality in things themselves: it exists merely in the mind which contemplates them; and each mind perceives a different beauty. One person may even perceive deformity, where another is sensible of beauty; and every individual ought to acquiesce in his own sentiment, without pretending to regulate those of others. To see the real beauty, or real deformity, is as fruitless an inquiry, as to pretend to ascertain the real sweet or real bitter.

(Hume 1741–2: 230)

Without any mind to perceive it, no one thing is any more beautiful than another: indeed there would be no beauty in the world. But hasn't Hume gone too far towards subjectivism? Does each mind really perceive a different beauty, just as the taste of one person could pronounce bitter when another pronounces sweet?

In the case of taste in the mouth, there tends to be a high degree of agreement over what is sweet and what is bitter. A fresh ripe apple tastes sweet to virtually everyone. If someone said honestly that they found this apple bitter we might suspect that their taste was somehow wired up wrongly, like other biological defects that people can have. Similarly, there is a high degree of agreement over aesthetic judgements. Perhaps the agreement is not quite as high as that in the case of the taste of our foods but nevertheless agreement is there. Sibley (1959) defends the idea that there is a clear distinction to be made between aesthetic and non-aesthetic properties. We can distinguish the sentimentality of a play, for instance, from one of its non-aesthetic properties, such as being two hours long, or the arrangement of colours in a painting from the weight of the painting. The weight of an art object seems one that is never considered to be among its aesthetic properties. Indeed it seems almost impossible that someone could consider the weight of a painting aesthetically. Weight may be important in design – the weight of a mobile phone may be praised, for instance – because of its practicality. But if someone admired the weight of a painting or sculpture aesthetically we might think them to be just as 'wrong-wired' as someone who found a fresh ripe apple bitter. The sort of division Sibley draws seems to have some validity, therefore. But how do we square this division with what Hume said, for it seems indeed that if there were no perceivers to behold these qualities their beauty would not be there?

One reply would be to allow that there was some degree of response-dependency in the perceiver that made some properties and not others aesthetic. Dewey (1958) suggested this approach, and we endorsed something like it in Chapter 3. These would be the properties that normal, well-placed observers found pleasurable. A partially clouded sky during a sunset, for instance, has such a spectacular array of colours and textures that we cannot help but find it a pleasure to see. This may well be a perception that is in our minds and it may well be a simple fact of biology or human nature, but there is little denying that we respond in a pleasurable way to it. Anyone who didn't see it as beautiful we would be likely to think of as incapacitated. Just as some people are red–green colour blind, we would be likely to dismiss as an incapacity any such failure to see this beauty.

Sibley's explanation is along these lines: the aesthetic properties require taste on the part of the observer to identify them and there is a degree of agreement among observers over matters of taste. It is nevertheless possible for some people to lack taste: they would be unable to perceive the aesthetic properties. Here, however, Sibley sees a possible ground for the aesthetic/non-aesthetic division. Everyone, he suggests, can see the non-aesthetic properties. No one could fail to observe the weight of a book if they picked it up but some may fail to discern the drama of the plot or the eloquence of the style. But is the division as sharp as Sibley suggests? In some conditions, I may fail to realise that the book is rectangular and think it square. And while I can tell that the book has some weight, I may make an inaccurate assessment of what particular weight it has. Cohen (1973) attacked a sharp division between aesthetic and non-aesthetic, noting that some terms such as daring and restful seem hard to push into either category. Let us not worry, therefore, too much about how sharp the dividing line is, as there may be more or less aesthetic properties that can be appreciated aesthetically to greater or lesser degrees.

This brings us back to the main issue, however. Is there an aesthetic way of perceiving some property or properties? The aesthetic properties would be those towards which normal humans tended to have pleasurable responses, and the non-aesthetic ones would be properties that tended to produce no such response. But does the having of a pleasurable response affect the character of the perception itself? Does one have a different kind of experience when one perceives aesthetically? Or is it merely that one perceives in the usual way but the perception is one that is accompanied by pleasure? If the latter option, then the security guard and the tourist see the fire extinguisher in the same way and it is merely that the perception elicits an accompanying pleasure in the tourist that the guard does not take.

It is clear now that there are two ways we could explain the nature of aesthetic experience. The first we can call the *perception theory*. This is the claim that there is a distinctive aesthetic mode of perception that one can adopt, deploy or enter into to gain an aesthetic experience. On this theory, the tourist perceiving aesthetically and the security guard perceiving purposively literally see different things. The second option is what we can call the *accompaniment theory*. This would mean that the tourist and guard see virtually the same things. The difference between them is not in the character of their perceptions. Rather, the difference is in something that merely accompanies that perception. This accompaniment might be some kind of pleasure or some thought about the object perceived.

Thus far, the prospects for the perception theory do not look good. There have been a number of attacks on the idea of there being a distinctly aesthetic attitude or aesthetic way of seeing. Dickie (1964) and Zemach (1997) are among those sceptical that there is a distinctive aesthetic experience. How, they query, would such a kind of perception be spelled out? What is its character?

To answer this, there is a tradition in which the aesthetic perception is outlined in terms of disinterest. The notion is to be found in Kant (1790) but appears also in Shaftesbury (see Stolnitz 1961) and in more modern times in Stolnitz (1960). The idea is that in aesthetic perception one has no interest in the prac-tical uses of the object being perceived (Goldman 2005: 263) but instead just enjoys the experience provided, abstracted away from all other considerations. One enjoys the object for what it is, not for what it can get you. Stolnitz defines disinterestedness as meaning 'no concern for any ulterior purpose' (Stolnitz 1960: 34–5). Schopenhauer (1818: vol. I, 185) uses this idea as a way of escaping the strivings of the will. The idea is to contemplate the Platonic forms and become a will-less subject of knowledge. And among philosophers of sport, Kupfer speaks of the aesthetic attitude in these terms:

> we can view a piece of land as an investment, a site for low-rent housing, or the scene of the Civil War battle. But when we attend to the piece of land simply for its appearance, its contours and colours, texture and rhythm, then we take the aesthetic attitude towards it. We turn away from a host of every-day interests and look for aesthetic relations and qualities.
>
> (Kupfer 1983: 469)

Hence, the tourist is doing no more than enjoying the experience provided by the observation of the fire extinguisher, while the security guard sees the same object as something that could put out a fire in an emergency and save the art collection, preserving a major financial asset. Dickie thinks this account has a major problem, however. A critic has an ulterior purpose: they need to write a review. But then that means they cannot perceive aesthetically (Dickie 1974: 128). A book reviewer is an obvious case. They read the book because they have to write a review, and they have to write a review to earn their pay. And it seems clear this doesn't prevent them from commenting on the aesthetic value of the work. Indeed, the reader of the review wants precisely that from the reviewer. They want a report of the aesthetic merits of the work. But according to the disinterestedness account, they cannot read the book aesthetically because they have an ulterior purpose.

Dickie is sceptical also for other reasons that there is a distinctly aesthetic per-ception consisting in disinterestedness. He considers two cases (1974: 116–18). Arthur and Zachary look at the same portrait of a man. Arthur looks at it aes-thetically but the man in the painting is Zachary's father, which provokes in him all sorts of other thoughts. Zachary is not, therefore, looking at it aesthetically. Dickie answers that Zachary is not attending to the portrait but to his own mus-ings. He is not attending to the portrait interestedly: he's not attending to it at all but to his own thoughts. In another case, Arthur and Marvin are listening to the same piece of music, Arthur again disinterestedly. But Marvin has to analyse it for an exam the next day. Again, Dickie denies that the individuals have sepa-rate interested and disinterested attentive powers. Rather, Marvin has an ulterior motive.

Despite the strength of considerations to the contrary, I want now to offer a justification of the perception theory as opposed to the accompaniment theory.

I will not be attempting to describe the character of aesthetic perception and how it differs from purposive perception, however. This will not be the point as it approaches the question from a viewpoint which I deny: a broadly Cartesian philosophy of mind. My task instead is to show that the proposal that an aesthetic perceiver and a purposive perceiver can actually perceive differently is more credible than it may first seem. The view that two normal perceivers observing the same object must see the same thing is one that we can question, for there is more to seeing than meets the eye – quite literally. This opens up the possibility that there are indeed distinct ways of seeing, the aesthetic being among them. To justify this, I will employ ideas developed in art criticism (Berger), psychology (Gregory) and philosophy (Dennett).

The philosophical account is the key, though it is an empirically informed account. Dennett (1991) points to a number of cases of perception that would raise problems if the mind worked as a Cartesian inner theatre. The Cartesian theatre is typified by transparency and incorrigibility. Transparency, in the case of perception, is the thesis that, if one sees P, one will believe that one sees P. Incorrigibility would be the thesis that, if one believes that one sees P, then one does indeed see P. The reason the mind is so transparent to us is that it is depicted as the inner theatre. All the mind's contents are played out in front of us, as if on the stage of a little theatre that we have inside our heads. Everything is there, on plain view, in front of us; nothing is hidden. Such a Cartesian view of the mind suggests that we are intimately acquainted with the contents of our own minds. Indeed, our minds are the things in all the world with which we are most intimately acquainted. We know better than anything else what is going on in our own minds. We simply introspect and find what is there, within ourselves, and we cannot be wrong. If I believe I am in pain, for instance, I cannot be wrong. No one, not even a medical professional, can tell me that I am not in pain if I believe that I am.

We may add to this Cartesian view of the mind another thesis, which we can call the naive realist theory of perception. There are various things that this could mean, but the claim that is most important for us here is that what we perceive is determined by the image hitting the retina, and nothing more. This is crucial in the argument because I do not deny, for instance, that the tourist and the security guard have the same, or almost the same, image hitting their eyes and projected onto the light receptors at the back of their eyeball. But the difference I allege between the tourist and the guard occurs after light has passed through the eye. The perception has not yet occurred, at least not completely so, until that light has been processed by the brain, and here is where things become more complicated.

Dennett invokes a number of examples in favour of his multiple drafts model of consciousness. I will pick three such. The first two show that there is more to seeing than meets the eye, and more to tasting than meets the tongue. These examples should soften up any temptations we might have towards Cartesianism. This then sets us up for the third example, which illustrates how two people listening to the same sounds could nevertheless have very different experiences.

When these cases are accepted, as I trust they will be, we see that the idea of two observers of the same object having different experiences is acceptable: one seeing in an aesthetic way and the other in a purposive way.

Dennett's first example concerns two rapidly flashing discs observed on a TV monitor:

> In the simplest case, if two or more small spots separated by as much as 4 degrees of visual angle are briefly lit in rapid succession, a single spot seems to move back and forth. [If the two spots were of different colours] … the first spot seemed to begin moving and then change colour abruptly in the middle of its illusory passage toward the second location.
>
> (Dennett 1991: 114)

This case is harder to describe in words than it is to see (I write as someone who has indeed seen this 'illusion', which is remarkably effective). The screen is otherwise blank. On the left side of it, a disc appears briefly then disappears. On the right side, another disc appears briefly then disappears. The two discs never appear at the same time: their brief appearances alternate. The experimenter can then increase the speed at which these discs alternately flash on. At a certain speed, the illusion occurs. Instead of looking like two separate left and right discs flashing on and off alternately, it starts to look like a single disc that moves from side to side, back and forth across the screen. This presents a major question (raised by Goodman 1978: 73), which it seems the Cartesian model of the mind cannot answer. When the disc appears to move from left to right, its 'appearance' (let us call it) at the mid-point seems to be caused by the flashing disc on the right-hand side. The proof is that, when the discs are finally stopped from flashing, it is not that the disc begins to move and then suddenly fades away, somewhere in the middle. So it is not as if our minds have just gained a habit of projecting an anticipation of the moving disc that then gets disappointed. Rather, the apparent single moving disc reaches the point of the last one to appear, either at the left or right side, and then vanishes at that point. What this tells us, then, is that the appearance of moving across the middle of the screen, from left to right, is caused by the flashing of the disc on the right-hand side. Yet here is the problem. The disc looks to us as if it is in the middle of the screen, moving left to right, before it appears on the right. But if our explanation is correct, the cause of that appearance occurs after that appearance. How, then, can our experience of the disc being in the middle occur before its cause? The experienced sequence of events is different from the actual sequence of events that caused the experience.

This example shows that we should be sceptical of the theses of transparency and incorrigibility. The contents of our own perceptions are far from open to us. We see the events as having occurred in a certain order in which they cannot have occurred, unless there is some kind of backwards causation. Dennett uses the case to motivate the multiple drafts model of consciousness in which the mind constructs a narrative of its experiences, which can be redrafted in the light of new experiences and, in a sense, backdated in the light of new information.

This information may be received in the order a at t_1, b at t_2 and c at t_3, but then the mind makes sense of it in a rearranged order as a being at t_1, c at t_2 and b at t_3.

The second case further undermines Cartesianism. It concerns your first taste of beer:

> Many people who like beer will acknowledge that beer is an acquired taste. One gradually trains oneself – or just comes – to enjoy that flavor. What flavor? The flavor of the first sip? No one could like *that* flavor [an experienced beer drinker might retort]. Beer tastes different to the experienced beer drinker. If beer went on tasting to me the way the first sip tasted, I would never have gone on drinking beer! Or, to put the same point the other way around, if my first sip of beer had tasted to me the same way my most recent sip just tasted, I would never have had to acquire the taste in the first place! I would have loved the first sip as much as the one I just enjoyed.
>
> (Dennett 1991: 395–6)

The example rings true and mundane to all who drink beer. But for Cartesianism, it is an embarrassment. There are two possible options for what has happened. Either the taste of beer now is the same as the first taste, and you have just grown to like it; or the taste of beer now is different from that first taste, because no one could like that. If the Cartesian theory of mind were true, there ought to be some determinate answer of which of these two options was correct. But there is no easy choice between these two options. Among other consequences, consideration of this example shows the problematic view that our minds are full of qualia: that the immediate objects of perception are internal qualities, transparently available to us through introspection.

Dennett's position, based on examples like these, leans in the direction of a view of perception supported by the psychologist Richard Gregory (1966). Perception is not just about light hitting the eye. An eye does not see. It is persons that see, and this involves an interaction between eye and brain, and similarly for the other sense faculties. Perception occurs through a combination of sense organ, or body generally, and the processing of information provided in the brain. But we should understand perception as not simply caused by the object of perception – the fire extinguisher, in our example – though perception is undoubtedly a causal notion. Rather, a perception is a mutual manifestation of the object's disposition to be seen and the perceiver's disposition to see. The notion of a mutual manifestation of reciprocal disposition partners, which I am using here, comes from Martin (2008: 3).

Dennett's third example is a musical one, concerning our perception of sound. It shows how we bring something to the perception. The perception is not just the causal effect of the object on our senses, but involves our own expectations and anticipations too. We bring some 'excess baggage' that shapes the experience in some way:

To see how crucial this excess baggage of ours is, imagine that musicologists unearthed a heretofore unknown Bach cantata, definitely by the great man, but hidden in a desk and probably never yet heard even by the composer himself. Everyone would be aching to hear it, to experience for the first time the 'qualia' that the Leipzigers would have known, had they only heard it, but this turns out to be impossible, for the main theme of the cantata, by an ugly coincidence, is the first seven notes of 'Rudolf the Red-Nosed Reindeer'! We who are burdened with that tune would never be able to hear Bach's version as he intended it or as the Leipzigers would have received it.

(Dennett 1991: 388)

Hence two observers of this piece, with different backgrounds, could seem to have different experiences. Suppose one resident of Leipzig had heard the cantata some centuries ago before it was lost. Their experience was surely not the same as that we would experience if we heard the world premiere now, in the twenty-first century. The Leipziger may have found it solemn and serious but we would struggle to suppress a titter. On the accompaniment account, the experience would have to be judged the same in both cases, merely accompanied by different thoughts. In the light of Dennett's stock of examples, how could it be asserted with any authority that this is indeed the case?

Our notion of experience may now have to be revised. I urge that we cast off the Cartesianism view of mind. This is not to deny that we are experiencers, and that we bring something to the experience, but that should not be cashed out in terms of qualia displayed on the stage of an inner theatre. The first taste of beer shows that the qualia story is inadequate because it suggests there should be a simple answer where clearly there isn't.

We are now in a position to take seriously the aforementioned contributions from psychology and art history. In defence of his view that perception involves an interaction between eye and brain (or ear and brain, tongue and brain, and so on), Gregory (1966) draws attention to a number of perceptual illusions. The most famous such cases are probably the Necker cube and the Müller-Lyer illusion (Figures 7.1 and 7.2). The Necker cube shows us that two observers who look at the same object in the same conditions do not necessarily see the same thing. For one person, the lower face of the cube may look to be the front one, while for another person the upper face may look to be at the front. It is not clear at all that this means they have different qualia. Indeed, one person can experience some kind of switch between these two ways of seeing the cube. At first, the bottom face looks to be at the front, and then suddenly the upper face looks to be at the front. There is certainly some difference between seeing the cube in these two ways, and one can almost feel the momentary switch between the two ways. But it seems to have little to do with the qualia, which as far as we can tell remain the same. Yet it is something to do with the perception and the experience rather than just thoughts or attitudes about that perception. One perceives either in a bottom-face-front way or in a top-face-front way.

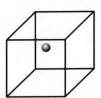

Figure 7.1 The Necker cube.

Figure 7.2 The Müller-Lyer illusion.

The Müller-Lyer illusion case is interesting for other reasons. With the perception of the Necker cube, the agent of perception seems to have some control over the way they see the cube. One can switch between the two ways of seeing voluntarily. But with the Müller-Lyer illusion, how one sees the figure is not within our direct control. The line on the right looks longer than the line on the left even after we have been told that they are the same length. But this is still not to allow that there is only one way in which the Müller-Lyer case can be seen. According to Gregory (1966: 148–50), the illusion may be culturally relative. People whose environment does not contain straight lines may not be susceptible to the illusion and may say honestly that the lines are of the same length. Again, the case then shows that two observers may look at the same object, receive very similar retinal images, yet perceive the object in two different ways.

Bringing the subject back to art, we find many relevant cases of ways of seeing in Berger's (1972) book. Art historians are already familiar with the idea that a work of art can be seen in a certain way and these ways can be informed by cultural, political and historical contexts. To take just one example (Berger 1972: 27–8), a painting of a pretty wheat field may seem like a pleasant landscape, but as soon as one is told that is was the final work painted by Van Gogh before he killed himself, one starts to see it in a different way. Those crows are no longer just hovering over the field: they are now coming towards Van Gogh to carry him away from the land of the living.

The ground has been laid for the possibility of the aesthetic and purposive being two ways of seeing the same object. We need not set this out in terms of those two ways of perceiving being different in character. Indeed, as Dickie suggested, one's motives and beliefs may explain the difference. But on the account of perception that has been developed here, which I would class as an adverbial theory (see, for instance, Lowe 1995: ch. 3), such motives and beliefs can indeed determine what is seen, or the way in which something is seen. In an adverbial theory of perception, instead of us seeing red, blue or square qualia, we are said to be able to see redly, see bluely, or see squarely. Seeing is an action that we perform, and an adverb modifies such an action. There are ways of seeing, and the aesthetic is one such way. The mistake of the accompaniment theory is to assume that motives and beliefs can be brought to bear on the perception after it has occurred. But if the account of perception developed here has some truth to it, they will to a degree determine what is seen. Thus one can indeed perceive aesthetically if one sets aside concern with the purpose of the object, or perceive purposively if one sets aside enjoyment of the perceived qualities.

This has been a circuitous journey into the philosophy of perception, so we shouldn't lose sight of our original purpose. The partisan was distinguished from the purist and a claim was made that, in a very real sense, those two types of observer see a different game. The purist is in the position of the tourist who views the fire extinguisher aesthetically. The partisan views the game purposively. It is all about gaining the victory. The purpose of competing is to win. But that does not prevent someone else seeing that same game in completely different terms. The purist just wants to contemplate the sporting contest for what it is in itself. Many of its aspects afford aesthetic experiences. And while sport certainly can provide victory, just as the extinguisher can put out flames, that is in no way inconsistent with a purely aesthetic perception for those who choose to enjoy it that way.

8   Ethics and aesthetics

Two reasons to watch sport are ethical and aesthetic. Thus far we have dealt exclusively with the aesthetic, showing that sport is a source of aesthetic experiences, available for our enjoyment. We will go on, in the following chapters, to consider questions of ethics, and how sport can provide ethical lessons for life more generally. But before we do that, it is worth considering how the ethical and aesthetic aspects of sport relate, if at all. Are they entirely distinct? Might one think of sport's moral dimension without considering its aesthetic dimension, and vice versa? In this chapter, I argue that one cannot do so insofar as ethical considerations intrude upon the aesthetic features of sport. Factors that are ethically bad can detract from sport's aesthetic value, and factors that are ethically good can improve sport's aesthetic value.

The argument for this is not new. It will merely be an application of recent claims that have emerged in aesthetics. What may be new, however, is the application of those claims to the case of sport. It is not a big step to make this application. Sport is a clear case where ethical considerations can invade the aesthetic. Except for some extraordinary and much discussed cases in the aesthetics literature, sport might be the best possible illustration of this close connection between ethics and aesthetics. Certainly it provides a very ordinary example, which everyone can grasp. And there may be cases where art does not always suffer aesthetically if it has bad moral content, whereas sport seems to suffer always in these circumstances.

What, then, is the issue? It has been claimed, for instance by Gaut (1998 and 2007: chs 7 and 8), that the aesthetic value of a work of art can be affected negatively if that work of art is morally flawed. On the other hand, a work of art that is morally virtuous can be aesthetically enhanced. This is a claim with which I broadly agree and I shall defend it in most cases, using some of the ideas that have already been developed in earlier chapters. Once it is defended, I shall apply it to the case of sport, which supplies very good examples of the thesis.

There might be a thought that the aesthetic properties of an object or work of art are simply those superficially observable properties that would be accessible to the senses of any observer. We saw that Davis (2001) made a claim like this (see Chapter 3). One might imagine a sculpture placed in a room in a museum, for instance, and one might find it reasonable to claim that if you were in the room, and free to explore the object, you could come to know all of its aesthetic features and qualities. One could examine its shape, texture, colour and so on, and then be in a fully informed position to make an aesthetic judgement about it. Having explored it, one might find it beautiful or ugly, or feel indifferent about it. There are other kinds of properties this sculpture might have. It could, for instance, have historical properties. It might be of a certain age, have been created in a certain city by a certain man, and so on. But one might maintain that these historical properties of the object are irrelevant to its aesthetic value. What counts, one might say, is only what can be observed and whether one has a positive or negative aesthetic reaction to what one sees.

A thought experiment might bolster this view. Suppose two artists, at different places and times, produced sculptures that were indistinguishable in terms of their intrinsic, observable properties. Wouldn't they be indistinguishable aesthetically? Would it really matter if one of those artists was a great philosopher while the other was an evil murderer? If you could not tell the objects apart, were they to be stood side by side in a museum, then how can you say that one is more aesthetically valuable – more beautiful – than the other? This is a line of thought promoted by positions such as formalism and aestheticism. A formalist, for example, would be one who looked to art to instantiate certain aesthetic forms: properties, shapes or patterns that naturally strike us as beautiful. One might subscribe to the old wisdom, for instance, that when photographing someone one should frame them in the picture so that they break the scene up into proportions of one-third and two-thirds. Similarly, in composing a painting, one might try to create those proportions. The focal point should be neither dead centre nor too near the edge.

If one thought that aesthetic value was basically about reproducing such forms, then it leaves no space for ethical considerations to affect aesthetic value. We can call this position autonomism: ethics and aesthetics are autonomous sets of values. This is not to deny that the same object or work of art could be a subject of both ethical and aesthetic values, but it is the claim that one doesn't affect the other. Hence, one might see that a certain sculpture is very beautiful but later find that it was made by slave labour, with captives forced to produce the object while their families were being held hostage. An autonomist would claim that the beauty of the object was a separate matter from the ethical concerns one has about its manner of production. Hence, on discovery of the dubious circumstances of its creation, an autonomist would not see any reason to alter their aesthetic assessment of the sculpture. They merely alter their ethical assessment of it. One may cite, for instance, the example of the ancient pyramids of Giza. In many ways, these are wondrous constructions. They may not have been intended primarily as works of art but they can certainly be admired aesthetically nevertheless. Their geometry is perfect and their scale is itself magnificent. But all those who admire their beauty do so despite knowledge that they were built with slave labour. Those who worked on the pyramids did so in cruel conditions of enforced labour with a short life expectancy. Many of them died during the construction. It was an atrocity. But that doesn't in any way, the autonomist says, diminish their aesthetic value. The lines of the Cheops pyramid's edges are still there. The perfect shape and simplicity of design remain the same whether their maker was evil or beneficent. Further, the cruelty behind their construction might never have come to light. Would that mean we were unable to make an accurate aesthetic evaluation of them? Surely not. The autonomist will say that, as long as we have the object before us, we have all the information we need in order to make an accurate aesthetic assessment.

In recent years, however, this kind of view, that separates ethical and aesthetic considerations, has been challenged. One key subject of debate is the much discussed film *Triumph of the Will* made by Leni Riefenstahl in 1934. In terms of its filmic qualities, this work deserves many plaudits. It was innovative both in terms of the techniques used to capture the images, but also in its editing and conception. Months were spent in preparation, including use of unusual camera angles, often from moving cameras (see Devereaux 1998 for details). The problem with the film, however, is that it was the official document of the Nuremberg rallies of the Nazi party under Adolf Hitler. The images seemed beautiful, and the film techniques revolutionary, but they were used throughout in glorification of the Führer. The film begins with his plane landing in Nuremberg, as if Hitler is a god descending from the heavens to be worshipped by his mortal subjects. We then have scenes of the choreographed marches that lasted seven days and had tens of thousands of participants. It seems hard to fault it as a documentary film of the rally. But there is, of course, a major ethical aspect that we simply cannot put out of our minds. This film was a glorification of Hitler and his Nazi ideals. It was propaganda for an ideology that led to the deaths of millions, either in war or the extermination camps. If anything has been morally bad, surely it has been the Nazis, and a work of art in their glory must also surely count as morally bad.

But what are we to make of this? The autonomist is unlikely to deny that the ethical message of *Triumph of the Will* is morally repugnant but that, they would insist, is a separate matter to its status as a work of art. It is ethically flawed, certainly: but that doesn't mean it is aesthetically flawed. How could this be challenged? How could the principle of autonomy be undermined?

The first thing to say is that the case for autonomism that has been developed thus far is clearly not conclusive. It is based on an intuition: that two objects that coincide in their superficial observable properties must also coincide in their aesthetic properties. But why should we trust this intuition? Intuitions are notoriously unreliable in philosophy and often don't stand up to scrutiny, as Socrates shows in the dialogues of Plato. And whether aesthetic value is determined in this way is a moot point. It all depends on what you take aesthetic value to consist in. Earlier (Chapter 3), I said that I would not be accepting that there are objectively real aesthetic properties, that exist mind-independently, waiting to be appreciated by us. Rather, I opted (in Chapter 7) for the idea that there was an aesthetic way of seeing, and this was in part determined by our own natures and what we responded positively to. If that is the case, then the question of what determines our aesthetic judgements is up for grabs. It may just be the properties that we see but there might also be wider considerations that enter the equation. This is what will be argued.

Despite the fact that *Triumph of the Will* is well shot and displays a lot of features that might in other circumstances give us aesthetic pleasure, it still seems plausible to say that it is spoiled for us as a work of art because it is promoting a morally abhorrent cause. It is uncomfortable to watch in a way it might not be if it was filmed in praise of Mahatma Gandhi rather than Adolf Hitler. An autonomist might say that the discomfort we feel in watching is only a moral discomfort, not an aesthetic one. But can we really separate these two kinds of value so easily? To see something aesthetically, we have said, is a particular way of seeing. The tourist sees the fire extinguisher aesthetically while the security guard sees it as something to put out fires. We deliberately did not say anything too specific about what aesthetic seeing consisted in. In particular, I did not attempt to distinguish aesthetic perception in terms of the quality of the perception. An attempt was made in Chapter 7 to steer away from accounts of perception in terms of qualia, mental sensations or raw feelings. It would be a mistake to think, therefore, that the aesthetic and non-aesthetic could be distinguished by the simple natures of the sensations that they involve. Similarly, it seems a mistake to distinguish memories of experiences from the experiences themselves by saying, as Hume did, that the former are fainter and less vivid than the latter. The account of what it was to sense something, because it dispenses with qualia, might better be thought of as cognitivist. Our beliefs, hopes and desires shape the way that we see. The tourist believes that the fire extinguisher has been placed there for their pleasure and they duly oblige in taking some. They think different thoughts about it than the security guard. They have perceptions, of course, and they can enjoy them. But they are all cognitively laden. They are all a result of the interaction of eye and brain, as we saw with examples produced by Dennett, Gregory and Berger in Chapter 7.

Although this also is not conclusive, it opens the way for a theory of the mechanism by which our aesthetic experience can be affected by our moral judgements. If aesthetic experience really were about sensations, understood as qualia, or retinal images, then it is hard to see how there ever could be an aesthetic difference between our two objects that are perceptually indistinguishable. An aesthetic experience would simply be the enjoyment of having such qualia. But we have rejected such a view. Experience must be understood more widely and as cognitively laden. In that case, my beliefs about the work can be part of my experience itself. So now let us consider again our two indistinguishable sculptures. Although I couldn't tell the works apart, suppose I am then told that the one on the left was made by an artist who was expressing his belief in liberty. It is called, I am told, 'Freedom is beautiful'. The one on the right, though by coincidence indistinguishable, was made by a murderer in praise of the suffering. I hear that its title is 'Make the innocent suffer and die'. This immediately changes my aesthetic experience of the two objects. I may now turn to the sculpture on the left and look at it more closely. I may consider its shapes and colours and think about how it relates to liberty. I may think of liberty itself. I know that this sculpture is available for my enjoyment, unhindered by any feeling of guilt that I am condoning evil. I may respect the artist who created it, and so on. This will all be a part of my aesthetic experience, understood in a broadly cognitivist way. Next I turn to the work in praise of suffering. I have no desire to contemplate its shape, form or texture. I don't want to think about a murderer having made it in a pathetic, self-justificatory attempt to praise suffering. I don't want to think of innocent people being tortured or killed. The object is a turn off. I do not want to contemplate it or enjoy my perceptual experience of it at all. It is a flawed work of art, given what I now know, and does not provide an experience I enjoy as a matter of fact or that I even want to enjoy. After all, who watches *Triumph of the Will* these days, other than aestheticians who want to understand the latest debates? And when those people do watch it, how many of them in good conscience want to enjoy it or can enjoy it? It is a work in praise of Hitler and Nazism and we see this as an aesthetic flaw: one that prevents us from enjoying it aesthetically. And it does seem to be specifically because it is a moral flaw that we cannot enjoy it. An alien that knows nothing of twentieth-century history may watch it and at the end say, to everyone else's embarrassment, 'Wow! What a fantastic and beautiful film: full of wonderful rich images and innovative filming.' Or a neo-Nazi, who misguidedly thinks that Hitler was right, might also maintain that it is beautiful. What the rest of us see, however, from a position of reasonableness and being fully informed, is tainted and spoiled.

Before applying this connection between ethics and aesthetics to the case of sport, where I will argue that it fits very well, it should be admitted that, in the case of art, there have to be some qualifications. The relationship between art and morality is a far from clear one, partly because its role is no longer that of simply providing beauty alone. Some art, including film, theatre, literature and poetry, aims to challenge us and some of our preconceptions, which might include moral preconceptions. Morality itself could be questioned, or the relationship between existence and morality. In *L'Étranger*, for instance, Camus has his protagonist commit a murder (Camus 1942). Furthermore, Camus depicts the act in a rather distanced, factual way, with no attempt to suggest the act was wrong. The book is all about the murderer: his decision to commit the act and live with it. It is arguable, therefore, that the abhorrent act of this work does not lessen it as a work of literature. Indeed, the act is integral to the whole point of the book. It wouldn't be a work of art without the murder, and depicted in that factual, non-judgemental way. Perhaps an even more controversial case is Nabokov's *Lolita*.

There are a variety of responses we could make to this kind of case. We might consider whether the novel is morally bad just because an act it depicts is. It is not clear that the book in question is morally flawed, so perhaps we need not consider whether it is duly aesthetically flawed. We might, on the other hand, just allow that there are some exceptions. Perhaps we can just say that moral flaws *tend* to produce aesthetic flaws, but not in every case. Or perhaps we could limit the scope of our claim and say that moral flaws affect only certain aesthetic features of a work and not others. Where the point of art is to be thought provoking, or questioning of morality, for instance, then it may have to involve immorality as its subject matter. If the work aims at beauty, however, then we may allow that moral flaws detract from it. This latter line shows some promise, but we need not settle this particular matter here. We can leave it to philosophers of art.

Instead, our aim should be to note that this same kind of connection between moral and aesthetic value can be found in sport. If one wishes to support the thesis, sport is an excellent source of examples. The most obvious case is the one where cheating – a moral flaw – detracts from the aesthetic value of a sporting performance. Cheating through the use of performance-enhancing drugs is a particularly interesting case, though the same thesis applies in other cases too. I am not going to justify the claim that cheating is a moral flaw, rather than merely an infringement of the rules. I believe that, in the context of sport, cheating is indeed a moral flaw, but I will simply assume this (see Loland 2002 for further discussion).

Suppose I watch a game of football in which a spectacular goal is scored at the end of a fine, flowing move. I may feel the highest degree of appreciation for the passing and movement that led to the goal and the final shot at the end of it, which involves a wonderful bodily form and a fierce, rasping movement of the ball into the back of the goal net. I walk home from the stadium enthusing about the goal, commenting to my friends that it was the most beautiful, magical and graceful goal I have ever had the privilege to watch. They are in a degree of agreement. On returning home, I turn on the TV to look for replays of the goal. To my horror I find that, where I thought a teammate had set up the scoring shot with a flick header, they had actually used their hand illegally to knock the ball on, away from a defender who would otherwise have ended the attack. The illusion of beauty, I suggest, is now lost to me. While there were some moments of beauty during the build up, and the shot itself, the goal as a whole is now flawed. The flaw is a moral one. The goal was scored through cheating. Without it, the defender would have prevented the shot on goal. But because of that moral flaw, the goal is also flawed aesthetically. I instantly remove it from the list of most beautiful goals I have seen. Indeed, I may feel I cannot classify it as a beautiful goal at all, in any degree.

One may counter that the flaw was a solely aesthetic one because use of the hand is not beautiful with respect to football. A legal goal could not have looked like this. But there is nothing unattractive about using the hand as such, as we find in basketball and volleyball, for instance. It must be specifically that the goal involved cheating – an unpunished illegal and, I say, immoral act with respect to this sport – that I no longer find it beautiful. Here, therefore, we seem to have a simple and relatively common example of an ethical flaw producing an aesthetic one.

Perhaps, however, it might be said that there is at least a visible difference between a goal scored using the hand and one scored legally. The cheating was an observable feature of the goal; it was just that at the stadium I was too far away to see it. So we don't really have the proof that the ethical flaw spoiled the aesthetics. But this is where the case of drugs cheating is so interesting. When Ben Johnson won the 1988 Olympic 100 metres gold, in a seeming world record time of 9.79 seconds, there was no visible sign of cheating. His performance looked immaculate and for three days we were able to admire it in aesthetic awe. The power of his body and rippling thigh muscles captivated us. We could watch a slow-motion replay of his whole race, with his face showing a look of concentration and unity of being. Had this been a fair contest, we might still marvel at that scene. But it is rarely replayed now. Few TV companies offer it for our aesthetic enjoyment. Johnson failed his drug test after the race. He had cheated and won with the aid of illegal performance enhancers. Here we have a case, then, where the race would have looked no different if he could have run just as fast legally. And had he done so, we would likely still be watching it and enjoying it. It would be one of our finest examples of aesthetics in sport. But it is specifically because of the ethical flaw of Johnson – that he had cheated – that we no longer see it as having aesthetic value. One might almost go as far as to say that, once we know the race was a cheat, it has no aesthetic value at all for us. Some might look at his run and admire certain features of it, but it is hard to think that anyone could know of the cheat and still think of his race as a whole as aesthetically enjoyable. You may, of course, see the race in ignorance of its history, and judge it beautiful. But you would be in the same position as the football fan who thought the goal was beautiful until he saw the cheat on the replay. As soon as we know of the cheat, our aesthetic judgement is altered.

As well as cheating, there could be other ways in which our ethical evaluations affect our aesthetic assessments. A player may not have cheated in terms of the rules of the game, but may have exhibited some other moral flaw of which we disapprove, and this too could affect the aesthetics of the situation. A player may, for instance, be very skilled but morally reprehensible. There have been cases of players supporting loathed political views: displaying open support for fascism, for instance. And players have sometimes exhibited contempt for other people, showing how complacent they have become in their rich superstar lifestyle. We will see later (Chapter 11) that the personal vices of sports stars may have some mitigation, and that their role as moral exemplars is a contentious matter, but that needn't impinge on our findings here. It is suggested that such moral flaws in athletes may indeed detract from the aesthetic value of what they produce on the sports field.

It need not be only individual players that we see as morally corrupt and therefore less able to produce aesthetic pleasure for us as viewers. There might be cases where some of the clubs or institutions are seen as morally flawed. We might think of a sports club as morally tarnished, for instance. Suppose they have success but it is based on the wealth of an individual owner. Now let us imagine that we also believe such wealth to have been acquired through corruption or organised crime, or that the owner has a questionable human rights record in a former political life. Even if the team plays good football, which would be aesthetically admirable in normal circumstances, we may feel it is less aesthetically valuable to watch once we understand that it was built on the ill-gotten gains of corrupt wealth. Similarly, we might feel that a whole competition could be tarnished if it is morally flawed. The purist would not want to watch a competition that has been 'sold out' to commercial interests, for instance, or whose hosts had been decided by corrupt practices within the governing body. Finally, we might allow that individual contests could in similar ways be aesthetically flawed because of moral flaws. Some of them could be corrupted in the ways just outlined. One interesting case in a slightly different category, however, was the infamous 'death match' of Dynamo Kiev during the Second World War (Dougan 2002). Players were forced to play against a Nazi team with death the price for winning. There may have been some beauty and profundity in Dynamo nevertheless winning the game, and accepting the fatal consequences. But this also could have been their last show of resistance in what they saw as a hopeless situation. In either case, it would have been wrong for us as spectators at such a match to sit and admire its beauty as a game if we were aware of the moral context in which it was conducted. The circumstances were morally abhorrent and it was consequently not something knowingly we should have admired aesthetically.

It is needless for us to multiply examples any further as it has been demonstrated how there are a variety of ways in which moral flaws can detract from aesthetic value in sport. What has not been shown yet, though, is that moral virtues can add to aesthetic value. But this is also not a difficult claim to defend. A very obvious example is that of Lance Armstrong's recovery from cancer to win the Tour de France in cycling. A similar but less heralded case was Bobby Moore's own recovery from cancer a year before being England's winning captain in the 1966 World Cup. Armstrong's win is something that strikes us as all the more wonderful because of the circumstances. Cycling is already a sport with a high aesthetic content, where we see the human body at its full limit of endurance. But to think that the win was due to good character defeating adversity makes it even more beautiful to us. Similarly, Bobby Moore's first battle with cancer is something that had been kept a private matter until recently. To English football fans, that 1966 win was already a thing of beauty. But to discover that the character of the England captain was even better than we thought enhances its aesthetics even further. Seeing him lift the trophy aloft, in one of football's most iconic images, now is endowed with stronger, deeper emotional content that adds to our aesthetic contemplation.

Thus far we have been concerned with the influence of moral considerations on aesthetic value. We have seen that ethical virtues and vices can have positive and negative effects respectively on aesthetic value in sport. We have shown that aesthetic value can depend on ethical value. But what of an influence in the opposite direction? Can we have cases where the aesthetic values affect the morality of sport? It is arguable that we can and that the two kinds of value are therefore interdependent.

In recent and ongoing work by Torres (unpublished), it is argued that some of the norms of sport are informed by aesthetic considerations. The starting point for this claim is Simon's (2001) interpretivism with respect to sporting norms. We should, according to this account, give the rules of sport their best interpretation. Russell has developed and defended a similar view in which the 'rules should be interpreted in such a manner that the excellences embodied in achieving the lusory goal of the game are not undermined but are maintained and fostered' (Russell 2007: 55). Torres goes on to show, for the cases of football and rugby, that some of those excellences have an aesthetic dimension as well as the usual ethical considerations, such as fair play and autonomy of the athlete. More precisely, there is an informal norm, or ethos: to play well, to play beautifully, to develop the aesthetic nature of the sport. In football, for instance, there are some ways of playing that seem more aesthetically pleasing than others. Adventurous football is encouraged and negative football discouraged. Sometimes the governing bodies of sport issue imperatives to score more goals in football, more tries in rugby and so on. The aesthetic virtues and excellences of sport thus inform some of its informal norms. We have a direction of influence from aesthetics to ethics. We have shown therefore that there is a close connection between ethical and aesthetic values in sport, with influences going in either direction and an interaction between types of value. The best way to characterise the relationship is therefore in terms of *interdependence*.

We have now almost finished with the topic of aesthetics in sport, as far as this particular book is concerned. We will henceforth be concerned more directly with some issues in ethics and in the philosophy of emotion so far as they are relevant to watching sport. But before leaving the topic, we have in this chapter erected a bridge from aesthetics to ethics and shown that these two topics are not distinct and autonomous but interdependent.

When Devereaux discussed the film *Triumph of the Will*, she raised a question about our negative reaction to what on the face of it might seem to be a beautiful work of art. She wondered whether we should say that there is more to art than aesthetics, or we should say there is more to aesthetics than beauty (Devereaux 1998: 246). She sided with the second option. We need to broaden our notion of the aesthetic beyond its traditional boundaries. It should be clear from all that has been said in this book so far that this broader notion of aesthetics is one that is supported in relation to sport. Mere enjoyment of sensations is too limited a notion of the aesthetic and, indeed, it is not a credible account of how we perceive aesthetically, or how we perceive at all. A more cognitivist line has emerged in which our experiences are usually heavily influenced by our thoughts, including beliefs, emotions and wishes. Naturally, we have plenty of these in relation to watching sport.

I began in Chapter 2 by considering some of the differences between partisan and purist ways of watching sport. These two kinds of fan will have different beliefs, emotions and wishes in watching sport and thus different kinds of aesthetic experience. Most sports fans will undoubtedly have some degree of partisan and some degree of purist inclinations within them. The total partisan and total purist are at the extreme ends of a scale. But now we are in a better position to understand the differences between those two tendencies in the way we watch sport and thus better placed to see those tendencies within ourselves.

9 Ethics in sport and life

The motives for watching sport are not restricted to matters of aesthetic enjoyment alone. It is arguable also that there are ethical reasons to watch sport. Sport, it will be claimed, can play a part in our moral education and continuing development.

There is a long tradition of claiming that sport morally enlightens us. The most famous such statement is probably that of Camus, who claimed: 'Everything I learnt about ethics, I learnt from football' (1960: 242). Less famous but perhaps more important for sport is the claim in De Coubertin's defence of the Olympic ideal, that it had a task of 'moral betterment and social peace' (2000: 537). But both of these claims were made in reference to the benefits of playing sport. There will be many such benefits of playing, of course, but they do not transfer straight over to the watching of sport: at least not all of them do. Sport produces physical fitness, but watching it doesn't – and in some cases watching sport has the opposite effect. Sport may improve our character and foster virtue through the self-discipline of training regimes but, again, the watching of sport is unlikely also to provide this. Some sports fans may be very undisciplined, and mixing within fan culture sometimes, but not always, has an ill effect on character. Clearly, therefore, where the watching rather than playing of sport is our topic, we need to look for some distinctive benefits of watching if we are to justify its morally educative role. Over the next chapters such a defence of watching sport will be offered.

Sport is full of moral content, openly available to us for consideration, comment, discussion and interpretation. We see that a team *deserves* to win, for instance, whether they do indeed win or not. I see cheating, bad fouls and overly physical conduct, but I may also see someone play the game how it should be played, who upholds the higher virtues of the sport. I see teams prosper through their wealth, sometimes due to rich owners of dubious character, but at other times I see sports clubs collapse when they reach for the sun only to fall back down to earth. I also see some teams triumph in adversity: David sometimes slaying Goliath. Does all this teach me anything? Could it be that, by reflecting on the moral content of sport, I can learn anything of use? Specifically, do I learn anything of use beyond sport: something I could apply to the rest of my life, outside of a sporting context? When I see a cheat initially prosper, for instance, but in the longer term fail, is that a lesson I could apply to the conduct of my career or to my interpersonal relationships?

There seems a good prima facie case for saying that this is so. Although sport is a very particular kind of context, any moral lessons to be found in it would seem to generalise. But there is a line of thought that would preclude this. It might be said that the norms of sport are purely for sport, which is a highly competitive situation in which winning is the ultimate goal. There is something very artificial and contrived about sport, it could be said. Might its connection with 'real life' be a rather tenuous one? In that case, how can we be so sure that those norms would apply outside of sport, in a world where cooperation is better than competition and helping others is more important than winning?

Suppose, for instance, that I am at the supermarket checkout, in a queue to pay, and the supervisor opens up a new counter. Those waiting in other lines can start a new queue at the new till. Is it right for me to quickly rush in as soon as I see the new checkout open, perhaps beating people there who have already waited in lines longer than me? It seems not. Yet in a sporting context, I am encouraged to take every advantage of my opponents' slowness and poor observation skills. If my opponent slips in football, I am expected to exploit it and go on to score a goal. I am not expected to wait for them to get up. In the supermarket, however, if someone slips on their way to the new queue, not only should I wait for them, I should positively help them to their feet and guide them to a place in front of me. Similarly, if one of the shoppers is elderly and slow, it is mean of me to use my superior, near-perfect physique to run ahead of them and beat them to the chase. Yet in sport, it is an essential part of the ethos that I always try my hardest against any opponent. It is regarded as an insult and patronising if I go easy on my rival: for instance, if I didn't try to win a race. Yet, as we move towards the new queue, I precisely should go slower than I could so that someone more deserving of an advanced position in the line gets it.

It shouldn't really be any surprise, therefore, to hear the philosophical view that there is a distinct morality or system of norms in sport that is internal to sport itself and from which we should not draw any general moral lessons. Simon has advanced this thesis, which he calls internalism. The idea is that there is an 'internal morality to sport' (Simon 2001: 36) and similar views have been suggested by Huizinga (1950) and Morgan's (1994) 'gratuitous logic' of sport. Pawlenka (2005) lists a number of other proponents. Sport, Simon says, 'has a significant degree of autonomy from the wider society and supports, stands for, or expresses a set of values of its own which may run counter to the values dominant in the culture' (Simon 2001: 35).

Simon's view is more nuanced than a simple internalism, as we shall see, so we might get a clearer idea of the claim if we look at one of its stronger presentations. Møller has what we might think of as a pessimistic view of the moral value of sport. He sees it as having its own character and values, though not particularly attractive ones. He points out the violence of boxing, ice hockey and rugby in which there are many acts that, were they committed outside of the context of sport, would be totally unacceptable (Møller 2009: 22). In boxing, I seek to stop an opponent at any cost, within the confines of the rules. If they falter, I must take full advantage and go for the quick finish. I seek to 'punish' and 'torture' them, and accept that they are trying to do the same to me, wearing down the other to the point of exhaustion and submission. Similarly in ice hockey and rugby, direct hits are not the explicit aim of the sports but they both nevertheless have an element of dominance and wearing down the opponent through imposing one's physical presence. Put in stark terms, Møller states that training in sport requires 'a gradual adaptation to brutality' (2009: 22), '... there are moral standards in sport. They are simply different from the moral standards of society at large' (2009: 23) and perhaps most strongly, 'Sport is a cultivation of the will to win taken to the threshold of evil' (2009: 24). One way to understand this would be that within sport a Nietzschean morality holds sway. The contests within sport are about sorting out the masters from the slaves, where our aim is to exploit and punish weakness. This is Møller's view:

> Nietzsche has given us a lens through which the unchristian element in sport can be viewed. Sport shares Nietzsche's contempt for the weak. The loser is relegated. There is no mercy. Once again boxing comes to mind as a clearcut example. When the stunned boxer is on his way to the floor, the referee has to step in to avoid the risk of the groggy boxer being given the *coup de grâce* by the winner, whose thoughts are only on finishing off the match. That classic ethical rule, 'Do as you would be done by', is foreign to sport. Here the opposite counts, namely that we should do to the other what we wish them *not* to do to us.
>
> (Møller 2009: 27)

Simon's (2001) brand of internalism proceeds from a far more positive view of sport, however. It is roughly the view that sport has its own internal system of norms and they are seen as generally good ones that allow sport to be played in the 'right spirit'. The rules provide some of this, but not all. The formal rules do not cover every eventuality, so there are some occasions where additional moral judgements have to be made. What if, for instance, one golfer arrives without their golf clubs, through no fault of their own, and their opponent has a spare, near identical set (Simon 2001: 37)? Should the opponent refuse to lend them the spare set, and gain a victory through default, or should they lend the set and play the game, even though they thereby risk losing? The rules of golf make no judgement on this. But Simon thinks there is nevertheless an answer to this question, provided by the nature of sport. The opponent should, in the spirit of sport, lend them the spare golf clubs and play the round. But this answer doesn't come from the stated rules of golf, so from where does it come?

A possible answer is to be found in conventionalism, which is the view that sport merely reflects the existing conventions of the society within which it is located. But Simon has reason to doubt that society outside sport could provide all the norms required of sport. Conventionalism, for instance, would suggest that all the existing conventions, such as those in sport, were immune from criticism.

How could we morally question and challenge a norm if it were merely a convention? But we evaluate rules in sport all the time and make changes when, among other reasons, they seem to favour a wrong outcome: allowing time wasters to prosper, for instance. Simon's solution to this problem is to opt for a *broad internalism*. There are wider norms in sport than just the rules, but these are still sport-specific norms. Hence, you should lend the opponent your spare clubs in the spirit of sport, so that the game can be played. One is adopting a lusory attitude, which is essential to sport in Suits's account, and it cannot be part of the rules of sport itself that one adopts this attitude. This sporting spirit and these norms are, nevertheless, rightly considered moral values.

> What gives moral force to the virtues and excellences required in sport is their connection within the practice to respect for certain qualities of human beings … if we regard competition in sport at its best as constituting a test of excellence through creation of challenges, principles requiring an ethic of respect for the opponent and a commitment to fair play are a consequence.
>
> (Simon 2001: 44)

The case for broad internalism is helped by the widely accepted idea that there is a sporting ethos (see Loland 2002: 6–9, for instance). The ethos seems to be a set of ethical considerations that are often not explicit – not stated directly in the rules – but are decidedly sport specific.

Whether we take the pessimistic Nietzschean view of sports morality, or the more moderate broad internalist view, the conclusion seems to be that we should not expect sport to provide anything of general moral educative value that we could apply outside the sporting context. The lessons of sport, it seems, should stay within sport. They are so sport specific that it would be inappropriate – almost a category mistake – to apply them in other contexts. Although it is not presented specifically in this way, Møller even has an explanation of how the norms of sport are separated from the wider norms of society. The transitions from a non-sporting context to a sporting one, and back again, are marked by rituals that occur at the boundaries. Those boundaries separate two distinct worlds:

> In practice, these two worlds are kept apart by means of rituals such as the change of clothing that signals the transition from member of society to athlete. Shaking hands after the match and thanking an opponent for the game is normally regarded as 'sporting'. Strictly speaking, however, this is not what it is, since it is precisely a demonstration of the acceptance that the sport is over and that players now return to being members of the wider society.
>
> (Møller 2009: 25)

This leads us to what Russell (2007: 51) calls the *separation thesis*. When we examine it, however, we will see that the division between sporting and non-sporting morality is not so impenetrable.

Russell sets the issue out in terms of a stark contrast between a thesis of separation and a thesis of continuity, which doesn't quite match the distinctions employed by Simon (for Russell is keen to show that Simon's broad internalism sits better with a continuity thesis). The key question is whether sport reflects the morality of the society in which it occurs or is at odds with it (Russell 2007: 51). Clearly there are two ways that sport might reflect wider morality, corresponding to what we might call a direction of influence. In one direction, we can consider whether some of the norms of society find their way into sport. Sport is, after all, a social enterprise, organised by its various institutions. These institutions are run by people who are members of the wider society and it would seem natural, therefore, to think that the norms of the society that forms the sporting institutions find their way into the institutions and practices of sport. In the opposite direction, we could have an influence going from the norms of sport into the norms of society. This is the kind of direction of influence that Møller, for instance, would want to resist. The suggestion, however, is that the norms that are played out in sport could indeed find their way into the non-sporting contexts of that society. This will be the claim that is developed in the next chapter.

First, though, how plausible would it be that there is no influence at all between the norms of sport and wider norms? Given how easily ideas spread between different contexts, it would seem prima facie that it would be hard to keep them separated. Consider, for instance, how quick people were to apply Darwinian ideas on biological evolution to the organisation of human societies. In the moral case, one may want generally that people get just deserts for their efforts and then devise the specific case of sport to reflect that norm. If sport revealed no correlation at all between effort and chance of success, we might feel that it is pointless. We don't want our winners to be randomly selected, as in a lottery, for instance. Sport includes certain athletic excellences that are to be encouraged and rewarded in the playing. Use of the appropriate skills, for instance, should tend towards success. There is a question, therefore, of why we would have had any interest in sport at all – why we would have institutionalised and fostered it – if its norms bore no relation to those we hold dear in wider life. There is a possible answer to this, however. We might believe that sport is retained as a segregated corner in which we are able to release the evil within us: let all the nasty, domineering sides of our nature have free reign so that we can get it out of our system. The purpose of sport would then be to offer a kind of catharsis.

Rather than base our view on intuitions we have or claims about human nature, let us instead look at some of the norms of sport so that we can consider whether they are to be found also in non-sporting contexts or whether they really are so distinctive that they are found nowhere else. Fortunately, Russell has already done much of our work and he concludes in favour of a continuity thesis: that the values of sport are continuous with wider morality, that they reflect and express it. He notes, for example, a Dworkinian interpretivism at play in the rules. They have to be interpreted in a way that emphasises the integrity of the sport's values.

Dworkin (1986) uses this interpretivist idea in the case of law, and the judgements that should be made in accordance with it. Thus, in respect of judges, 'in an adjudicative context the moral virtue of integrity requires that judges try to give a coherent, principled account of the system of law' (Russell 2007: 56). Russell argues we have to do the same with sports and consider their rules to be part of a coherent and principled system. What we get from that is a principle of sport that its 'rules should be interpreted in such a manner that the excellences involved in achieving the lusory goal of the game are not undermined but are maintained and fostered' (Russell 2007: 56). Hence, there is no explicit rule forbidding a football player from carrying a baseball bat with which to club opponents away. But the governing body responsible for interpreting and implementing the rules of the game, indeed anyone who plays any kind of game of football, no matter how informal, operate with this principle. Russell calls it sport's *internal principle*, which tells us that it is of course undermining of the excellences involved in football if players were to stop each other with blows from baseball bats. Nothing about the carrying of the bat would maintain or foster the skills that are seen as integral to the sport: accurate passing, fluid movement, ball control, changes of tempo and so on.

Russell also identifies an *external principle* of sport. While the internal principle governs the sport once it is being played, the external principle concerns the conditions under which someone is deemed to be playing sport: what it is to join or leave a game. The external principle is based around the notion of consent. As Suits summed it up, a game is 'a voluntary attempt to overcome unnecessary obstacles' (2005: 55). One must consent to take part in the game, for anyone who was being forced to participate would not be adopting the requisite lusory attitude. They would not be game playing. When one enters consensually into the game one does so under a certain understanding, which includes an understanding of the boundaries of acceptable and unacceptable behaviour. As Russell says, this includes an understanding of acceptable force that is appropriate for that sport. The level of appropriate force is much higher in rugby than it is in basketball, for instance, but even in rugby there is an upper boundary. A rugby player knows that hard tackles are one of the 'excellences' tested in the sport and thus consents to be on the receiving end of them, if they come. But, picking up on the themes of Chapter 6, a punch in the face is considered beyond that boundary and it is thus not considered a part of the sport, hence not what you agreed to when you consented to play. We may say the same of so-called *sledging*, for instance, and other personal verbal attacks. One player may pass a comment to undermine another's confidence, which may be seen as part of the psychological aspect of the game, but there is still a boundary around what is acceptable. Racially abusing another player is beyond that boundary, for no player consents to it, not even tacitly, when they enter the game. The external principle manifests itself in a host of norms, for instance that 'participants are entitled to equal concern and respect' (2007: 56), or that the aim of game playing is to promote human excellences (2007: 57).

The question now is whether such values are to be found in wider society or whether they evince a sport-specific morality. There was the aforementioned thought that, prima facie, people were likely to set up sports that reflected their moral values and we can now look to corroborate that view by finding values in sport that indeed correspond with non-sporting values. There is a slight complication, however. This would not, of course, *prove* that the morals of society had influenced society, or vice versa, as it is possible they could have developed concurrently but independently and merely happened to coincide. Such a possibility does not matter for the debate in which Simon and Russell are involved. Their concern is only with whether sport has a distinct morality. Finding that the moral values of sport coincided with wider morals would be enough to refute such distinctness. But for the concern of the present book, the question of influence passing between the morals of sport and wider morals is indeed pertinent. If we wish to claim that sport plays a morally educative role then we need to show that there can be influence from sporting to non-sporting values. Finding some common ground in the two does not quite prove that this occurs but it is at least consistent with it and would probably be the best explanation of how there is coincidence, rather than it being a pure accident.

Russell makes the case for both his external and internal principles of sport being continuous with the ethics of society at large. The external principle, which we saw made consent an essential requirement of being a player, Russell claims reflects a general Kantian morality in which each person should be taken as ends in themselves, never as means. This is the *second maxim* of Kant's moral philosophy (Kant 1785: 30). Now, it would be misleading to say that society at large runs according to Kantian ethics. However, this particular Kantian maxim, treating individual people as ends rather than means, is one that does have a widespread appeal in many societies as one of the basic principles that ought to be respected. The ideas that all people are entitled to equal consideration and that certain acts should be voluntary and consensual are clearly principles with a wider appeal. Each person's vote usually counts the same in a legitimate democracy and we feel we have a right to withhold consent from various activities in life. We feel that sex, for instance, is something that should be a voluntary matter and for which we should be able to withhold consent. Without consenting, we are not a genuine participant in a sexual encounter. If coerced, it is regarded as a sexual assault, just as we are playing a game only if we are doing so voluntarily. Russell concludes, therefore: 'It is difficult to think of a human institution that has a more profound commitment to a Kantian consent principle than sport and games generally' (2007: 59). The principle of consent is vital for sport and has general application. We have found an issue, therefore, where the ethics of sport and wider society coincide. Both appeal to the importance of consent.

In respect of the internal principle, Russell draws a similar conclusion. The rules should be interpreted, according to his Dworkinian interpretivism, so as to maintain and foster the game's excellences, rather than undermine them. One can see immediately that the interpretivist approach has application outside sport, given that it is a theory that comes from the philosophy of law. Dworkin had argued that applications of law should be interpreted this way, so the law has a broad set of norms that corresponds with the broad norms of sport.

These may not be fundamental norms, however. There could be a further reason why we feel that sport (and the law) has a commitment to this norm. Russell thinks it is based on something more basic: 'This principle seems clearly drawn from a general moral ideal of promoting human flourishing. That is, the internal principle requires the fostering of special contexts for the development, creative exercise, and enjoyment of distinctive human capacities and character traits' (Russell 2007: 61).

Sport encourages human flourishing by rewarding the exercise of virtue. The desire for victory offers one motivation. And even competitors who know they have little chance of winning, as with most runners of a marathon, seek to display the best of their abilities. Although one may be unable to win the marathon, one may desire as high a placing as possible. Playing itself provides 'a competitive context in which excellences can be displayed and measured' (Russell 2007: 57), but even this is not specific to sport. One is often in situations outside of sport in which abilities are compared and judged: in the workplace, for example. Russell concludes, therefore, in favour of the continuity thesis over the separation thesis:

> the external and internal principles, the principle of integrity, and in related commitments to fairness, impartiality, and moral equality ... show that sport is profoundly informed by ideals that are continuous with and represent, reflect, extend, and reinforce more basic moral values found outside sport in everyday life.
>
> (Russell 2007: 61)

Russell has given us a strong argument for the continuity thesis. But the separation thesis might not be defeated conclusively. There remains the possibility of offering a more sophisticated separation thesis that explains why some of the morals of sport can be found outside of it, and vice versa, but at the same time claiming that the dominant sporting ethos is a distinctive one. Møller's defence of separation seems to be making this kind of tweak to the theory by allowing that there can be some seepage of morals from non-sporting life to sporting life that may influence certain aspects of the sport without changing its fundamental nature. Hence, he argues:

> Despite the fact that these two worlds differ as far as morality, values and norms are concerned, they are not entirely separate. To some extent they exert an influence on each other. The public's idealisation of 'sporting' behaviour has, for example, left its marks in the form of symbolic actions within sport. An obvious example is to be found in football, where it has become common practice to throw the ball in to the opposing team if they have kicked the ball into touch in order to secure treatment for an injured player. This is now an unwritten rule symbolising fair play. But it just does not alter the overall system of values and norms in sport. As soon as the

opponent has got the ball back again, it is no longer the extraneous ideals of fair play that prevail but the will to win, and the players go at each other again just as hard as before.

(Møller 2009: 25)

Can we, however, dismiss Russell's external and internal principles as mere details of sport? Are they outside the 'overall system of values and norms in sport'? Russell has given us a systematic account of the norms involved in entering into sport and the norms that apply once involved in sport. If he is right, then these are fundamental to what it is to play and cannot be dismissed as a merely incidental detail. The norms Russell has identified are working at all times during sport, even when, to return to Møller's example, the ball is back on the field and the players go at each other again.

There are further issues raised by Møller's view, however. Even if we are not persuaded by a separation thesis, the pessimistic view of sport can still be taken seriously. The issues of competition and winning at all permissible costs may be common to both Russell's positive account of sport and Møller's negative account. Is this, then, just a matter of whether we consider competition itself as a negative or positive factor? In Russell's case, competition is seen as something that encourages human flourishing because it incentivises excellence. For Møller, however, it is depicted as something that brings out the worst in us, encouraging us to push the boundaries of legality within the sport. Sport can make the winners flourish, but what about the losers? The less athletic children forced to do sport at school may see it as something that tends away from their flourishing. It may be something they associate with failure or bullying. And even the winners, who flourish to the extent that they are rewarded, have won because of their superior evil and will to power. The moral character of sport's values is something that can be contested, therefore. Whether it produces human flourishing or its opposite is a judgement that is up for debate (see, for instance, Carr 1998: 120–1).

Another thought that comes out of Møller's position, therefore, is that, even if we were to side eventually with Russell's continuity thesis, we have no right to assume that the morality of sport is a good one. If sport does reflect and reinforce the wider morality of the society in which it is located, that gives us no right to assume it must be a desirable morality. If Møller is right that there is a ruthless morality in sport, might that be because the morality of society itself contains ruthlessness? Certainly, I am likely to stop and help an elderly person who is trying to join a queue, but might this be analogous to Møller's example of stopping the football match so an injured player can be treated? Once they are back in the game, the ruthless competition recommences. Similarly, once the elderly person is back on their feet, they may be just another economic competitor against me for resources in a society that revolves around the satisfaction of selfish desires (note how *rational* for economists basically means *selfish*). In more recent work, Russell has also conceded that some of the values of sport may be morally dubious (Russell 2010), but this need not undermine his continuity thesis if the morals of society at large are also dubious.

This discussion has now given us enough to proceed. In the following chapter we will be looking further at the way in which the watching of sport can play a role in moral education. In order to allow that as a possibility, we needed to know that the morality of sport was not something completely distinctive to sport, that could have no possible application outside of it. We have seen enough now to conclude that this is not the case. Based on Russell's response to Simon, we can see that some of the most fundamental principles of sport reflect a morality that is to be found in society at large. We can thus support Russell's continuity thesis: the morals of sport are continuous with those of the society in which they occur, instead of separate from them. But merely from our support for a continuity thesis, we are in no position to presume the positive nature of those morals. Sport created in a bad society may reflect those bad morals. As an example of this, we might consider the corrupt nature of football in a host of eastern European countries during the so-called communist era, some details of which are documented by Wilson (2006). In the next chapter, however, we will look further into the nature of virtue and vice in sport and it will be argued that, in this respect at least, sport has a distinct capacity for encouraging virtue and discouraging vice. Given our support for the continuity thesis, this is significant because it makes sport a legitimate arena in which we can learn virtue.

10 Contests of virtue

We saw in the preceding chapter that there were reasons to support some form of continuity thesis, in which the morals and norms of sport were not completely isolated from those of wider society. Some of the morals that we found in sport reflect those we might hold generally, such as respect for the consent of individuals. The emphasis there was on the morals of wider society finding their way into sport, and we argued that they did, or at least this was the most likely explanation of their coincidence. But the purpose of rejecting a strict internalism about sporting values was so that we might consider the morally educative value of sport. Here, the concern is with a direction of influence that might go from sport back to the rest of society. If this can be established, we would have shown that sport is both informed by the morality of society but also, in turn, informs that wider societal morality. This will indeed be the claim. But there is also a stronger thesis we should investigate. Might it be that watching sport produces some real moral benefit and enhancement to those who study and understand it? Might it be not simply that sport reflects back the same morality that came to it from outside, as if it were nothing but a mirror, but that it could actually enhance those morals to some beneficial effect, as if it were more of a magnifying glass?

How could we argue for this and what would it mean? If certain claims can be upheld about sport being a good source of moral education, or what McFee (2004: ch. 8) calls a moral laboratory, then we can argue that sport has the potential to improve those who watch it. It could allow us to reflect on morality and form judgements about what is good or bad. It might even inculcate in us good moral habits; in other words, the acquisition of virtue. This, it will be argued, is the case. Sport contrives scenarios for us to watch that we might liken to a contest of the virtues. When we see the virtues in action, we are able to see their successes and follow their example. The argument of the previous chapter is crucial here because, given the truth of some form of continuity thesis, those virtues that we see succeeding in sport can then be applied in our everyday lives, even in non-sporting contexts. In that case, the morality we get out of sport might not be just the morality that we as a society put into it. There would be nothing morally to be gained from watching sport if it simply reflected back what it received. Rather, sport is interesting because it brings morality to the fore. It provides a moral focus because it is full of conflict between virtue and vice. Desert seems to be one of the key notions within sport, accompanied with the judgements of observers as to whether those deserts are just or not.

We should step back from this conclusion however and consider more carefully the arguments that would stand in its favour. We shall henceforth assume some version of the continuity thesis to be correct and move on to the other issues. In particular, we need to clarify and justify the notion of sport as a contest of virtues and then we should seek to understand the role of virtues in morality and how the watching of sport can lead to their cultivation.

The idea that sport provides a contest of the virtues is an ancient one, though it might not always have been named in such terms. Reid (2010) details some thoughts of Seneca that are comparable to the idea of sport as the contest of virtues. The gladiator's display of valour, for instance, is considered by Seneca as 'inspiring instruction in the Stoic's daily pursuit of virtue and understanding' (Reid 2010: 210). Some benefit is assumed here, but how does that occur? What is it that is intrinsic to sport that allows it to play this role of inspiring instruction?

To answer this we must return again to the nature of sport itself. Our notion of sport was a social one: an institutional theory where those institutions grew around games and athleticism. We also saw that Suits defined games as voluntary attempts to overcome unnecessary obstacles. The latter part of the definition of game is useful for our purposes. The notion of unnecessary obstacles shows us that game playing, and thus sport (because all sports are games), involves an element of artifice or contrivance. There is no particular reason why we should want these small white balls to go into only slightly larger holes in the ground, or why we should want to jump over a high bar instead of walking under it, or why we should fight over an oval ball as if it meant the world. Sport involves competition in most cases, admittedly not all, but where the competition has no real point outside the context of sport. Yes, winning can make you rich, if you compete at the highest level in a major sport. But it is not as if it is useful in itself to be able to sink a golf ball with the fewest shots or to be able to jump over a bar rather than go under it. Skills and capacities are displayed in sport, and some of those very same skills might, in theory, be adaptable to real-life situations. The long-jumper may at some point have to jump to save their life, for instance. But in playing the game one adopts a lusory attitude to one's activity. One tackles the unnecessary obstacles, rather than just avoiding them or moving them out of the way, precisely so that one can play the game. There is a sense, therefore, in which the contest is artificial. One is competing to be the best at something that is valuable only within the sporting contest itself. It is not as if the rugby ball that is fought over contains within it some cure for cancer, for instance, or that carrying it across the goal line makes that cure available to the people. The reasons for fighting over the ball are contained entirely within the adoption of a lusory attitude towards that activity.

We know why the participants adopt this lusory attitude: so that they can play games, which is an intrinsically valuable thing to do. But why should we as spectators have any interest in watching other people play games? We don't get the health benefits or fun the players have in fighting over an oval ball. And we also know that nothing really hinges on the fight, given the artificiality of the contest. The winner of the game gets to win the game, and little else. Why should it matter to us who gets the ball in the end, given that the getting of the ball has importance only within the game itself? We, as spectators, are not really even part of the game, so why should it be of any interest at all to us what the outcome is? The remainder of this book might provide some answers. One kind of answer will be in terms of our emotional attachments in sport but another kind of answer is here: our interest in sport is a moral interest.

The fact that the obstacles of sport are unnecessary could, then, be an explanation of our interest in sport rather than being undermining of it. The moral interest we have in sport could be facilitated by its very artificiality. There are of course many other areas of contest in our lives, and we are very often participants in those contests: for wealth, for work, for happiness, for sexual partners. In these cases, it seems that there is something very real at stake. Our quality of life can be seriously affected by how we fare in these contests. Sport, however, is something we can watch with a relative level of disinterest. Its outcomes can be very important to some people, such as the partisan supporters, but even then it does not affect in any immediate way their wealth nor seriously their long-term happiness. Is there any evidence, for instance, that supporters of Manchester United (a successful team) are happier than supporters of Rochdale (a relatively unsuccessful team)? And if there is greater happiness, would that survive if we factor out other influences such as wealth? Because of the artificiality of the sporting contest, it is arguable that we are able to place it into a moral quarantine and disconnect it from outside concerns. There are boundaries between sport and everyday life and these are often marked by rituals, of the kind Møller discussed (see previous chapter). But those rituals, we can argue, do not mark specific moral boundaries, as an internalist claims. They do mark something, but this is best understood in different ways, as we can now consider.

The notions of overcoming obstacles, and of the competition to do so most effectively, create the possibility of victory and defeat in sport, but we are yet to explain the notion of just desert. In doing so, we will reveal what is so apt in sport for the role of moral educator. I will now present a meta-interpretation of sport that explains why it is fit to serve the purpose of a moral laboratory (McFee 2004: ch. 8) or a modern morality play (McNamee 2008: 1). Once we see this, we will see why it is morally so significant.

The idea to be exploited is that sport be understood as a contest of virtues. Each participant brings their virtue to the arena and what interests us as spectators is not directly the competition between individuals but, rather, the competition between the virtues those individuals embody. This is a more abstract and metaphysical interpretation of sport than, for instance, Suits's account of what it is to play a game, which is why it might best be described as a meta-interpretation: keeping it apart from more concrete interpretations of what constitutes sport. The account is no less important to us for being abstract, however, for at this level its moral fascination to us is revealed.

What do we mean by a virtue? There is a tradition of virtue ethics that stretches back to Aristotle's *Ethics* but continues into contemporary moral philosophy (for an example, see Hursthouse 1999). The first thing to note is that *virtue* falls within the disposition family of concepts. To have a virtue is to have a disposition that can manifest itself in appropriate circumstances. If we assume empathy to be a virtue, for instance, then it might manifest itself when one meets someone who is stressed or upset about something one personally feels to be unimportant. The empathic person may understand the distress of another even though the cause of that distress in the other would not be a cause of distress in them. Without empathy, one may see that the other person is distressed but be dismissive of it, thinking it irrational. Note, however, that it is not until encountering someone in such a condition that empathy reveals itself. Only when certain situations arise do we see who is and isn't empathic. This is not to say that people are only empathic at the time they are manifesting it, however. It is characteristic of a disposition, and thus of a virtue, that it can be possessed while it is not manifested. A glass can be fragile without being broken, for instance. Similarly, one's virtue may be exercised only at certain times. One might expect it to be exercised during certain moments but it is nevertheless arguable that there is no conclusive test for possession of a disposition. Perhaps we think that a brave person should always manifest their bravery when in a dangerous situation. But as Wright (1991) argues, even if they fail to manifest that bravery, there could be some other explanation than that they are not brave: they were ill at the time, for instance, or drunk. And nor should we assume that possession of a trait is a simple matter. As Butler (1988) has shown, virtues such as bravery may be complex in nature. The brave person must first have a disposition to recognise certain situations as dangerous – a foolish or rash person may not have this, although a coward does – but then be disposed also to behave accordingly by not giving in to the fear.

Virtue, and its opposite vice, are, however, dispositions of a particular kind. They may both be thought of as character traits (see Butler 1988) but are also morally loaded. Clearly, a virtue is a disposition it is good to have and a vice is a disposition it is bad to have. We may think therefore of disposition as the genus of which there are several species. An ability, for instance, is a disposition it is useful to have and a liability is a disposition it is useless to have. Virtue and vice are varieties of disposition, therefore, but that still leaves many questions to be resolved. What is meant by good and bad, for instance, if it is only in relation to these notions that we are able to distinguish virtue and vice? One sensible approach seems to be to adopt pluralism (Swanton 2003), which allows that what counts as good and bad can vary according to different contexts. There can be individual sporting virtues that are not especially moral. We can distinguish these as specifically athletic virtues. Stamina is a virtue for lone-distance runners, for instance, while height counts as an athletic virtue for basketball players. These are virtues in the sense that they tend towards success within those sports. In different sports, of course, they could be liabilities. The height of a basketball player would be a serious disadvantage in sprint races. There are, however, other virtues that come into play in sport that have a more overt moral sense, and it is these that will interest us more.

The idea is, then, that in sport, each competitor brings their relative virtues to the contest and uses them to battle with the virtues of others. Some of these are merely athletic virtues, but not all of them. Other virtues that the athlete brings to the contest include dedication to their sport. This is a virtue that is exercised by the athlete not just in the contest itself but is a virtue that can allow them to develop the excellences of the sport through training and practice. Again, these count as virtues for the sport because they tend towards success. The better one's training regime, and the more one practises, the more one tends towards success. Other virtues, however, have to be exhibited during the contest itself, such as determination and strength of will. Some athletes and teams seem to have greater mental strength than others, which allows them to improve their performance when under pressure. Someone of a weaker character might buckle under the stress of the competitive situation, which would be considered a vice. A number of the virtues that tend towards success in sport will involve a mental, intellectual aspect: keeping calm in the heat of the contest, or having a greater understanding of how the game is developing.

When we watch sport, we watch this contest of the virtues play out. We see them pitted against each other and are able to see what character traits tend towards success and what character traits tend towards defeat. Here, it is important that we understand the truly dispositional nature of the virtues. They bring us only a tendency to victory, not a guarantee of it. A disposition doesn't necessitate its manifestation, even when it is tested for it, but it also tends towards that manifestation in a stronger way than a pure possibility (Mumford and Anjum 2011). Hence, one increases the chances of success the greater one's virtues, but we all know in sport that the better team does sometimes nevertheless lose. Rather than being a flaw (Kretchmar 2005), this provides one of the great beauties of sport. It is not simply that in watching sport we always want the best team or player to win. Part of its appeal is to see that the weaker can occasionally triumph over the stronger. And this itself may teach us something about morality and character. It shows us that it is possible to win against the odds, and it also shows us the vices of overconfidence, complacency and hubris, which all tend towards defeat. Our notion of a virtue, therefore, is not determined solely by the outcome of the disposition. There must be some independent notion of virtue that is not merely attached to the result, and that is how we are able to allow that the better team nevertheless can lose even though they will have a tendency to win.

The way in which this can provide moral education, therefore, is that the lessons we learn about the virtues and vices in a sporting context can transfer outside to other contexts. Virtue is a particularly important notion in this respect. There is a concern in rule-based systems of ethics about how we can apply a moral rule or law in a new situation that we encounter. This is one of the motivations for moral particularism, which states that moral assessments cannot be general but must be made on a case-by-case basis (Dancy 1993, 2004). While it is not within the scope of this book to commit to a detailed ethical theory, we can note that the challenge of particularism leaves us with a problem in want of a solution. The problem with rules or principles is that they can often come into conflict. If we believe that we should always both tell the truth and be kind, there can be situations in which it is not possible to satisfy both principles. In addition, such a general principle is not responsive enough to changes in context, which we think can alter the moral features of a situation. As Plato showed in the *Republic*, while we think we should pay our debts, there are at least some situations in which it is preferable not to, for instance when the person to whom a debt is owed has in the meantime gone mad. We need not pursue the case for and against particularism here, but we can note that at least these two problems are avoided by forms of virtue ethics. Instead of morality being about the application of strict, universal principles, it is about the cultivation of good habits: of empathy, kindness, consideration, bravery, determination, honesty, integrity, faithfulness and so on. And once acquired, these good habits can be brought to bear on situations that are completely new in our experience, that are not covered by any principles we know.

The idea of a tendency, being something more than a pure possibility but less than an absolute necessity, is illuminating in this context. The principle 'Always tell a truth' does not admit exceptions. One falsehood constitutes a violation. And thus, there can be situations where there are conflicting principles, some of which then have to be broken. In the case of the virtues, however, they can be held, and brought to bear on a situation, without universality. The honest woman might, on occasion, lie, if she has other virtues that tend more strongly in the opposite direction. In one situation, kindness might win out, but in another situation, telling the truth might be the strongest habit. This is not to suggest that the habits alone dictate behaviour. On the contrary, there is a role for context and situation. One must also be able to respond appropriately to the situation one is in. But, as with Butler's claim of the complexity of character traits, part of what it is to be a kind person is to recognise the sort of situation and circumstances in which kindness is appropriate. Unless one had this disposition, one could not truly be considered a kind person. Suppose someone never helped a friend in need and still insisted they were really a kind person: they were just bad at noticing friends in need. In this case, we would have good reason to doubt that they were really kind.

Because of its dispositional nature, then, habits allow us to explain the two cases that were problems for rule-based morals. Paying our debts may be good but there can be some situations in which we should not do it. Having the virtue of being a good debtor is consistent with sometimes withholding your debts, and so on *mutatis mutandis* for every virtue. And it is also perfectly possible that the virtues conflict and the course of action is determined by which one is stronger: there might be a stronger inclination towards kindness than truth, for instance.

There is an objection to the whole dispositional and virtue approach to morality in sport that was raised by Heather Reid (in discussion). What can we really know of virtue and vice? All that is available to us is evidence of the outcomes in sport: who wins and who loses, and where someone is placed. How then could we learn anything about the virtues themselves by watching sport when all we see is their effects? I don't know whether Reid is sceptical of dispositions generally but this is certainly a question that should be asked as it gets to the heart of an important matter. With dispositions generally, and not just virtues specifically, we know them through their manifestations. We know of fragility, for instance, through seeing things break, and we know of solubility by seeing things dissolve. But does this mean that the dispositions themselves are unknown? Are only their manifestations knowable? But then what is our basis for believing there to be some enduring state or property of a thing – its fragility or solubility – that is supposed to persist even when it is not manifested? Why believe in dispositions at all? Why not just believe in the events that occur – the breaking or the dis-solving – and not speculate as to their hidden origins? This is a view that many empiricists have taken towards dispositions, as detailed by Wright (1991). But the case for dispositions can nevertheless be made.

Our reasons for believing that there are enduring dispositions that are at least partly responsible for their manifestations are to an extent theoretical but they are nevertheless sound. We note that all sugar is able to dissolve in liquid, for instance, and that all wine glasses can break. And if we see a glass that is barely distinguishable from the many others that have been dropped and broken, isn't it a reasonable supposition that it would do the same? This broadly inductive evi-dence is backed by other empirical knowledge about the structure of glass, which explains its brittleness. And when we get to the specific case of the virtues, we see that there are some similar considerations. We may only see the manifestations of a person's kindness but we can have good theoretical reasons for taking it to be an enduring habit or disposition of that person. There may be some constancy in their character, for instance. The idea that character exhibits constancy has been challenged by Doris (2002), but not on solid grounds. We have seen above that, although a disposition tends towards certain manifestations, it does not neces-sitate them and does not require that they be manifested on every occasion they are tested. Constancy of character does not require absolute uniformity and is not, therefore, falsified just because contexts can be found where an honest per-son, for instance, acts dishonestly. What we do know, however, is that people tend to manifest a pattern of behaviour in a variety of circumstances. This reveals their virtues and vices and is some inductive evidence that they have a good or bad habit integrated into their character. The structural evidence, akin to the structural explanation of the brittleness of glass, is not, however, on the whole available. We just don't know enough about how humans, especially their brains, physically embody habits. This makes character traits very difficult to know in this structural way. For purely athletic virtues, we do have such evidence, how-ever. We can see that certain basketball players find the game easier because they are tall, and certain runners are better at sprinting because of their muscle bulk.

These considerations give us reason to believe in enduring virtues and vices and not just the results of their exercise. But there are also good reasons to believe that it is the virtue and vice that is important for us, rather than just their result, which adds evidence to the claim that our interest in sport is a moral interest.

The evidence for this claim is the way in which we are so keen to test the veracity of victory. We are very keen, for instance, to have a regime of drug testing so as to tell whether victory was achieved unfairly through banned performance enhancements. A reasonable explanation of this is that we want to know that the victory was a genuine result of virtue, rather than a triumph of vice. Cheats can sometimes win. In the case of drug taking, offenders can be stripped of their title, but even in cases where this does not occur, we are still keen to see cheats exposed. In football, for instance, a foul play can be missed by the presiding officials and the rules do not permit a retrospective change of decision. But we are nevertheless very keen that cheating be exposed. Thierry Henry, for instance, was roundly condemned for setting up a goal by handling the ball that saw France qualify for the 2010 football World Cup in the place of Ireland. This incident was played over and over on TV and Henry's action discussed at length and condemned. Although France scored the goal, it seemed extremely important to all interested observers to let it be noted that it was an unfair and undeserved goal. This gives us a basis for answering the challenge to virtue in sport that was posed by Reid. It is not just the result of virtue that interests us and it is not all that we can know. There are various ways in which we can test whether an outcome in sport really was a result of virtue or nefariousness. In modern times, TV directors clearly are keen to expose cheating in replays, and any other way of exposing cheats is encouraged. Drug testing is an obvious case while even more dramatic has been the occasional exposure of sporting conspiracies, such as match fixing for betting scams or, in one infamous case, an ice skater arranging for her rival to be kneecapped.

Desert is thus a key concern in watching sport. We don't want to know only who won, but whether they deserved to win. The result alone tells us so little. Indeed, we don't particularly watch sport to find out the result: there are now far more efficient ways to know results. We watch sport to find out how the result was achieved. Did the runner come from behind in the final straight to win from a seemingly impossible position? Did the losing team in football have their shots hit the post on a number of occasions, and were they cheated out of a penalty kick? Did the winning boxer really deserve the points decision awarded in their favour by the judges? And so on. Seeing how victory was achieved is of course not solely a moral interest. We may be interested from a coaching perspective, or just for the intellectual pleasure of understanding tactics. But moral interest is often a reason for many who watch sport, and it is hard not to be captivated by the moral debates surrounding it. This is not just over the final victory and defeat, of course. There may be many incidents during a game that are fit for moral consideration. Was a particular tackle during a game excessively violent, for instance, or was an instance of retaliation malicious rather than warranted?

If we see sport in this way, as testing out various issues of virtue, vice and desert for success and failure, then we can see why McFee likens sport to a moral laboratory. It is in sport that we are able to reflect on all these moral incidents that we see in a relatively harmless and inconsequential environment. And when we observe the success of certain virtues, such as courage and determination, we see the advantage of cultivating it for ourselves so that we can use it in the rest of our lives. Seeing victory 'snatched from the jaws of defeat', for instance, shows us that, if we don't give up, we can achieve our goals, whether they are sporting goals or otherwise. And seeing courage exhibited in a hopeless situation might be of use to us when we face our own hopeless situations.

Is this educative role unique to sport? Does it provide something that could be gained just as well elsewhere? This is a concern for McFee, who, in seeking a justification of sport, interprets it as requiring that sport provide something nothing else can. That would be a strong justification. Many would think that an activity is justifiable just by its being useful. Whether that thing serves a purpose that nothing else could serve might strike us as an exceptionally high standard of justification. And it might be intrinsic to the nature of sport that it provides a moral laboratory without being intrinsic in the sense of being the only moral laboratory (see Culbertson 2008 for a discussion; and also the reply from McFee 2009). There seems nothing wrong as such with the idea of sport being one among many moral laboratories. Fiction, for instance, can serve a similar purpose to sport. If we consider the novels of Charles Dickens, for example, they are full of battles of virtue and vice. Oliver Twist's virtue, for instance, wins out over Fagin's vice. For Dickens, the characters of his cast are the key drivers of the plot and the moral of the story. *A Christmas Carol* tells us how Scrooge's vice is replaced with virtue. On stage and screen too we may be encouraged to reflect on matters of morality.

McNamee (2008: 1) builds on this theme, likening sport to the modern morality play. The original was a medieval method of spreading catholic morality to an almost entirely illiterate people. A band of actors would come into town and act out a story with an obvious moral at the end. Certainly this can play the morally educative role that we now find in sport. But there is a major difference between sport and fiction, written or dramatised. What makes sport so interesting is that it is a genuine contest of virtues. The outcomes in fiction are contrived by the author, while the outcomes in sport are the authentic results of pitting the virtues against each other. The moral of the story in fiction may be simplistic or idealistic. It might show that the good guy always wins, as they do in Dickens. In the religious morality play, good always triumphs over evil. And even if a good person suffers, they get their eventual reward in heaven. But one valuable moral lesson is that undeserved triumphs and failures can happen, and that setbacks and defeats are at least as common as successes (Skillen 1998). Of course, more modern fiction indeed deals with the theme of suffering injustice, as in Orwell's *1984* or Solzhenitsyn's *One Day in the Life of Ivan Denisovich*. But even here, we are getting one author's take on the morality of the situation. We can argue, then, that what is important in the idea of a moral laboratory is that we have a genuine empirical experiment in how the virtues and vices interact. We can thus liken the outcome of a sporting contest to an experimental outcome. Fiction might also allow us to contemplate morality, but its contrivance can be likened to a thought experiment instead of a genuine one. We are dependent on the author's intuitions, beliefs and desires about what the outcome should be rather than what the outcomes actually are when the experiment is run.

Sport differs from fiction in another respect, to which we have already alluded. Fiction can deal with some of the great themes of human existence: love, death, life, money and power. Sport does not deal with morality this directly. It deals with morality at a harmless distance because, as mentioned before, its ends are entirely fabricated. Kupfer has made this point well, saying that sports set up a 'shared delusion'. 'In this respect, sport takes the pretense of theatre one step further. Where theatre presents real ends and activities within a pretend setting, the significance of even the ends and activities are pretended in sport' (Kupfer 1983: 457).

This nevertheless might be seen as an asset with respect to the use of sport in moral education. It can be hard at first to deal directly with certain moral questions. And it can be difficult to cultivate virtue if one immediately starts with the hardest, most testing and emotive moral problems. Just as one learns to swim first in the shallow end of the pool, so virtue can be learnt and tested in a safe context before being brought to bear on the more serious matters of life.

We can now start to gather together the themes in this chapter and explain the core idea of sport as a contest of virtues that may then play a morally educative role. Sport involves an artificial contest over fabricated goals. Among others, a reason for doing this is that it sets up for us the possibility of moral conflict, where each participant brings to the contest the sum of their virtues. We see these pitted against each other and we often reflect at length on some of the key incidents of such conflict, where issues of just desert and reward are to the fore. Sport thus creates the possibility for us of moral reflection in a safe, segregated and, we might say, laboratory situation. But it is only a possibility of reflection. We cannot guarantee that everyone who watches sport will use it for personal improvement, and nor can we guarantee what sort of moral lessons a particular game will provide. The outcomes in sport are not predetermined, and this is a feature that makes it of particular interest.

Given our observation of the moral laboratory within sport, we are then able to apply that morality outside, in wider contexts. In the previous chapter, the continuity thesis was supported. Arguments that the morality of sport is distinct and isolated from the morality of wider society were rejected. But we allowed there was at least the unlikely possibility of a pure coincidence of sporting and wider morality. How could we show that they did actually interact and inform one another? One way would be to show that there was a plausible mechanism by which the morality of sport 'gets out', back into society. In this chapter, a mechanism has been suggested. The witnessing of virtue in action teaches us what virtues we ourselves should cultivate: virtues such as honesty, fairness, dedication and determination. We have seen the positive benefit of such virtues in action. We have seen in sport, in its artificial and isolated moral laboratory, that they tend towards success. And reflection allows us to see that we should cultivate such virtues in the hope, often corroborated, that they will tend to success in non-sporting contexts also. Furthermore, there is good empirical evidence that morality derived from sport has made its way outside of the sporting situation. McFee argues that 'metaphors – of fair play and level playing field – are (among) the things ethics gets from sport. I suggest that a value of sport resides precisely here' (2004: 137). Having seen the idea of a level playing field in sport, where for a true contest the conditions must be the same or similar enough for all parties, we can apply this to the competitions of wider society: judging between job applicants, for instance, or tenders for a contract. And how such a metaphor comes into play in our lives generally, it has been argued, is that we integrate it within our character as a virtue: a disposition to set up equal conditions for all contestants. Such a dispositional account was offered as a way to explain how moral lessons learnt in one context could transfer to others. Rather than having a rule-based system of morals, in which difficult questions can be asked about how those rules are to be applied in new, previously unencountered contexts, an idea in virtue ethics is that we should aim to cultivate virtues so that we automatically respond in the virtuous way, whatever the circumstances. It was also said, however, that one's action will be determined by many virtues, often competing against each other, such that in different circumstances we get different outcomes. A virtue thus only tends towards a certain form of action. It never guarantees it.

There is a further argument to be had, though not one that will be pursued here. There is of a course a thought that the playing of sport is also morally improving (Carr 1998; Gough 1998). It might then be wondered whether in merely watching sport, and not being a participant, one is losing out in some respect. Is there something to be gained from playing that cannot be gained from merely watching? Indeed, is it regrettable that we become less active participants and more passive observers? It may be, but it is not a new problem or theme. As Reid's study of Greek and Roman sporting morality shows, the significant shift probably occurred long before our time:

> It has been said that sport in Rome, with its emphasis on spectacle and entertainment, comes much closer to our own culture than that found among the Ancient Greeks. In some ways, this is unfortunate. The educational benefits of sport as touted by the classical Greek philosophers clearly require some level of participation and perhaps even competition. Roman citizens' lack of athletic participation reflected reduction in civic participation; something else we struggle with today. Becoming a nation of spectators is hardly a social ideal; but neither need it be a barrier to a good life. Roman Stoicism and Epicureanism show that philosophical spectatorship can contribute to the pursuit of virtue and happiness as long as we maintain the proper attitude. Furthermore, sport may be used politically as it was in Rome, not just to promote government interests but also philosophical ideals such as cosmopolitanism. The overarching lesson is that even though sport is entertaining, it never needs to be merely entertainment.
>
> (Reid 2010: 225–6)

Even if mere spectatorship cannot duplicate the benefits of participation, there is no reason to think that it doesn't nevertheless still have a role to play in the cultivation of virtue. Reid allows this, 'as long as we consider the spectacles rationally and try to learn from the lessons they teach' (Reid 2010: 226). And the defence of watching sport that is offered in this book must always come with this kind of proviso. The watching of sport need not benefit everyone. Its benefits are always premised on the adoption of an appropriate aesthetic and ethical perception.

Appropriately viewed, therefore, sport is available for the moral enhancement of those who watch. We began by wondering whether sport merely reflects back the morality that society at large puts into it or whether it enhances it before giving it back. Is sport merely a moral mirror or more a magnifying glass? Some reasons have been given for the latter. In being a contest of virtue, sport allows us to learn about and understand morality better. It puts ethical concerns into sharp focus and is thus well placed to teach us to some extent how to live our lives.

11   Should athletes be role models?

Any successful athlete must display a considerable degree of virtue. As such, it seems they would be good examples to follow. But does that mean we should adopt them as our role models? This is the question to which we now turn.

The question seems to be one that we cannot avoid. The argument of the previous chapter raises it naturally. It was argued that sport should, and does, play a beneficial, morally educative role. It provides a genuine contest of the virtues, where virtue tends towards success and vice tends away from it. Some virtues, it was allowed, may be relevant purely to the sporting situation but others, it was argued, were transferable to non-sporting contexts. Players or teams are disposed towards success when they train the hardest, prepare the best, practise their techniques and tactics, have a steely resolve to face challenges, have inner mental strength, and so on. By contrast, the vicious competitor decreases their chances through laziness, weakness of will and complacency. It might be thought natural, then, that successful athletes should be role models. If we aspire to be like them in our own lives then are we not entitled to think that we can share in their success? Can't we exhibit the same virtues and reap the consequent benefits?

If this is so, a further moral question is raised. Given their alleged potential educative influence, doesn't this place an obligation on the athlete to be a good role model? That is, to exhibit virtue at all times, in their professional and private lives. Successful athletes have what we may call (following Tymowski) a greater sphere of influence than regular people. Others will imitate them, especially the young and impressionable. And does this give them a moral duty to use that sphere of influence for good rather than ill? Just as every parent knows their behaviour will be followed by their children, the athlete should know that they set an example many others will follow, and this places on them a far greater obligation to behave well than someone who is not in the spotlight.

I will argue, however, that matters are not so simple and that we should always try to separate virtue in the abstract from the various successful athletes who at times display it. I will argue, further, that there is no moral obligation on athletes to be role models. We cannot say that they should be positive role models even if some of them are and even if it is praiseworthy in those cases. To be a positive role model, I will argue, would be an act of supererogation, which therefore involves no obligation even if it can produce good. The demands on being a role model are too strenuous, I argue, and cannot fairly be foisted on an athlete.

This carries with it some degree of controversy. As part of an advertising campaign, basketball player Charles Barkley claimed he was not a role model (see Reid 2010: 125). Assuming he was being serious, rather than just saying it for advertising purposes, it raises the question of whether someone has the right to disown or renounce their position as role model. Tymowski (unpublished) says not. Whether one is a role model or not is not a matter of choice, one could argue. If people start to imitate you, you are a role model whether you like it or not. It is not a position you can walk away from. It is disingenuous, it could be alleged, to pretend that one has no responsibility for those who imitate you. The elite athlete knows that they are watched by large audiences. They know as a sociological fact that sports stars are among the heroes of many people. They furthermore know, or should know, that it is a fact of psychology that many people imitate the behaviour of their heroes. Taken together, all this would seem to suggest some degree of moral obligation on the part of the athlete to use their influence for good. And that suggests they must behave in an exemplary fashion. This will extend outside the sporting and professional sphere. Those who are easily influenced are just as likely to imitate the general lifestyle, including the private lives of their heroes, and thus the athlete cannot display vice when they have the ability to spread it widely.

I will argue, however, that there are a number of mistaken claims in this line of thinking. Although virtue can be learnt through watching sport, role models do not need to be the vehicle through which such virtue is spread. I will advance the following claims:

1   Role models are a bad way of imparting moral lessons.
2   The status of role model is unreasonably conferred by others on to the athlete whether they want it or not.
3   The role of role model is too demanding for anyone to fulfil.

These lead me to conclude that there is not, after all, an obligation on athletes to be role models. Setting aside the issue of role models directly, I then argue in addition:

4   Athletes do not have (total) responsibility if others follow their example.

I will conclude by ruling out what I call the perfectionist conception of the role model, but I will allow that there is a weaker conception in which there can be imperfect role models. Athletes may provide some good examples of role models in this latter sense precisely because they are imperfect. In seeing their mistakes and their reactions to them, we can learn much about life.

First, then, we need to look at the notion of a role model and see how important it would be in conveying the moral lessons that sport no doubt contains. As it is used in moral parlance, the idea of a role model is that it is an individual who is set as an exemplar for others to study and imitate. The role model is some-one we should try to be like. There is also an assumption that the role model is virtuous so that in imitating them one can exhibit the same virtue. This need not always be the case, however. There is at least the theoretical possibility of a negative role model: someone who is bad but admired by those who are also bad. A scoundrel might take as their role model an even greater scoundrel, so it seems that it not a matter of necessity that the notion is a morally positive one. There is nevertheless always some idea that the role model does what they do in the right way. There is a sense of good in which the scoundrel role model is a good scoundrel: they know how to be a proper scoundrel, such that anyone who aspires to being a scoundrel would do well to be like them. To be a scoundrel, it seems, one must acquire the correct set of virtues required to be one. The notions of role model and virtue still have some connection even in this case, therefore. The role model knows what skills are appropriate for the kind of role model they are. But we would do well to take as our paradigm case the role model who is a positive exemplar, rather than a negative one.

Let us now examine this ideal of a role model critically. There is a major question to be asked. Do we really need role models? Are they an efficient way of imparting moral lessons? One thing in their favour is that they are a very concrete instantiation of virtue and, it might be thought, thereby an easy and convenient way of displaying morality for others to see. One can simply tell a student 'be like X', where X is someone we can trust to always display virtue and nothing but virtue. But, on the other hand, one should not forget there could be other ways in which moral lessons are conveyed that are less concrete but perhaps more reliable. This is what, I argue, we should allow to be the case.

The problem with role models is indeed their unreliability. A role model is to be exemplary. They are to be emulated because they are completely or ideally good. But no one is likely ever to be able to live up to that ideal and, when they do mess up in some way, we feel badly let down. A generation of young Americans, for instance, have been brought up to think of Tiger Woods as the perfect sporting role model. Yet in 2009 his life and career unravelled when it was revealed that he did not live up to the image that had been projected of the perfect dedicated sportsman and husband. Salacious revelations left him entirely discredited as a role model. What were all those young people to think in whom hero worship of Tiger had been inculcated? Should they think that a raunchy personal life is good? That a high sex drive produces sporting excellence? Or, instead, that there are no true heroes any more? That everyone has got something to hide? That morality involves only shades of grey? That no one can be moral? The perfectionist role model ideal has no ruling on such cases. There is no contingency for the possibility that the moral exemplar turns out to be less than perfect.

One can hardly condemn Tiger Woods especially. Could we plausibly claim that any sports star meets the required standard? Indeed, could any human be all and nothing but good? Isn't it a normal part of being human that we make mistakes, do things we wish we had not, we succumb to temptation, decide on changes of direction in our lives, or put ourselves before the needs of others? For any role model, isn't it inevitable that there be some such failing, and also inevitable in contemporary society that the failing come to light?

The sporting case, however, magnifies these points several fold. A sports star faces far more temptation than the regular person. With wealth and fame, all manner of potential problems come an athlete's way. Sex, recreational drugs, performance-enhancing drugs and many other temptations will be within their ambit, and we have no reason to expect their resistance will be stronger than that of any other mortal. Second, of course, if the athlete does succumb to one of the vices on offer, it is far more likely to be exposed by the media than if a regular person did the same. Many people experience infidelity or recreational drugs but, of course, no one wants to hear about it. But if an athlete does any of those things – a famous athlete, perhaps a role model athlete – then upon discovery the full exposure of the media tends to follow. The Tiger Woods story ran for many months, his personal failings receiving an almost surgical scrutiny and daily updates.

The example concerns what we may think of as a private vice, which had nothing to do with that fact that he was a sportsman. That is debatable, but the point must be well taken that any person, in any walk of life, could suffer from sex addiction, for instance. But if we need to look for cases of role models letting themselves down within the playing of sport, we will not have a difficult job. The case of Ben Johnson has already been considered in Chapter 8. Briefly a national hero in Canada, he then failed a drugs test and he was stripped of the medal and banned from the sport. It was a huge let down to those who had supported him, admired him and gloried in his ultimately pyrrhic victory. His mistake was to be a cheat and contribute to a widely growing cynicism about sports that is spreading. Similar cases, affecting athletics and cycling especially, have led some to believe that 'everyone is at it' and that those being caught are just the stupid ones who can't follow the correct instructions from their coaches for disguising their drug cheating. Johnson is a case of a cheating athlete who got caught, but there are many others who cheat and nevertheless succeed. Because they succeed, they might still be taken as positive role models and spread a lesson that winning is all that counts, regardless of the methods. This might also foster a rather cynical attitude in society. Maradona's 'hand of God' goal at the 1986 World Cup is an obvious example of successful cheating. At the same time, however, the goal in question tarnished his image in many places. And when there are people who disregard this, and still admire him, is it only because of a morally bankrupt culture in which we already believe in 'success at all costs'? Doesn't the successful cheat contribute further to that moral bankruptcy?

Sporting superstars, indeed any rich and famous celebrities, make bad role models, then. If we were to have role models at all, we should choose sports stars and other celebrities last of all. But, we seem at least entitled to ask, what is the other option? How else can we learn moral lessons, and in particular lessons from sport? There is an alternative, however, and we can venture that it has only been in recent times that it has fallen into neglect as a way of thinking about morality. This is the tradition that can be found as far back as Aristotle's

Nicomachean Ethics that deals with virtue and vice in the abstract. One needs, in this tradition, to study the virtues directly, rather than via some person who is supposed to exemplify them. Against the ideal of role models, there is a whole tradition of philosophical ethics that deals in abstractions of good and bad, virtue and vice, and rights and obligations, that does not concern itself primarily with the concrete. Isn't this a far more reliable way of considering ethics, given that it is not hostage to the weakness of will of the role model? Why, then, have we come to concentrate on the role model so much? Might we speculate that it has something to do with the rising power of the media and the celebrity culture it has spawned? As this is not a philosophical hypothesis – it is an empirical, socio-logical one – I will not dissect it further but it is a charge I will repeat below.

The more philosophical point is that it is not clear that we need role models even if we find it easier to learn about virtue through its concrete instantiations. I may see virtue displayed in this or that action, and similarly for vice. And I may be able to abstract from that a notion of general virtue or virtue on its own. The problem with role models is the seemingly groundless hope or assumption that the virtuous acts are all to be found in single individuals. Experience suggests on the contrary, however, that it is almost unknown for a human to be always virtu-ous and never vicious. People are usually some mixture of both. Admittedly, some can be more one than the other, but virtually everyone has at least some virtue and at least some vice. To take single individuals as moral exemplars, therefore, seems foolhardy and sets us up for disappointment. The actions from which we can abstract a notion of virtue in general can, instead, be performed by a range of different people rather than one or two, and similarly for vice.

The ability to abstract from our experience is not, of course, some very special ability for which we need philosophical training. It is done naturally by anyone who is able to understand what a shape is or what a number is, for both of these involve universals rather than particulars (see Armstrong 1989 and 1997). They could not be grasped by us unless we were able to abstract from our experience. But even very young children understand shapes and numbers. If one wants to see children's ability to abstract morally, one need only cut a cake for two of them and make one piece smaller than the other. The very abstract and complex concept of fairness will no doubt be raised very quickly.

It is hoped that the first claim has been established, by a weight of considera-tions, that role models are a bad way of imparting moral lessons. The second claim concerned how an individual becomes a role model. The point that the status of role model is conferred by society on the individual should itself be uncontrover-sial, so we will spend more time considering the ethics of such a conferral.

It seems that only a fool would declare themselves to be a role model, though it is at least a possibility. Perhaps a parent might tell their children to be like them. It is likely, however, that anyone who did this might be considered ego-tistical, complacent and self-satisfied, all of which are vices. So it is almost as if self-declaration of role model status proves that one is not in fact a role model. But whether or not that is the case, it is clear that role model status is almost always conferred by others. The Charles Barkley case shows, if we take it at face value, that this need not even be done with consent. It also shows, irrespective of the rights and wrongs of it, that the subject seems unable to resign the role of role model. Those who confer the status in the first place seem the only ones able to remove the status, which they can do. Arguably, the Tiger Woods case is one where the role model status has been withdrawn. Woods is no longer offered as a role model but, rather, more as an example of how a life of vice will eventually catch up with you.

We have not yet been very specific about who confers the status in question. To say that society confers the status is rather vague, yet it is hard to make much more precise. Certainly the media plays a big role, but only insofar as we let it do so by consuming their products. Players' agents are also complicit in that they have often encouraged the release of certain stories and images that cultivate the image of a morally upstanding family man, for instance, as in the Tiger Woods case. The media tend to be happy to collude in the building up of a role model. Might this be because they can sell even more papers and get more viewers when a role model inevitably comes unstuck and is exposed by some folly?

Do we, however, have the right as a society to confer such a status, with all the weight of expectation it carries, upon certain individuals, who tend to be young and faced with various temptations? Can I not ask to be admired for my sporting prowess alone, irrespective of anything I do in other parts of my life? Can I not admire the footballer Paul Gascoigne *as* a footballer, for all he was able to do on the field of play, irrespective of the fact that he is a deeply flawed and troubled individual in other respects? Why should his personal life be a matter for my judgement and why should my judgement of that part of him matter to my judgement of him as an athlete?

Suppose, for instance, a young athlete realises that they have some aptitude for a certain sport and are judged by their coach to have the potential to succeed at an elite level. At the same time, however, they also realise that they have some compulsive personal vice that they cannot control. Or perhaps there is merely some aspect of their life – one that is not at all vicious – that they would prefer not to disclose (many gay athletes have felt in this position). What are they then to do? Should they withdraw from sport and decline to go as far as they could, simply for fear of exposure? But that would mean that the sport could lose a potentially good competitor, and the athlete would lose what might be a major part of a rewarding life, including the livelihood and rewarding experiences it might bring. For all we know, a successful sports career might actually assist in the athlete's personal coming to terms with a vice, and this option would be being denied them. In short, it seems a violation of the athlete's right to flourish if they have some uncontrollable part of their life that excludes them from the sport. If being successful in sport carries a danger of being made a role model, and being a role model carries danger of personal details of one's life being exposed, then this seems oppressive of athletes in that position. In that case, therefore, it seems that we do not have the right to expect certain forms of behaviour from athletes, for it could exclude from the sport, for non-sporting reasons, people who are unable to behave in the expected way. And we can say, following from that, that we should not have a right to make such an individual a role model, for that may be the first stage of a process that could result in their exposure and accusations that they have let down their fans and admirers.

The third contention was that the role of role model is too demanding for anyone to fulfil. This has already been supported with the claim that no one is perfectly good, so no one could meet the required standard. That is a descriptive claim, and it might be argued that it is giving in to human failing far too readily. It might be urged instead that there is nevertheless a moral obligation on athletes to be good irrespective of their failings and thus to overcome them. This is a normative rather than descriptive claim. An argument (which I attribute to Tymowski) is that, because the athlete has such a large sphere of influence, they are capable by their example of producing much good and virtue. This, it could be said, puts an extra obligation on them that regular people do not have. Few others follow my example, for instance, because I am not well known and have no sporting success or anything else that makes me widely admired. This frees me of an obligation to use my influence, as I have very little. But we know that many impressionable people will imitate their sporting heroes. If they behave badly, others will too, but if they behave well, their virtue can spread among their fans.

Nevertheless, the normative argument can be resisted. The fact that we are able to do good does not entail that we are obliged to do so. There are some types of act that are known as supererogatory (a term first used philosophically by Urmson 1958). This means that, although it is praiseworthy to perform such an act, it is not blameworthy if one doesn't. For example, suppose I am back in the queue at the supermarket checkout. The person in front of me, we suppose, finds that they do not have enough money to pay their shopping bill. No one would blame me for taking no heed and keeping out of their business. But suppose instead I give this stranger 20 pounds in cash for them to settle their bill. Many would think this a praiseworthy act. But it is an act of supererogation because, while it would probably be considered worthy of praise, no one would blame me for not doing it.

What has supererogation to do with athletes as role models? The point is that, if an athlete (or anyone else) sets a perfect example for others to follow, it could indeed be considered praiseworthy. But we cannot blame someone because they are unable to set such an example, despite Tymowski's point that they have a huge sphere of influence and capacity to spread virtue. Why, then, is there no such obligation? A plausible reason is that the role of role model is too demanding. We may be pleased if someone plays the role but we can't expect that they do. It is an unreasonable demand, so no one has a duty to satisfy it. What is behind this is a general criticism of overly demanding or perfectionist systems of ethics (discussed in Mulgan 2001), for example utilitarianism. It can be said that a pure utilitarianism is an unreasonable and unworkable moral code. It tells us that what is good is that which procures the greatest happiness of the greatest number (for example, Mill 1861). But with a little thought, we see that this is a near hopeless formula. To be good is to be nothing less than perfect. There is only one possible future action for me that procures the greatest happiness of the greatest number.

Many of my actions will procure some happiness of some number of people, but there is only one good, right thing for me to do (or perhaps more than one action tied for first place as the best). We can see that this is far too demanding, hence the term perfectionism. It allows me no leeway to do something that gains a lot of, but less than maximal, happiness. Unless it is the most happiness, I am on this moral code blameworthy. And everyone is indeed likely to do something less than perfect, for they are unlikely to be able to correctly calculate exactly how they should act so as to obtain that ideal outcome. Even if they did correctly discover that right act, it is almost certain to require so much personal sacrifice to achieve that one would think it an unreasonable demand of anyone.

Utilitarianism can be dismissed on grounds of perfectionism, therefore. At the very least, it requires a reformulation. The same perfectionist charge, I argue, can also be brought against the demands on a role model. It also requires too much. Any slight failing is seen as a disappointment and a dereliction of one's duty as role model. This is too strenuous a morality, requiring exemplary behaviour in public and private life. It is a form of perfectionism in that, if we are to follow the logic of the argument, because one has a large sphere of influence, one has the capacity to spread virtue. But if there is an obligation, for this reason, to spread some virtue, there should be an obligation to spread the most virtue. The premise being assumed is that, if one has an ability to do good, one ought to do good, and clearly doing most good is better than doing some good. So, like utilitarianism, the role model has to behave perfectly, by the sphere of influence argument, which is a moral code no one could hope to fulfil.

The arguments thus far are enough to establish, we should believe, that there is no obligation on athletes to be role models. To repeat, however, we may still claim that sport can play a morally educative role in displaying virtue in action, but there is no reason why this should require focus on individuals rather than on virtue in the abstract. But there remains one further argument that we need to counter. Immediately above, the discussion centred on Tymowski's suggestion that the obligation to be a role model is provided by the athlete's wide sphere of influence, which gives them an opportunity to spread virtue. It was said that no obligation followed from this. But there is the opposite side of the coin to consider. Tymowski also points out the opportunity the athlete has to spread vice. The sphere of influence works both ways. Just as good behaviour will be imitated so, too, will bad behaviour. It might be argued then that, even if the athlete has no duty to be an exemplary role model because such a role is supererogatory, they might nevertheless have a duty not to spread harm through their influence. The thought is that, though they don't have to do good, they shouldn't do harm. It is easy to see the argument for the bad influence of bad behaviour. The impressionable may copy the behaviour of their role models, as we have already conceded, and just as they may copy good behaviour, they may also copy bad behaviour. It could then be argued that the wrong-doing athlete has responsibility for the bad behaviour of their imitators.

But are athletes really responsible for such behaviour? Let us consider again one infamous incident of an influential sportsman behaving badly. In the 2006

World Cup Final, Zinedine Zidane headbutted Marco Materazzi and was sent off from the field, with his depleted side eventually losing the game in a penalty-kick competition. Zidane had been a hugely influential player for the national team during his career. He inspired France to their 1998 World Cup win and, because of his north African origin, it did much to unite for a time France's diverse society. For fans of French football, Zidane was as much of a role model as one could find. In the 2006 incident, however, he lost his cool, publically showed aggression and violence, severely lessened his team's chances of winning, and exited his last ever game of football in shame. This sad end to his career was mirrored at the same time in French society as disorder was on the increase. Can one say, therefore, that Zidane was at fault in showing a bad example to all his followers? His defence was that he had been provoked, but wasn't that a terrible example to show to people of how one should handle provocation? Might others who also feel ill-treated respond violently, having seen Zidane's reaction?

Nevertheless, one can argue that the individual player does not have total responsibility for his or her imitator's bad actions. The TV pictures of the headbutt were shown over and over again, from every available angle, together with comments on how bad it was of Zidane to have done it and statements of what a bad example he was setting. But why blame Zidane alone for any such influence? His action was able to influence only those people who knew about it. Apart from those in the stadium, the world was only able to know about it because of the media's detailed coverage. The incident had not been broadcast in the original live transmission of the game. It occurred away from the ball so the camera was focused elsewhere. When the nearby linesman brought it to the attention of the referee, the TV director had to review action from the other off-air cameras to find the confrontation and, once found, it was then aired subsequently from every available angle. It seems, therefore, somewhat unfair on the player to speak of his sphere of bad influence when it is only through the subsequent actions of the media that it was able to have any significant influence at all. Had the incident not been played over and over again, it would have had a far more limited sphere of influence. It is arguable, therefore, that the media's actions are more responsible for any imitation than the player's, for they have set up the context in which there can be publicity of bad behaviour. In the days before TV and a global media, far fewer people were able to be influenced by sports stars. There seems to be some hypocrisy, therefore, if the media harks on about the bad influence of such incidents given that there would be no such bad influence without their coverage of it. By way of contrast, we can compare the dissemination of Zidane's error with a more sensible approach to on-screen violence adopted by the UK government in the 1980s. With a rise in spectator violence in stadiums, a rule was agreed prohibiting broadcasters from showing any stadium unrest on screen. Not only did this starve the culprits of publicity for their misdemeanours, which they seemed to crave, but it also stopped a bad influence on anyone who might be impressed and influenced by what they saw. Perhaps it worked. Since the 1980s, UK football hooliganism has been in decline. A responsible media, therefore, or a responsible regulator of the media, could have taken the decision that any bad behaviour on the sports field should not be shown, or at least not be gratuitously re-shown.

There is a further defence that could be mounted of Zidane, and any other sports star judged to be badly behaved in the performance of sport. The best athletes will be those who have a high level of physical and emotional commitment when playing. A game such as football involves much pressure, passion and emotion. By the end of a match, a top-level athlete will be physically and mentally exhausted. An occasional aberration such as Zidane's ought, in such circumstances, be understood and excused. It was a big error, not least because it seemed to end his side's chance of winning the World Cup, but it is one we ought to excuse because of the highly pressured and stressful circumstances in which it occurred. Anyone would be susceptible to mistakes in such a situation. Forgiveness ought not to come too hard, therefore. But what this also shows is again the point that athletes are among some of the very last people we should look at to be role models. The very performance of their sport makes them vulnerable to errors of judgement during play. We may broaden this out along lines already mentioned above. Professional errors in sport are one thing and may be explained and excused by the stress of the situation, but can't one say the same about any errors in the athlete's private life? It was suggested earlier that the superstar athlete will be exposed to greater temptation than most regular people. But we can also add to this point that the stress of playing elite-level sport is bound to affect the athlete's whole life. It does not begin and end when they enter and leave the field of play. The life of an elite sports star is highly pressured because of the high stakes of success and failure and, indeed, the very media exposure that makes them role models. Constant attention and expectation is sure to lead to stress, and all too often that can lead to errors, failings and vice in one's personal life.

These considerations weigh in favour of the conclusion that we should not hold athletes responsible for any negative sphere of influence they have and therefore not responsible for any imitations of their negative acts. And it then seems that the case for athletes being role models is looking weak indeed. We have seen why having role models is not a good idea insofar as it is not a reliable way of imparting a moral education. We have seen also that the status of role model is something assigned to individuals whether they want it or not. One might even say that it is inflicted upon them. It was then argued that the role of role model is too demanding as it requires too high a standard of behaviour and does not acknowledge human failings. Sports stars, it seems, are likely to be even more susceptible to such failings than others. An ethics of role models is a variety of overly demanding, perfectionist ethics that no one could realistically hope to satisfy. It was shown that the sphere of influence can in theory lead to either the spread of virtue or the spread of vice. But it was argued that neither case leads to obligations on the part of the athlete. Although they may have an ability to spread virtue, to do so could be understood as supererogation. And while they are able also to spread vice, they should not be held responsible for doing so given that it can occur only with the full complicity of the media. Indeed, the media might be thought of as the main driver of the spread of bad examples.

Before ending, however, another possibility should be noted. The perfectionist notion of a role model is one that is categorically rejected here. We are all imperfect. But that does not mean that we cannot learn from other people and how they deal with the trials of their lives. People who have experienced shame and troubles, and wrestled with inner demons, may be able to teach us more about our own lives and how to handle our problems than any media-manufactured image of perfection we are given. Real people face real temptations and make frequent mistakes. How one responds to such defeats in life is often how character is built. Because sports stars face temptation and pressure, and occasionally succumb to it, we may be able to learn life lessons from their mistakes. Defeat teaches us as much about life as victory. Athletes are some of the last persons on earth who should be role models, but that doesn't mean that we cannot learn from them and how they cope with their defeats, both professional and personal.

12 Collective emotion

Thus far we have concentrated on aesthetic reasons and what we may call broadly educative reasons to watch sport. But for many sports fans these do not tell the full story of why they support their team. By concentrating on the purist tendency, it might be said, we have over-intellectualised the watching of sport. Sports fans speak instead of an attachment to their team, a deep bond that they feel in their hearts, which compels them to love and support their chosen side. For many, the experience of watching sport is an emotional experience.

There are doubtlessly different kinds of emotional involvement and engagement one can have while watching sport. As argued in Chapter 2, the purist will experience a different type of pleasure from watching sport than does the partisan. Using Hume's distinction, we might say that the purist experiences calm passions and the partisan violent passions. This chapter will be concerned mainly with the latter. The aesthetic pleasure of the purist is not what the average sports fan would take as a central case of emotional experience in sport. Instead, emotions will be associated with the joy of victory and pain of defeat, plus all the minor, inconclusive victories and defeats along the way as the game unfolds. There will be hope, tension, surprise, wonder, awe, relief, frustration, despair and anger, and every other emotion. By the end of some big games, the sports fan may feel they have been through the whole gamut.

There is a view that depicts sport as a leisure product to be consumed (see Crawford 2004). The consumer goods are not, of course, physical objects that can be taken home and stored but something less tangible. One pays for the experience: to 'be there' as a first-hand witness when the game is played out. The purist will see this experience more as an aesthetic one and the partisan more as an emotional one. One major reason why a partisan consumes sport, we may contend, is that they seek to 'buy' an emotional experience. The argument of this chapter is that there is something characteristic about the emotional experience of sport. It is regarded by many as an intense experience, and there are reasons for this. Sport often provides a shared experience that seems all the richer and stronger for being shared. I argue that this is because it is a collective experience involving a plural subject of emotion. I argue further that, in being part of a collective, those emotional experiences compose in a non-linear fashion. The effect is that the sum total intensity of emotion in watching sport collectively is greater than the sum total intensity there would have been had each individual watched alone.

There has been some philosophical work on collective action and belief but surprisingly little on collective emotions. Standard books on philosophy of emotion, for instance, concentrate on the individual as the subject or bearer of emotions (see, for example, Kenny 1963; De Sousa 1987; Gordon 1987; and also the Calhoun and Solomon 1984 anthology of historical writings). And in the major work on collective belief and action (Gilbert 1989), emotions are not discussed. Sports do, however, seem a clear case where a collective outlook is taken, among fans of the same team, for instance. The pronoun 'we' is used to refer to one's collective side, or 'us', with 'they' as the opposition. Gilbert's notion of a plural subject seems to be found as clearly here as anywhere and, if she is right that plural subjects can be ascribed beliefs (1989: 2), then there seems no reason why we should not extend this also to the case of collective emotions.

If we consider how groups operate then there are at least two opposed views we can distinguish, though no doubt with room for other views in between. *Singularism* is the view that takes the individual human being as the subject of belief, desire and action (we will set aside non-human collectives for the moment, though one will be discussed shortly). When one talks of groups, on this view, one could never more than quantify over the singular beliefs of people in that group. Opposed to that is a position I will call *collectivism* in which beliefs, desires and actions could be ascribed to a whole collective, which Gilbert terms the plural subject. The idea is that it can be correct to say that a whole group believes something or committed an action. This is Gilbert's view: 'there is an important and theoretically respectable sense in which collectivities can act, and, indeed, think, have attitudes, and hold to principles of their own' (1989: 15).

The appeal of singularism is to be found in a broader philosophical thesis of individualism. Gilbert attributes this view to Mill (1843: 6.7.1), where he says that individuals in a group do not form a new substance, and to social theorist Max Weber (1922: 101–2). The greatest proponent of philosophical individualism, however, is surely Hobbes (1651). Hobbes's project can be understood as an attempt to explain the workings of a society from the bottom up (see Macpherson 1962). Employing the resolutive-compositive method of the Paduan school, intellectually taking apart and then reassembling, Hobbes resolves a society into individual persons and their selfish appetites and aversions. He then recomposes them into a group and concludes how a society must operate, with a strong rule of law necessary to keep selfishness in check. By contrast, Gilbert follows a tradition expounded by Durkheim (1895) that is also found in a later work of Mill (1861) and even as far back as Plato (*Republic*: §463–6), writing on the unity of the state. This is the idea that we can see ourselves as part of a collective, a plural subject: a man 'never conceives himself otherwise than as a member of a body' (Mill 1861: ch. 3, 231). We give ourselves to that plural subject and willingly take part in its actions, beliefs and desires. At a sports stadium, for instance, the fans applaud or boo in unison. They often sing chants and lengthy songs together. In some of its most spectacular and flamboyant manifestations, collective support for a team involves use of musical instruments, flags and flares in a choreographed display of colour and sound. Fans are happy to sing as if with one great voice and sometimes to move with their arms or whole bodies in a collective way so as to appear as a single entity. Similarly, the fans will also experience joy and sorrow collectively. Before talking of emotions specifically, however, there is more to be said on plural subjects and what it takes for one to be constituted.

It is clear that there needs to be some principle of unity that makes a subject plural, and thus eligible to hold a collective belief or have a collective emotion. Any old set of individuals will not do. As Gilbert (1989: 9) explains, 'the population consisting of Rudyard Kipling, Julius Caesar and David Hume' is not a plural subject. Why not? For a start, Kipling, Caesar and Hume are separated by both space and time. This seems an important factor, though it might not be decisive. There is no reason in principle why a plural subject couldn't be spread over a spatial or temporal region. A society, for instance, may spread throughout the area of a nation's borders. But Kipling, Caesar and Hume seem far too spatiotemporally disconnected. Caesar was dead, for instance, long before Hume was born. But even if a population shares an extended spatiotemporal location, that would also be insufficient to make a plural subject. The left-handed people of a city do not automatically form a plural subject, for instance (Gilbert 1989: 9). They may never speak with a collective voice or hold any collective beliefs. So what extra would be needed to make them so?

Gilbert's own solution is to argue for intentionalism, which says roughly that

> it is necessary that the participants express to each other willingness to be part of a plural subject for a certain goal, for instance the goal that A walks in the woods and B walks in the woods and that they so do in one another's company.
> (1989: 17)

Each person consents to being a part of the collective, just as Rousseau suggests that we consent to being part of the General Will (Rousseau 1762: bk I, ch. 6). This raises a problem, however, of whether the account still remains individualistic at its base. The single person is still the starting point in Gilbert's account for they are making the deliberate and individual decision whether to participate or not, rather than the plural subject itself taking a decision. But what, one might think, is the alternative?

It seems possible to argue for a more thoroughgoing holism that takes us even further from the intended consent of individuals. Certainly an individual spectator might enter a sports stadium voluntarily and may have some expectations about what will happen once they are inside. But it seems we have to allow the possibility that someone might unintentionally be swept away in the crowd's passion and become part of a plural subject unexpectedly. A tourist, for instance, may call in to see a game and yet find that the emotion of the crowd draws them in and makes them feel part of the collective no matter how much they would prefer to resist. The general will of the crowd might be infectious and, when they cheer a goal, our unwitting tourist may cheer too. When the crowd rises to its feet, so too does our visitor. It may be only after they return to their hotel room that they realise what has happened. Without giving any knowing consent, they had become part of the plural subject. They lost a degree of their individuality, being partially subsumed into the collective. Could this really happen or is it a philosophical flight of fancy?

Research on crowd dynamics (Still 2010) suggests that a group of people crossing a street will tend to behave collectively in a certain way, without any deliberate intention to do so from any of them and without any leader. When the lights change, people on opposite sides need to negotiate the obstacles presented by the other pedestrians. Groups moving in opposite directions will form interlocking streams. Crowd behaviour emerges from simple principles. People find it easier to follow the path of someone moving in the same direction, rather than cutting their own route through the oncoming throng, so they begin to walk in criss-crossing alternate lines going in either direction, simply moving into the space that the person in front vacates. No one is doing this by explicit consent. They are likely not to be conscious of having a strategy for crossing the road, nor that they are part of an emerging pattern that can be observed from above, and nor even that there is a group dynamic in operation. This is collective action. It is an action towards which a number of people contribute, mostly unknowingly, and something that can only be performed by a group. One individual acting alone could not have achieved this. Can something similar be found for the examples of belief and emotion, which seem to be more purely mental than involving physical movement?

Gilbert considers two options for joint beliefs: summativism and correlativism. Summativism says that, for the collective to hold a belief, all or most of the members constituting the collective must hold that belief. Correlativism says that, for the collective to hold a belief, at least one member of the collective must hold that belief. But, we can argue, this still places importance on belief at the level of the individual. In complete contrast, we can offer the story of Aunt Hillary told by Hofstadter (1979: 311–36). It is suggested that Aunt Hillary is a thinking, conscious subject, capable of beliefs and so on. Aunt Hillary is actually an ant colony. None of the individual ants that compose the colony is capable of holding beliefs but the colony as a whole is, Hofstadter ventures. The whole exhibits vast complexity in its behaviour such that it is capable of instantiating mental states. Hofstadter uses the example to illustrate the different holistic and reductionist outlooks. To think of Aunt Hillary as a person, we have to view the colony holistically: as a single subject, though a plural one in Gilbert's terminology. If we view it as a collection of parts, we will see nothing but millions of stupid ants wandering around seemingly at random. A crucial point is that none of the individual ants that compose Aunt Hillary is aware of the beliefs that Aunt Hillary as a whole holds. Our brains are in much the same situation. As a whole, we are capable of holding beliefs, though none of the individual neurons out of which a brain is composed can hold a belief: they are too simple for that.

A truly holistic approach should allow, therefore, that a collective, plural subject composed by persons might hold a belief that none of the individual composing persons holds. Neither summativism nor correlativism allows this. Gilbert goes only half way towards the holism suggested by the Aunt Hillary case, therefore. She argues for a view of collective, group belief where 'a group belief is a *jointly accepted view*. That is, it is a view that each of a set of persons has shown willingness to accept jointly with the others' (1989: 20). But it has been argued above that a member of a plural subject need not willingly and intentionally accept membership of the collective and nor need they accept a view that the collective jointly holds. What, then, holds the plural together, allowing it to jointly hold beliefs or jointly act? There need only be acquiescence, it can be argued, which amounts to nothing more than playing the part that is needed from the individual in that collective and continuing to do so. As we saw in the case of road crossing, individuals just take what seems the quickest and easiest route across the street, unaware that they are contributing to a pattern. Similarly, one might acquiesce in, and participate in, membership of a group that has a collective will, belief or emotion.

How will this work in the case of emotion? How can there be collective emotional states? As mentioned at the beginning of this chapter, there is some plausibility to the idea that emotions are felt more intensely when with a group than when watching alone. The larger the crowd, the more excited the spectators can become. At amateur football, for instance, with very small crowds, one's team's attack on goal might provoke some excitement, but it is rare one sees people at such events at any great height of arousal. The level of excitement seems to grow as the size of the crowd grows. A thought experiment would seem to confirm this to anyone who has watched sport with crowds of varying sizes. One may see a very thrilled crowd supporting a team to victory in front of, let us say, 60,000 spectators. One sees how excited each spectator is as the ball nears the opposition goal. They scream as the ball is shot, they kick out in their seats, vicariously trying to prod the ball home, and their ultimate ecstasy is the goal itself. On the other hand, a late equaliser would be seen as a tragedy that would ruin the weekend irrevocably. Now imagine that one such spectator was watching that very same game, from the same seat, but almost alone in the stadium. Perhaps the game had been ordered to be played behind closed doors, for instance, and this person was able to pull some strings to negotiate an exception. Would that same individual jump in their seat with the same excitement? Would they go quite so crazy when the goal is scored? We surely think not, and anyone who has attended amateur football before sparse crowds will have found it confirmed. It seems, therefore, that at least a part of the cause of the emotion, and certainly a determinant of its intensity, is the surrounding crowd of which the individual is a part.

How does this work? It is suggested here that the degree of emotion is a result of a non-linear composition of causes. In linear composition, the degree of the total output is directly proportionate to the degree of the inputs. When we calculate resultant forces, for instance, we simply add all the component forces, subtracting any countervailing forces. Addition is a linear function. But in non-linear composition, the output is not proportionate to the input (see Mumford and Anjum 2011: ch. 4). Consider, for instance, the causal connection between money and

happiness. There seems to be some connection, at least in the way most societies are organised, but it is not a linear one. When a relatively financially poor
person doubles their income, say from £10,000 to £20,000 per annum, they are
overjoyed. But that same quantity of extra income means very little to one who is
already rich and may have only a negligible effect. To one who earns £1 million,
an extra £10,000 is barely noticed. And there is plausibility in the idea that, at
a certain point, extra income decreases happiness, as pop star Michael Jackson
found. Life can become more complicated and one can start to wonder whether
one's entourage is really made up of true friends. If we plot happiness against
wealth, therefore, we are likely to get a curve. With linear composition, such as
with composition of forces, we get a straight line. The hypothesis ventured is that
the intensity of emotion in a crowd increases in such a non-linear fashion. It is a
kind of non-linearity for which we have an explanation, however.

Consider the decibel volume of people talking. Two people conversing in a
room may produce noise in the magnitude of around 60 decibels. Suppose, however, that these were only the first guests at a party and, as the night progresses,
others join them. Multiple conversations begin. But as they do, our original couple start struggling to hear each other at 60 decibels. They raise their voices. But
then all the other couples in return raise their own voices so that they can hear
each other too. As a result, our original couple raise their voices even further.
The individual components – the noise levels of the persons speaking – begin
to interact and affect each other. People start to speak at 65 or more decibels,
which they would never have thought of doing if the room contained one other
person only. The result is that the noise produced in the room is greater than
the sum total there would have been had each of the conversations taken place
in isolation. Had they done so, it seems plausible, each would have been held at
around the 60-decibel mark. But because they are in a context of surrounding
noise from other conversations, they are each conducted at 65 decibels. (For all
sorts of other reasons, sound levels do not in any case compose in a linear fashion.
Three conversations held at 65 decibels would not produce a total volume of 195
decibels – the loudest possible sound being only 194 decibels.)

This same kind of interaction occurs in the case of composing emotions, it is
contended. Being in a context in which there are other alike factors affects the
original contribution. It is not, of course, only in sport that one experiences this
kind of effect. A similar emotional response could be gained in listening to a
piece of music in a crowd at a concert. Or one might attend the funeral of a complete stranger and feel oneself saddened just by being surrounded by the misery
of others. Humans are capable of empathy: a sense that allows us to perceive the
emotions of others, identify with them and feel the same. Emotions thus have an
infectious nature. They have a social aspect to them, as a way of communicating
with others. And there is a certain language of emotional expression that we must
learn in order to take part in that communication. Communication is possible
only through an interaction, and this is how we are able to make each other's
emotions more and more intense. Just as the other conversations at the party

lead to a raise in volume of all the individual conversations, so in expressing one's emotions one encourages others to do the same as a way of engaging, sharing and communicating one's sporting experience.

This is not to deny that emotions have a rational structure (De Sousa 1987); they are not a form of hysteria. If one is sad that p, one must believe that p is the case and prefer that it were not the case. But the intensity of the sadness that p is something that we can characterise as infectious. It is thus often crucial that we distinguish the intentional object of an emotion from the cause of it. If we ask the fan in the stadium why they are elated, they will say it's because their team has scored, they have won and so on. But our thought-experiment concluded that they might not be elated if they were the only one watching the game. This suggests that there is another answer to the question of why they are elated. An answer might be that they are elated because everyone around them is elated too. The thought-experiment would support this conclusion. But there is also something misleading about the answer. The joy is directed towards the goal or the victory. The win is what the emotion is about: its intentional object. The emotions of neighbours may have a causal influence over one's emotions, making them more intense, but one's happiness is not directed at or about the behaviour of one's neighbours: it is about the sport. One is happy that one's team has scored, not that the other fans are happy. Of course, a humanitarian may well be happy when other people are happy, but this is not, we should assume, what is taking place in the sporting case. And indirectly one could be happy when one's fellow fans are happy because, if you support the same team, the reason they are happy would also be a reason for you to be happy. But, we should maintain, what the emotion is about directly is the win or the goal.

There has been a divide historically between sensation theories of emotion and more rational and cognitive theories. William James (1884), for instance, argued that an emotion is some bodily disturbance, or at least the perception of it. One first cries, or frowns, or smiles, or feels a burning within one's stomach, and the perception of such sensations and bodily states is the emotion. Hence, one does not cry because one is sad: one is sad because one cries. Although this reverses the common sense order of explanation, there is some appeal to the account. Emotions are not rationally bounded, according to James's theory. They are immediate and visceral, and this may accord with the experience of the sports fan. Emotions are not thought through: they occur without any control of the agent, in response to goals scored. For this reason, we are often depicted as passive with respect to our emotions: they are passions rather than actions. Philosophers such as Hume have seen this division, ruling that reason is and only ought ever to be the slave of the passions (Hume 1739–40: II, iii, 3). But the philosophers' divide also exaggerates the irrationality of emotion. There is a rational structure too that cannot be ignored easily. What distinguishes emotions from moods, at least according to Wittgenstein (1980: §148), is that emotions are directed towards an intentional object, whereas moods are not about anything. To be sad, therefore, is to be sad that p: that someone has died, that your team has lost and so on. But then one must also believe p to be the case: one cannot be sad that p while also believing that p is not so. And one must also prefer that p were not the case. All these points are matters of conceptual necessity. If someone said that they were sad that p but didn't believe that p, or had no preference whether p was the case, we would say that they were guilty of a conceptual confusion. Unless one prefers p not to be the case, one cannot be sad that p. Perhaps one misnames some other emotion. To be happy, for instance, is to be happy that something is the case, q, believe that q is indeed the case, and have a preference that had q not been the case one would like it to be the case. For hope, by contrast, where one hopes that r, one cannot believe that r is already the case. Again, if someone hopes for something they believe is already true, then we could accuse them of a conceptual error (or some other rational failing). Whatever their emotion is, it is not hope. To understand emotions is to know these conceptual constraints and thus to understand a rationally bounded domain. Certainly reason alone cannot tell us what to desire or what to be happy and sad about, and to that extent Hume was right. But reason can bound our emotions to the extent that they have to have some rational coherence with our beliefs and other psychological states. We can say there is something wrong, indeed incoherent, about being happy that p but not believing that p is the case. This is a normative constraint. Occasionally someone may fail to conform with the rational structure of emotions, if they are psychologically ill or just plain irrational, so this is not a descriptive account of the actual psychology of emotion. For a variety of reasons people may not obey the rational constraints of emotion. But because there is indeed such a rational structure we may then have difficulty in understanding and classifying the emotions of such a person. If someone says they are sad that q but prefer q to be the case, are they really sad or are they happy? Do they misunderstand sadness? Or do they misunderstand happiness? It becomes hard for us to give a rational answer when such questions concern irrationality.

The initial appeal of the Jamesian account is to be rejected, therefore. Certainly one may respond emotionally and immediately to some incident. And there may indeed be accompanying bodily disturbances such as tears or smiles. But one should not mistake the bodily disturbance for the emotion, even if it were to accompany it every time. Emotions can be just as immediate if they have a rational and cognitive basis. One sees that the goal is scored, for instance, and it is something one wanted to be the case. One is happy because the desire is satisfied. One believes that something good has happened. It is difficult to see how a bodily disturbance alone could have carried this content.

A position has been developed in which there is a rational aspect to emotion concerning its intentional objects. In the case of collective emotions, however, a non-rational and causal factor has been introduced. The intensity of emotional experience can be an infectious matter based on empathy and interaction. It has been argued that the intensity of emotion composes among multiple persons in a non-linear way. We need to return, however, to Gilbert's question of when and how a group of persons constitutes a collectivity or plural subject. We did not resolve this matter.

It was argued above that the intentionalist account does not ring true. But what alternative can be given? We need one in which participants need not deliberately consent to becoming part of a plural subject but instead may merely acquiesce, perhaps unconsciously, in that plural-subject parthood, as we may call it. For this to happen, it seems that we need some notion of joint activity, which we should construe broadly and allow it to include joint purposes, actions, beliefs and emotions. The fans at the stadium all want more or less the same thing: to see their team win and to support them in their efforts. The joint purpose that unites them need not be a purpose of each individual who becomes part of the plural subject. The purpose could be something that emerges only at the collective level. But, it is claimed, joint activity of some kind is what binds them together as a cohesive group. We should not, therefore, begin with the notion of a plural subject in order to explain what a collective action is. Contributing to the same collective activity is all that binds together a group of people into a plural subject. The so-called Mexican wave, for instance, that may begin spontaneously at some indefinable and imprecise area of the stadium but then travels around the whole, is what unites its participants into a plural subject. They produce an action jointly – and it looks to be a single action of a plural subject – that none of them could have produced alone. Similarly, the heights of goal celebrations and lows of sorrow in defeat are joint activities in which individuals participate and interact, producing an intensity that none would have experienced if alone. Manifesting such emotions should thus count as a joint activity that unites a collection of people into a plural subject. By contrast, there was no joint activity ever undertaken by the trio of Rudyard Kipling, Julius Caesar and David Hume. In summary: don't start with a plural subject to explain joint action or emotion; start with the joint action or emotion to explain plural subjecthood.

Although being among a crowd can intensify an emotional response, the same effect can occur when one is watching on TV. One can be part of a plural subject that is not spatially co-located but can nevertheless be engaged in a joint activity. We see that this is so when we consider a well-known phenomenon in watching TV sport. When one watches a live TV game, it can be very exciting: almost as exciting as being there in the stadium. Sometimes one may not be able to watch the game live and instead have to record it to watch later. As every sports fan knows, however, watching a recording later, even if it is a recording of a live airing of the game and one has no knowledge of the outcome, is never as exciting as watching it live. How can this be so? We venture that this is a well-confirmed case that shows in reality what was shown in the earlier thought-experiment. There, it was suggested that watching alone would not be as exciting as watching the very same game with 60,000 others. While we could only consider the watching-alone case as a thought-experiment, we can now see that the sports fan watching the live recording after the event is in almost that exact same position. They are watching alone what others have previously watched together. This accords with the interpretation of the puzzle offered persuasively by Fisher (2005). The reason, he suggests, that the recording is never as exciting as watching live is that, when watching at the same time as others, one is involved in a shared emotional experience, in 'shared time' as he says. We want to watch in shared time because this means we are experiencing the emotional highs and lows of the game simultaneously with many others. Our interest is increased because of the more intense emotional experiences we can have (Fisher 2005: 189–90).

Fisher further argues that there is a kind of interactive phenomenon between those watching that produces a non-linear increase in intensity. Our emotions are more intense, he ventures, because we believe that watching in shared time licenses our emotions, where licensing means: 'I believe that other[s] experience *x* intensely, so I may experience *x* intensely' (2005: 190). This suggests a form of intersubjective validation and affirmation of one's emotional responses. Fisher does not use exactly those terms but does say: 'There is a joint accountability in the emotional reactions we have' (2005: 190). The TV case shows, therefore, that the intuitions we had about the thought-experiment case are largely valid. It shows also that it is not necessary to be part of a plural subject that the individuals are all gathered in one place. We can empathise over a distance. A joint activity, purpose or emotion can be realised by a spatially disparate plural subject. Fisher explains these group emotional responses in terms of social psychology. This seems right. When we watch sport, we learn the appropriate emotional vocabulary and how to use it correctly at certain key moments of the game. This vocabulary can change. Since 1990, English football fans, having seen Paul Gascoigne cry after defeat in a World Cup semi-final, added crying to that vocabulary. At the end of each Premier League season, some fans of relegated teams cry openly in the stadium to show how deep their love is for their team. TV images reinforce this as standard behaviour: an accepted response to the situation. Prior to 1990, it would have been thought unmanly and weak to have cried over such defeat. The appropriate response then was usually anger which sometimes manifested itself in violence and rioting. In some cultures, anger remains an accepted reaction within the group norms (Fenerbahçe supporters in 2010 set fire to their own stadium when they failed to win their final game of the season, losing the league title as a result). As Fisher says, the appropriate emotional responses are controlled through 'evaluation apprehension' (2005: 192). If we do not behave appropriately, the crowd will think we are uncommitted. If we behave appropriately, they will mirror our behaviour. Such behavioural reinforcement is a breeding ground for collective behaviour and an increasing intensity of emotions. Those who celebrate wildly are praised. Those who don't are condemned for under-commitment. Many fans submit willingly to this kind of experience, seeing the intensity and collectivity as desirable. While an intensification of positive emotions seems hard to denounce, we ought also to bear in mind that cheering a team involves a risk. And if the emotions produced are negative, their intensification is far from pleasant and occasionally dangerous.

Although we have found a reason why people watch sport, we can see that it is not a reason that is intrinsic to sport itself. The intense experience of collective emotion is something people may seek out, but there are of course other places that they could find it. Wherever groups come together there is the opportunity for collectivity of emotion. Many see sports as an easily accessible source of such emotions. But one might also argue that the nature of sport particularly lends itself to the emotional roller coaster, so we should not underestimate the importance of the emotions for the watching of sport.

13 Allegiance and identity

It might be argued that our investigation into the emotional experience of watching sport has concentrated on only part of it, and it is not even the most important part. The partisan sports fan will speak of their love for their team, for instance, and thus far we have neglected that. They may feel very deeply for the club they support, thinking of it as deep an emotional attachment as any other they have in their lives. We noted that emotions have intentional objects – something to which they are directed – but so far we have considered only the cases where the object is a win, a defeat, a goal having been scored or a near miss. These are events or incidents, and they can be intentional objects of emotions such as happiness, sadness, hope and despair. But when we come to emotions such as love, hatred, reverence, obsession and so on, it will not normally be events or incidents that are the objects of these emotions. Rather, it will be some particular subject towards which the emotion is directed: a particular sporting club or individual player. Certainly, the club or player may have been involved in many incidents in sport, and some of them might be among the reasons someone chooses them to like. But the allegiance in sport is mainly to the club or player. One first and foremost loves a team or club, for instance, and only derivatively loves, or takes joy in, the sporting incidents produced by members of that team or club.

Allegiances are not, of course, the sole preserve of sports. One may feel an allegiance to a partner or spouse, a political party, a nation and so on. But allegiances in sport do raise some distinct and barely explored philosophical and psychological issues, as I hope to demonstrate. For one thing, sporting allegiances often involve a persistent and intense emotional investment, which many believe enhances the experience of watching sport (Dixon 2001). Often a relationship with a sporting club is a lifelong experience. Lifelong relationships in marriage occur, though there are also many cases where a sporting allegiance outlives an interpersonal relationship. As I will argue, however, sporting allegiances can raise a class of problem that is unknown in the cases of relationships with persons, except in science fiction or counterfactual contexts. Because the sporting clubs that are the objects of allegiances permit major qualitative and compositional change through time, there are cases where the identity through time of such a club can be questionable. This may leave the sports fan in doubt as to where their sporting allegiance should properly be directed. I will not, in this chapter, be offering a complete solution to such problems of identity. Rather, I will be explaining how the problems arise and how, nevertheless, allegiances continue to be maintained.

I take it that an allegiance is an emotional attachment, certainly in the case of sports, involving some notion of support, interest for well-being, and loyalty. There may be cases of forced allegiances, such as when someone is forced to join a political party in a one-party state, and cases of obliged allegiances if someone has an obligation of allegiance to their country of birth. But the allegiances that are the subject of this chapter – sporting allegiances – are distinct from these cases in being formed voluntarily and maintained willingly. Hence they cannot be forced or acquired without consent. This is not to deny that there can be cases where one professes to support a team for no other reason than peer pressure alone. These will not be genuine cases of sporting allegiance, however, if there is no real emotional attachment.

The allegiances are typically formed as a result of some accident. For example, one may support a sports team on the basis of a family tie, geographical location or a religious/cultural affiliation. They are formed accidentally in the sense that the allegiance formation cannot be accounted for in solely rational terms. Reason simply seems to have no place here. One may *rationalise* one's allegiance; for example: one supports the team a parent supported. But reason alone does not dictate that one should support the team of one's parents. This is simply to apply the fact/value dichotomy. Allegiance falls on the side of value, so cannot be rationally dictated by any fact. As Hume said, 'reason alone can never produce any action, or give rise to volition' (Hume 1739–40: II, iii, 3, p. 414). The fact/value dichotomy is, it should be conceded, philosophically controversial.

However, we already saw that the fact that allegiances are formed by accident in no way undermines them. One typically meets one's partner through some accident – some contingent circumstance – but one would rarely see this as rational grounds for questioning the veracity of the emotional bond or abandoning it. Rather, one is likely to regard the development of a relationship over time as a central component of the personal allegiance. The contingent circumstance of the initial meeting is of relatively little importance to the fact that one has a relationship that undergoes development and growth.

This raises two further points that are crucial to the logic of allegiance and which will play key roles in the argument of this chapter. First, allegiance is an intentional concept; that is, an allegiance must always have an intentional object. Second, an allegiance must, of conceptual necessity, be extended through time. I will expand upon both these ideas.

Many psychological phenomena are intentional; that is, directed towards an object. If one follows Brentano (1874), such intentionality is the mark of the psychological (Brentano's criterion of the psychological is not uncontroversial; see Molnar 2003: ch. 3). Certainly, if one views an allegiance as an emotion, and one follows a broadly cognitivist account of the emotions (see De Sousa 1987: ch. 5; Gordon 1987: 22–3; and Chapter 12 above), one would consider allegiance to be intentional. The intentional object is that to which the allegiance is felt. It is not entirely clear precisely what this object is, however, as we will see below. Prima facie, however, we might say that it is a sporting club or team. One curious datum is that sporting allegiances are more commonly directed at teams rather than individuals. One may have a favourite tennis player, for instance, though it is rarer to speak of having an allegiance to, or being a supporter of, an individual player. Supporters or fans will almost always be attached to teams rather than individuals, and there will be a brief speculation later as to why this is.

The second crucial point on the logic of allegiance is that an allegiance must extend through time. The notion of a fleeting or momentary allegiance would be practically an oxymoron. This is because the concept of an allegiance is of a strong and persistent, at least semi-permanent, emotional attachment. Allegiance would thus behave like love (indeed, one might say that sporting allegiance involves a variety of love), which cannot properly be a brief episode but conceptually must be extended over time. To say that an allegiance, or love, must be permanent would be too strict, however. Despite the depth and the non-momentary nature of these emotions, people can fall out of love or lose their allegiances. Some cases are lifelong, but not all, which the idea of semi-permanence is meant to allow.

If we bring together these two notions, of an allegiance being necessarily extended through time and necessarily having an intentional object, we find what might be called the rational component of allegiance: allegiance must pre-suppose the identity through time of its object. Because an allegiance must be extended through time, one could not have an allegiance to some object that lacked identity through that time, or lacked *diachronic* identity. (There is, of course, a distinct but no doubt connected question of *synchronic* identity. This second question concerns the issue of what the intentional object of allegiance is *at* a time. What follows below will also provide an account of synchronic identity.) Allegiance is an emotion, therefore, whose object must endure or persist (pleonastically) through time. I will be ignoring the details of the exact nature of persistence, for which see Hawley (2001). Hence when I use the term *endurance* I am not using it in the technical sense, in which it is contrasted with a *perdurance* theory of how things persist.

This raises the question of what the identity through time of the object consists in. Where we have an allegiance to an individual, as in the case of a personal relationship (if this is properly classified as an allegiance), the diachronic identity conditions of the intentional object consist in personal identity. What the identity conditions are for persons is no simple matter (see Noonan 1989). But in the case of sporting allegiances, we have extra complications because, as remarked above, sporting allegiances are rarely to individual persons. They are more frequently to complex particulars such as clubs or teams.

Sporting allegiances typically presuppose the identity through time, therefore, of the clubs or teams that are their intentional objects. This leaves us with the question of what the identity through time of such a sporting club or team consists in. Such a question is no simple matter because of the evident changes, or discontinuities, through time that such complex particulars undergo.

By a *permissible* discontinuity we mean a change through which identity is preserved. More will be said generally, later in the chapter, about what is occurring in such cases. But first we can concern ourselves with practical examples. It should be clear at this early stage that by identity we mean numerical identity rather than qualitative identity (see Lowe 2002: ch. 2). Two things are qualitatively identical when they share all their non-relational qualities or properties, in the same sense in which all ten bowling pins or skittles should be identical. This means that they should all have the same weight, shape, colour and so on. Numerical identity means that we have one and the same thing; for example: when I say that the pen on my table is the same one as – is identical with – the pen I left there yesterday. The case of the bowling pins shows that qualitative identity is not sufficient for numerical identity as the pins are qualitatively identical yet ten numerically distinct particulars. Nor is (diachronic) qualitative identity necessary for numeric identity because things may change over time yet nevertheless be numerically the same particular, as when I say that the tall plant in my room was only 12 inches high when first I got it.

When we say that identity can be preserved through change, therefore, clearly we mean numerical identity. To say that qualitative identity could be maintained through a real change would be a contradiction, because this means a change in non-relational qualities. A *permissible discontinuity* is just such a change: a qualitative change through which numerical identity is preserved (see Lowe 2002: pt 1).

Sporting clubs have, in this sense of preserving numerical identity, endured through many changes. Consequently, sporting allegiances have endured through many changes in their intentional objects. Here are some examples, taken mainly from British football clubs. There have been changes in name, as when Newton Heath became Manchester United. There are frequent changes in club members, as when the composition of the team changes through time, or the board of directors at the club, or the body of supporters. There are changes in the base or location of a club: for example, Arsenal moved north of the River Thames to Highbury from Woolwich in 1913. There can also be changes in an ideology of a club. Ideological associations are rare in all British sport, but they are more common in continental Europe and Central and South America. AC Milan, of Italy, was once the club for the Milanese upper crust. Over time it gained a more working-class supporter base, but more recently it has regained its right-wing associations because it was taken over by Silvio Berlusconi. Left-wing Milanese are now more likely to identify with Internazionale because of the ideology they represent. Such major changes are not exclusively restricted to soccer, nor to Britain, of course. Examples are easy to find in the United States or other countries, such as when the Cleveland Browns moved to Baltimore and became the Ravens or when the Washington Senators in baseball moved to Minnesota and became the Twins.

One may surmise that diachronic identity can be preserved because there are gradual changes in some of the above factors, at different times. Hence, while a club changes name, it nevertheless remains at the same stadium with most of the same team, and so on. At a later stage it might move to a new stadium, but only while maintaining the same name, executives and ideology. Hence, one might say that, as long as changes are gradual, the diachronic identity of the club is preserved relatively unproblematically. This continuity might be like the continuity Wittgenstein describes through a rope (1958: 87) where both ends belong to the same rope even though the rope consists in a series of overlapping fibres, none of which stretch from one end to the other. However, there seem even to be cases where identity is preserved, or is understood to be preserved, through radical discontinuities. Many sports clubs have had temporal gaps in existence. For example, some British soccer clubs closed down for the Second World War or have had other breaks in existence. The supporter may well have wondered whether it was warranted to direct their allegiance towards the new club: the club that claims to be re-forming the old one. They could puzzle over what the endurance of a club, through a break in existence, consists in. Hence they may wonder whether their allegiance has been to the same intentional object at different times, thus whether it is properly the same allegiance at all.

I argue that there are circumstances, under each of these categories of change, in which it is rational to suppose the endurance of one's intentional object of allegiance. There are conceivable and actual cases in which these changing clubs are numerically the same. Moving from the concrete to the abstract, we need to analyse what is happening when such changes occur.

It should be clear, I hope, that identity and continuity are being distinguished. There may be numerical identity despite discontinuity or change, or indeed some continuity but without identity. It is useful to be able to separate degree of change – degree of continuity/discontinuity – from identity, which appears not to admit of degrees. Hence we may find that some discontinuities are of a low degree and allow the preservation of identity, and some are of a high degree and end identity.

A sporting club is evidently a complex particular. It has many constituent parts and it can endure through change in, or loss of, one or more of its constituent parts. This seems to be what is happening in the permissible discontinuity cases. However, what those cases also seem to indicate is that there plausibly is no single constituent of the club that is necessary for its persistence or diachronic identity. Nothing seems to be individually indispensable to it. If it may change its name, its location, its fan base and so on, one may doubt whether there is anything it could not give up yet still be the club it is. If so, this is a particular with no essential qualities or components. There are even cases of clubs switching sports: many British soccer clubs switched to soccer from cricket or rugby, as in the case of Bradford City FC, when the new game gained in popularity. But also, there does not seem to be a single constituent of the club that is individually sufficient for diachronic identity. A number of distinct clubs of the same name have existed, for instance, and there are many cases of distinct clubs using the same stadium. However, this is not to suggest that there cannot be a group of conditions (or group of constituents) that are jointly sufficient for diachronic identity, otherwise it would be a mystery how any club maintained identity through time. But this does not mean, either, that it is a simple matter to state this group of conditions. Indeed, it is argued towards the end of the chapter that these identity conditions are complex and, to at least some extent, conspiratorial in nature.

Despite sporting allegiance being a commonplace, therefore, and despite its rationality resting on the endurance of its intentional object, it is by no means simple to state what the endurance of its object consists in. Even a gap in existence seems to be no insurmountable obstacle to identity. We have seen that clubs have gone out of, and have returned to, existence. But the notion of a temporally gappy existence is respectable in metaphysics (Simons 2000) as, for example, when a watch is disassembled and its components dispersed and it is then reassembled at a later time.

Nevertheless, despite all these permissible changes, it is clear that there must be some preservation of numerical identity through such change. This is supported by the conceptual point that change itself must assume diachronic identity. As Aristotle noted (*Physics*: V. 4), for there to be change, there must be an underlying subject of change that preserves its numerical identity through the change in qualities. For example, where there is a man x with hair at t_1 and a man y without hair at t_2, we can only say that a change has occurred (namely, a man has become bald) if x at t_1 is numerically the same man as y at t_2. The paradigm of genuine change, therefore, occurs to an object that endures through that change. (A class of exceptions must be admitted, however. An object coming into or going out of existence will also be a change, though not a change *in* a thing, as passing from existence to non-existence is not a change in the qualities of some object.) Even though we cannot easily identify the necessary and sufficient conditions for the endurance of sports clubs, therefore, there are compelling reasons to believe that they do endure. We can thus continue to look for what their endurance consists in.

There is another reason why we might continue to seek an account of the endurance of such objects, namely that it is not the case that *anything goes*. While identity can be preserved through many discontinuities, it cannot be preserved through all discontinuities. Some changes are so big that that they make their subject cease to be, and clubs can be discontinuous enough that they are distinct rather than identical. We had indeed better have an account in which not anything goes, otherwise every club would be identical with every other, which evidently they are not. There are many distinct clubs, so there are evidently constraints on identity.

Some non-trivial account of such persistence must be possible, therefore. Our account must allow that it is possible that two clubs be distinct and that a club can cease to exist as, for example, where it folds completely or merges with another club. There are many actual cases in both these categories. Middlesbrough Ironopolis and New Brighton are clubs that have folded some time ago, without any hope (or even possibility) of resurrection. When a thing has ceased to be for a considerable time, and all its component parts have ceased to be, it seems that there comes a point when it is no longer a possibility that the very same thing can come back into existence. This is not to deny, however, that a distinct entity that resembles our first could come into existence. This same issue would strike against resurrection of persons as well as sports clubs. Rushden and Diamonds are a club that were formed when two former clubs merged. The only reasonable conclusion about the former clubs is that they are identical with no current club, in other words they no longer exist. Could the former clubs be numerically identical with the current merged club, Rushden and Diamonds? No. If both are identical with the current club, then by the transitivity of identity, they would have to be identical with each other, which they are not. Identity is a one-to-one relation, so club x at t_2 cannot be identical with two distinct things, y and z, at t_1.

While not anything goes, therefore, it is nevertheless difficult to specify further substantial constraints on identity. Many changes seem to be permitted, as we have seen. An account will be offered of why such sports clubs can survive so many changes but, before that, some more problem cases will concern us. Problem cases are interesting because they allow us to explore the boundary between identity and distinctness. They allow us to consider whether this boundary is precise or vague and whether it is fully known or only partially known. In these problem cases, it will be argued that it is contestable, in varying degrees, whether the identity of a club has been preserved through certain changes. Because it is uncertain whether or not club a at t_1 is identical with club b at t_2, the supporter is correspondingly uncertain where their allegiance lies. The examples again come from British football.

The first example is one where a number of clubs of the same name, and based in the same vicinity, exist but with lengthy periods of inexistence between. This has actually occurred in the case of Bootle Football Club, of which there have been three incarnations. Is the current Bootle identical with the first Bootle? Arguably not. On the spectrum of continuities and discontinuities, there are few continuities and many discontinuities. For instance, there was a large gap, between 1893 and 1947, between the first and second Bootles. Furthermore, the third Bootle overlapped slightly, under another name, with the second Bootle. There are some continuities, in that the clubs represent that same geographical area and may have had some supporters in common, but we would most likely conclude that these continuities are inadequate to constitute identity. This example is reasonably straightforward, so we move to one that is not.

The second example concerns the re-formation of clubs that have been forced to fold due to insolvency. In recent times, this has happened in the cases of Newport County and Aldershot Town. In both instances, large numbers of supporters and executives were left with no club onto which they could direct their allegiance. After a brief period, they came together to form new clubs playing at the same venues, with the same colours, and with similar names. British insolvency laws prevent a club having exactly the same name as a folded club for a period of at least ten years. Newport County reclaimed the former name almost as soon as this period had elapsed. Legally and financially, the clubs before and after insolvency were certainly distinct entities. Yet with almost all the same supporters and the same heritage, it was far more natural to think of there being a single club having had a brief break in existence. It is, further, quite plausible to suppose that, with the passage of time, such breaks in continuity will become less important or forgotten completely. Such cases seem very close to the borderline between identity and distinctness. They seem to be good examples of where there is an indeterminacy of identity. These are cases where we can know all the available facts of the matter yet still not be sure whether *a* is identical with *b*. Any theory of the identity of clubs ought to allow that there can be such indeterminate cases.

A third class of problem concerns those cases where, for whatever reason, there is a breakaway club. These are some of the most controversial cases precisely because the correct object of allegiance is being contested. They are cases of disputed identity. A current British example is the case of Wimbledon FC. Wimbledon were a small south London club that rose to prominence in the 1980s, culminating in winning the 1988 FA Cup, one of the highest honours in British football. New owners decided, in the hope of financial gain, to relocate the club to Milton Keynes in the Midlands where they thought there was a greater potential supporter base. Understandably, the south London-based supporters objected that they were effectively losing their club to another town. The sports franchise, though a common concept in America, is still resisted in Britain. The supporters accordingly set up their own club, which they named AFC Wimbledon. This raises the question of whether Wimbledon FC or AFC Wimbledon are identical with the club that won the 1988 FA Cup. AFC Wimbledon have most of the original supporters, are committed to staying in south London, claim the FA Cup among their honours, and kept the original badge. The club badge was a double-headed eagle that was associated with the original home: the borough of Merton. It was inapplicable for (and, by order of the Borough Council, could not be used by) the Milton Keynes club. Wimbledon FC kept the original name though little else. But significantly, they kept the Football League place that had been held by the original Wimbledon.

In the terms used by Parfit (1984: pt III), in relation to personal identity, this is a case of a fission of a particular. Cases where clubs merge are fusions. However, unlike Parfit's cases of person fissions and fusions, these sports club cases are actual rather than counterfactual or science fictional. Passions have run high because the proper object of allegiance hinges on the correct identity of the club through time. Hence, for many supporters it has been a very difficult decision where they should direct their allegiance. Most have gone with the new club, AFC Wimbledon, because of its commitment to stay in the locality and despite having to begin from scratch. British football clubs have to begin at the bottom of a pyramid and can reach the top levels only through being promoted on their league record. They cannot be elected directly to the higher, professional levels of the pyramid no matter how wealthy or well supported they are. But some supporters, though small in number, have found it difficult to give up on their attachment to the old Football League club. A very similar case has occurred with the smaller club Enfield, which has had an offshoot club, Enfield Town, formed by disgruntled supporters. The division in support between the two remaining clubs has been nearer to equal than in the Wimbledon case. Again, supporters have agonised over where their allegiance properly lies.

It seems, therefore, that our theory will have to allow degrees of continuity, which do not always determine identity. There may be cases of definite identity, and cases of definite non-identity, but apparently also an indeterminate area between. We need an account of what the identity of a sports club consists in that allows there to be cases of at least these three categories. A sketch of such an account will now be presented.

Identity, in the purely metaphysical sense, is understood as something that is all or nothing. Yet we seem to have found cases, concerning the intentional objects of sporting allegiance, where it is unclear whether things are determinately identical. The aim now is to offer an explanation of how this can be so. To begin with, we should consider again what kind of object a sports club is. Clearly a sports club is a particular, but we can say more than this as particularity is a very general term that might be used to categorise abstract entities, such as numbers, or even universals. A first-order universal is a second-order particular, as when we treat redness as a particular (Armstrong 1978: 163). To be more precise, therefore, we can understand sporting clubs to be complex concrete substances. Substance is a technical term of metaphysics, best understood as meaning something that is capable of independent existence within its own ontological category (following Hoffman and Rosenkrantz 1997). This means that a substance exists in logical independence from other substances. Because of the unity and connectedness of the parts of a sports club, it seems appropriate to classify it as a complex substance rather than as a mereological complex, such as a pile of (unconnected) stones. Hoffman and Rosenkrantz do not consider whether social institutions are substances or mereological sums.

I argue that while we often have a great deal of passion associated with the identity of such a substance, especially as I have argued in the case of sporting allegiance, that identity is nevertheless to a degree a conventional and conspiratorial matter. This demonstrates that sporting clubs have to be treated as *social* substances. Their identity through time depends not just on the metaphysical facts: the (weakly) mind-independent facts of where they are based, their colours and so on. It also depends crucially on facts about the behaviour of people, including facts about the allegiances of their supporters. Whether identity conditions are mind-dependent or mind-independent may provide a criterion for whether or not a substance is a social substance. To at least some degree, it is argued, facts about allegiance are constitutive of the identity of the club. Bearing in mind that sports clubs are complex substances, having many integrated parts or components, then one of the components that is constitutive of the substance, and its persistence through time, is the intentional allegiances of which they are the object. There are, therefore, many facts that contribute to the persistence of such a social substance, but one category of such facts is conspiratorial, hence strongly mind-dependent. Sport itself is a strongly mind-dependent phenomenon, of course, as sport essentially concerns intentions of its participants. Hence, even if a sports team has no supporters, it is a strongly mind-dependent substance in virtue of its participants.

A notion of mind-dependence (and independence) is being employed here, and contrasting weak and strong forms distinguished. Social substances contrast with non-social substances, such as a rock or a dog. The identity through time of a rock, for example, is in no way mind-dependent because its identity does not entail the existence of any mind. The persistence of a social substance does, however, entail the existence of a mind. Indeed, one can argue that a social substance entails the existence of many minds because it can only exist and persist through the intentions of a community of thinkers. A phenomenon is weakly mind-dependent where it entails the existence of minds only if accompanied by contingent, true and non-redundant premises (see Molnar 2003: 112, on weak and strong anthropocentricity).

Also employed has been a notion of conspiracy, about which more needs to be said. This is a notion that must be freed of its negative, pejorative connotations, as it is intended to mean, following Lewis (1993), any phenomenon, good, bad or neither, that requires the participation of more than one thinker. Such a conspiracy is pertinent for the case of a complex social substance where the shared intentions of the supporters (and other observers) are strong enough to overcome certain classes of discontinuities. It is, therefore, agreement among a community of onlookers that identity has been preserved through a range of discontinuities that is in part constitutive of that identity through change. Effectively, though not necessarily consciously and deliberately, it is the conspiracy that creates the permissible discontinuities discussed above. A sports club may move to a new stadium, for example, perhaps changing its team colours and name in the process. Nevertheless, it may survive such major changes if the community of onlookers, including the supporters directing their allegiances, permit the discontinuity. Permission, in this context, means accepting the preservation of identity through these discontinuities rather than judging the case to be the ending of one sports club and the beginning of a new, distinct one. And such permission may, of course, be a joint action of a plural subject, in the sense discussed in Chapter 12.

Some essential points of detail may be drawn out. First, the conspiratorial and conventional nature of such permission means that it cannot usually be granted by one person alone, nor in the face of near-unanimous opposition from the community of onlookers. Suppose I judge that club b at time t_2 is identical with club a at t_1 but I am alone in making this judgement. All others in my community judge a and b to be distinct. Does the fact of my belief grant the identity of a and b? Not on this account. The fact that the community has not been persuaded will be in part constitutive of the distinctness of a and b. What is needed is that enough people join the conspiracy to make it defeat rival views. If enough people are in the conspiracy, it may, therefore, be sufficient for the club to be a logical subject of Aristotelian change: a persisting substance. I can, of course, choose to support b in these circumstances nevertheless. But this would have to count as a change of allegiance.

Second, for a conspiracy to be successful, there must be at least some metaphysical grounding to it – some mind-independent basis – that will persuade enough people that the conspiracy is sufficiently rational. This explains why it is not the case that anything goes and why beliefs and intentions of the community alone cannot dictate identity. The community is made up of rational agents who wish their beliefs to fit the facts. They require that identity be grounded in something other than their own beliefs. Rationality requires, for identity, that there is some mind-independent thing, the substance, which is the persisting particular. The conspiracy allows, however, some looseness or vagueness over what this persisting thing is. We have seen that there are a variety of facts, of components, that constitute the sports club, and it seems that none of these components alone is necessary or sufficient for the club's persistence. But we would not be persuaded of the rationality of an identity between a and b, at distinct but adjacent times, where not a single component or quality was common to a and b. Where there is a lengthy passage of time, however, a and b may well be numerically identical, though nothing about b is the same as a. This would be where a gradual series of changes had occurred; for example: one year the club changed its name, the next year it changed its team colours, the next year it changed its geographical base and so on.

Third, it remains a possibility, in this account, that there be no consensus in the community whether or not a and b are identical. This is the situation that occurs in the indeterminate problem cases. There are some metaphysical facts – continuities – that would support the identity of a and b, but some discontinuities that do not. Identity in these cases is indeterminate because there is insufficient metaphysical grounding for the rationality of either the distinctness or identity of a and b.

One case in which there is a lack of consensus is where there are two separate sub-communities persuaded of the rationality of opposing stances on the issue. This seems to be the situation with the disputed identity of Wimbledon. The sub-community that is constituted by the supporters of the old club are persuaded that AFC Wimbledon is identical with the old club. This is because AFC Wimbledon is committed to remaining in the borough and maintaining the traditions of the old club. It is also the club that the majority of the previous supporters have decided now to watch. Such a factor, which might be the result of a bandwagon effect, is no doubt a highly valued factor for those supporters because one of the key attractions of their experience is the social interaction it brings with each other. They are brought together by having the same allegiance. Because the club is a complex social substance, it is in part constituted by that body of support, so part of the object of allegiance is a group having a shared allegiance to each other, *qua* components of the club. This factor, however, carries less significance among the community of non-supporting onlookers, such as the sports media and supporters of other teams. For this other group, the notion that the Milton Keynes-based club is identical with the old Wimbledon has remained sufficiently rational.

A final note is one that was promised earlier. An account could come out of this analysis that explains why allegiance to teams is more prevalent than allegiance to individuals in sport. Because sports teams or clubs are complex social substances, the supporters themselves, through their allegiance, can feel part of the club. In many cases, supporters can become official members. Whether they do or not, part of the object of the allegiance is the supporters themselves: they support an entity of which they are a part. In the case of non-team sports, there is very little rational sense in which I can be a part of the thing I am supporting. Hence, I may wish that Andy Murray wins at tennis but I am unlikely to have the same kind of intense allegiance to him as I could have to a team. Murray is not a complex particular, in the philosophical sense, so I can in no way be a part of that which I would support. I can have a favourite player, therefore, but it does not seem appropriate or entirely natural to speak of having an allegiance to an individual. If it is not natural to have an allegiance to an individual, what of the cases of marriage and other personal relationships that seem to involve some kind of allegiance? In such cases it seems rational to speak of having emotions for, or loyalty to, a spouse, for instance. These cases are perhaps best described as cases where parties to the relationship are allies. The idea of allies suggests an equal relationship between the parties, but when I have an allegiance I have a loyalty that need not be reciprocated. Hence I can have an allegiance to my club without expecting that it have an allegiance to me. To be an ally suggests that any support would be reciprocated.

We have analysed the concept of allegiance, which appears to be an important aspect is many people's experience of sport. We analysed it as an emotional, at least semi-permanent, bond. As such, it must be understood as having an intentional object that persists over a period of time. We then tried to explain what this intentional object is and what its conditions are of diachronic identity. We said that the object of allegiance was a complex concrete social substance. Its identity through time was in part constituted by mind-independent facts about it, but in part by conventional and conspiratorial facts. These issues are important because we will want to know what it is that our sporting allegiance is an allegiance to, and what justifies our continued allegiance through changes in that object. This is just one issue that arises when we consider the philosophy of sport through the experience of the observer rather than through the experience of the participant player.

14 Why do we care?

We are coming to the end of our study. We have been examining various philosophical issues that arise from watching sport, and throughout the book a concern, never far in the background, has been with why we watch sport. In this final chapter, the aim is to bring that question to centre stage. The purpose will be to consider why sport specifically is something that we like to watch. Is there something in its intrinsic nature that enthrals us? Does it give us anything that nothing else could? And why are there some people who simply have no interest in sport? This last question should not be ignored, because it has to be conceded that, while the watching of sport is a very popular pastime, it is not one enjoyed universally. Sport strikes some people as far from fascinating to watch but, rather, an utter waste of time. Is there something such people are missing? Do they misconceive sport such that if its appeal were explained adequately they would then understand its importance? Or is it simply a matter of subjective taste whether one enjoys sport or not? During this book, we have been keen to separate watching sport from participating in sport and, again, we need to make sure we have these two activities separate in our minds. We may play sport for fitness and well-being. We do not automatically gain those benefits merely in virtue of watching sport. As it will be argued, however, there may be some relation to be found between the two activities. Part of the value of watching sport may indeed derive from the value of playing it.

Playing games, it has been suggested, is an end in itself. It is something we do for its own sake. Its lusory goals are pointless. They are artificial in the sense that they are things we want to do only because it is a way of creating a contest. We wouldn't ordinarily want to hit so many golf balls into holes, for instance, unless it was as part of a game. Why then should we, if we are not even contestants, be interested in watching other people knock golf balls into holes? Why should we care about someone participating in so pointless an activity? There are, of course, the aesthetic, ethical and emotional reasons why we watch sport, that have been discussed in the preceding chapters, but we still may feel we haven't justified the interest of sport.

It has been suggested that watching sport may give us an increased sense of well-being and that it is simply pleasurable to watch even if one is not a participant. Gumbrecht reports that he wasn't very good at sport, for instance.

He lacked the required competence. But still he nevertheless takes pleasure in watching it (Gumbrecht 2006: 31). He is reluctant to intellectualise his activity, however: 'I also want to emphasize that when I am actually watching sport, I am not pursuing any intellectually (or even ethically) edifying ends. I simply enjoy the moments of intensity that such events provide' (Gumbrecht 2006: 31–2). But he goes on to cite factors that do seem more edifying, mentioning a 'feeling of communion' with the athletes he watches, who do have the required competences. He claims that 'the distance between myself and my athletic heroes seems to become smaller' and 'watching sports can allow us to be suddenly, somehow, one with those beautiful and beautifully transfigured bodies' (2006: 32).

Whether the pleasure is an intellectual one or not, Gumbrecht is convinced that you will feel 'on a high when you leave the stadium after an exciting match and you may even feel your self-esteem boosted' (2006: 40). Perhaps whether your self-esteem is boosted will depend on whether your team has won, if you are a partisan. If you are a purist, perhaps your self-esteem is boosted because you have been aesthetically enriched by your experience. But Gumbrecht does not explain how this boost of self-esteem comes about. What would the mechanism be and is it something intrinsic to sport that has encouraged it? If one feels associated closely with a team, perhaps one feels their victories are also your victories. This has become known as BIRG-ing: basking in reflected glories. Then again, for every winner in sport, there is at least one loser. And in many sports, the losers far outnumber the winners, so it would seem by parity of reasoning that sport at least as often would lower the self-esteem of those who watch it. That would seem to create a mystery, however. If sport did tend to lower self-esteem, it sounds like a less enjoyable experience than many people find it. The joy of victory must outweigh the sadness of defeat, if we are to say that watching sport is overall pleasurable. We are, of course, bracketing the purist here, for whom the only thing corresponding to the defeat of the partisan would be a poor contest that offered little by way of aesthetic interest. There might be an explanation, however. We have a problem only if there is an equal and opposite reaction to BIRG-ing in the case of defeat: a kind of reflected shame in defeat. Instead, however, there is a different phenomenon of CORF-ing: cutting off from reflected failure. This means that sport could still tend to produce happiness overall because we associate ourselves with victory, and boost our self-esteem, but distance ourselves from defeats by dissociating from them.

We have found something, then, that does seem intrinsic to sport and which might be a reason we find it interesting. It is intrinsic to sport that we have contests, even if they are ultimately meaningless contests, and through them we can gain an increased sense of self-esteem through associating with their victories. But this is all rather speculative. And nor does it say much about the state of humanity that our self-esteem should be boosted by beating others. Shouldn't cooperation make us feel better than competition? And why should association with victory in a meaningless contest make us feel any better? Aren't sports contests like two blind men fighting over a pair of spectacles? Why should the win mean anything to us? Even more to the point, why should we feel better because the blind man we have cheered on is the one who eventually wears the spectacles?

There is at least some plausible account of how association with a victorious team can work. The winning athlete has probably displayed superior physical and mental virtue to win, in which case their self-esteem might be boosted through having confirmation of their prowess. But we saw in the previous chapter that, in the case of sports clubs, we have complex social entities of which the supporters are a part. In belonging to the club, the association with success can be real. The supporters have not displayed any physical or mental prowess themselves, but they could be part of a sporting club containing another part – the players – that has.

But, again, how does this mean anything? A complaint of non-sports fans is often that it is all so pointless. Why be associated with a meaningless victory? Perhaps this point can be answered. Morgan says that many of us do indeed care about sports. We really care: we love them. And there need be nothing irrational in choosing to care about something that is ultimately meaningless. Sport is 'instrumentally barren' in that it is not for anything else (Morgan 2007: 17). Yet we can make it a final end, rather than a means to anything more valuable. And it being so can be one of our choices. This, according to Morgan, is one of the things that makes us human: we choose our final ends rather than discover them. Morgan is following Harry Frankfurt's rejection of 'pan-rationalist' accounts of how we should lead our lives. How we do so cannot just be about the properties of things in the world – that they are 'careworthy', perhaps – but also has to be about how we relate to the world. Hence, we need to find what is truly valued by us as final ends. Caring is essential to good living. It gives purpose and meaning to our lives. What you care about, you have to think of as important: 'If we care for nothing at all our lives would not be worth a damn' (Morgan 2007: 11). It is our own caring about things that confers value on them (2007: 12). And when things such as sport are important to us, they become active in our lives. Hence, they shape our social loves, for instance, and the use of our leisure time and our habits of consumption. Morgan dissents from Frankfurt's subjectivism on one point. He insists that our cares must be intersubjective (2007: 14). We must come together and decide jointly to care for something. Thus, the institutionalisation of sport is evidence that it is intersubjectively valued. A number of people have conspired together to choose sport as something to be valued. It is a mistake of someone to say simply that they cannot find any meaning in sport, therefore. Morgan is right. Such meaning has not been discovered but has been chosen. We care because we have chosen to care.

This still leaves the question of what exactly we care about. Presumably it is not all aspects of sport that we value. And why is this a care that many people have chosen not to have? I will venture a couple of hypotheses. One of the things we have chosen to care about is the contest itself: not because its prelusory goals are important but simply because the contests are fun. And they are fun precisely because those prelusory goals are unimportant and who achieves them first or best is of no consequence. Hence, we prefer towns and nations to compete over the inconsequential contests of sport than in more serious matters such as wealth or war. The latter competitions cannot be fun because too much is at stake. In the case of war, the campaign can be protracted, strategic and ruthlessly competitive but the very existence of a nation, or at least its political regime, might be at stake. We cannot possibly treat this as a light-hearted and frivolous diversion. It is far too serious. In sports, however, it is fun to see winners and losers, and various tactics for winning being tried, with successful teams being built and broken apart, precisely because nothing is really at stake. The winnings are fantasy. The losers are not put to death. It is therefore permissible and appropriate to take joy in a victory and perhaps even laugh at the defeated, which would be an entirely inappropriate thing to do to prisoners of war, for instance (which is not to deny that prisoners of war have indeed often been humiliated and mistreated). Similarly, it is appropriate to take aesthetic pleasure in many aspects of sport, whereas it would not usually be appropriate to take aesthetic pleasure in war. A goalkeeper in football may leap across the penalty area, reaching with every inch of his or her arms to get to the ball and prevent the goal. Their body is fully extended and seems almost to fly through the air. Various aesthetic qualities of the human form and its motion are evinced. But now imagine that this body is in the theatre of war: a soldier jumping for their life. Again, they run with all their speed and dive out of the way of gunfire, their body fully extended. How inappropriate it would now be for us to take aesthetic pleasure from this human form. War is sometimes the subject of art, of course. There are often official war artists appointed. But this seems a different matter. Their job is usually to document. They may sometimes take heroism as their subject matter, but merely watching some poor soul reach to their full extent to save their life is not something we would want to enjoy aesthetically. A first reason why we might have chosen sport to care about, therefore, might be its very triviality. This makes it appropriate as a leisure activity, a pastime, a hobby. But there is a further reason, which is perhaps more profound.

Best (1978: 117) says that sport is not about anything: art can be about sport but sport cannot be about art. But maybe there is, after all, something that sport is about and it may be something very important to us. We exist as physically embodied beings: causal agents and patients in the world. We manipulate things and suffer changes done to us. It is through our bodies that all this happens. Anything we do as causal agents, we do with our bodies. Schiller (1882) says that we need to strike the right balance between the formal impulse (from our rational nature) and the sensual impulse (from our physical nature). These are both essential parts of our being and, like the Aristotelian mean, we need to find a harmonious state of wholeness between them. In games, and sport, these two impulses come together to form the play instinct: 'man only plays when in the full meaning of the word he is a man, and he is only completely a man when he plays' (Schiller 1882: 453). Hegel also saw that sport displayed our freedom as embodied agents. He saw that sports are organs of spirit, as he says in a passage cited by Morgan (2007: 14):

if we look at the inner nature ... of sports, we observe first how sport itself is opposed to serious business, to dependence and need ... Serious occupation is labour that has reference to some need. Man or nature must succumb; if one is to love, the other must fall. In contrast with this kind of seriousness sport presents the higher seriousness; for in it nature is wrought into sport. In this exercise of physical powers, man shows his freedom, he shows that he has transformed his body into an organ of spirit.

(Hegel 1830: 55)

In Marx this idea appears less explicitly. But in the same tradition as Hegel, Morgan (2007: 15) interprets sports as being in Marx's realm of freedom rather than the realm of necessity, the latter being work.

Could, therefore, sport be about our existence as physically embodied rational creatures? Sport might be a celebration of the body: an arena in which we can admire the body and the extent of its physical capacities, under our rational control. In competition, participants are encouraged to test the limits of those capacities for us as spectators to see. Sport may be the best display in which we may see and learn about embodied mind. To play it, and to watch it, may be our best insight into this vital aspect of our existence. Yet embodiment is a subject on which philosophers have rarely concentrated. The life of the mind, rationality and consciousness have been given far greater attention. Among major philosophers, only Merleau-Ponty (1945) has given embodiment serious consideration and even here we find the topic of sport neglected. This is unfortunate because sport may well be the crucial instance which teaches us about the nature of our embodied existence.

Contrary to Best's allegation, then, we may well be able to say that sport is about something: it's about our existence as physically embodied beings, able to exercise various mental and physical powers. There are, of course, other ways in which we come to understand this aspect of our situation. Work and sex also show us the nature of our physical embodiment, but sport does so in a significantly different way. I can come to see the power of the body even when those powers are not my own. I cannot jump 2.35 metres high but I can see others do it. I can watch sport, and learn about the body, in ways that are socially acceptable. Of course, I could watch people work, but they might regard that as a private matter for which they do not want an audience. And I could watch other people having sex but that may be regarded as voyeuristic or, if I watch pornography, it might bring disapproval. To learn anything worthwhile about work and sex, I usually have to do them. But the case of sport is different insofar as it is socially acceptable and often encouraged to watch others perform. Watching sport, therefore, provides us with possibly our best way to find out about embodiment vicariously. I can observe the body performing the various excellences of sport, but it is not my own. My empirical knowledge of embodiment is not, therefore, restricted to the first person.

Given such attractions, why does sport not appeal to everyone? Why have some chosen not to care about it? There is almost certainly no single reason.

Different things may turn different people away from sport. Many of these reasons will be non-philosophical ones and merely extrinsic to sport. Some people are less competitive than others and dislike the whole notion of defeating another. Sport might be thought to create a macho environment and thus be a less pleasant way of exploring embodiment than, for instance, sex. There are also a number of issues specifically about watching sport that turn some people away. Sports stadiums have at times been refuges of racism, sexism and homophobia. Why should anyone want to attend sporting events if they feel they would be victimised in any of these respects, or have to witness prejudice against other groups? Certainly we would have no business thinking someone wrong for avoiding sports for these reasons. Many such people may be participants in sport, or at least have gym memberships that show they have an interest in physical fitness, yet nevertheless find supporter culture and the stadium atmosphere repellent. These are indeed genuine concerns, and at different times, in different places, sports events have been more or often less pleasant places to be. This may be especially felt by someone in the purist camp, who seeks an edifying aesthetic experience. They may far prefer to gain their aesthetic pleasure in the civilised and sophisticated confines of an art gallery than in a sports stadium. Indeed, if they want to appreciate sporting beauty, they may even prefer to see it at an art exhibition of sporting images than at a real-life event.

But this only increases the moral imperative on us to make sports events welcoming to all people, irrespective of race, gender and sexual orientation. Sport, it has been argued, can offer us insights into embodiment, agency, freedom and the limits of human potential. It is wrong of us to tolerate situations in which large classes of people are informally excluded from witnessing those insights because of a perceived hostility to their presence. It may be that some of the contingent and extrinsic but dominant values around the watching of sport are what deter people from interest, rather than anything essential to the watching of sport. It is one thing to be uninterested because of a dislike of competition but altogether a different thing to be uninterested because of a dislike of homophobia. Competition is a vital component of sport; homophobia is not. Similarly, sport may be seen as overly commercialised (Morgan 2006) or in some cases corrupt. These are again factors that surround sport and may put people off. But, again, that gives us an imperative to remove corruption and the power of commercial excess if they are deterring people from enjoying what may be a rewarding experience.

When it comes to a matter that is a central component of sport, we of course cannot expect that it appeals to everyone who sees it. But Van Gogh, although he appeals to many appreciators of art, does not appeal to them all. We do have variation in our aesthetic sensibilities, as was discussed in Chapter 3. Certain qualities tend to produce aesthetic satisfaction. But because this is a response within us, and human nature shows some variation, then we cannot expect that everyone will take that same aesthetic pleasure. Many people find it pleasing, aesthetically, intellectually and emotionally, to watch athletes struggling in a contest, but not all do. And just as we might try to persuade someone with no appreciation of Van Gogh of the virtues of his paintings, so we might do in the case of sport. Indeed, this book might be seen as an attempt to do so. We have pointed out aesthetic ways of seeing sport that might not have occurred to some. There is, of course, one final yet major issue upon which we have not yet commented. Like any form of aesthetic experience, sport has an ability to provide us with a kind of release. Many sports promote what Kant (1790: §25) calls the sublime, in the sense that they 'threaten to overwhelm us', and sport 'brings with it a feeling of the promotion of life' (Gumbrecht 2006: 47, quoting Kant). Schopenhauer (1818) made use of this notion. In his development of Kantian metaphysics, he sees us as being controlled by a will that is never at rest but constantly striving for satisfaction. This leaves us in a constant state of dissatisfaction because our striving either goes unfulfilled or, if it is fulfilled, it only makes us greedier for more. Because of this effect on us, Schopenhauer characterises the will as evil.

Schopenhauer offers us one glimmer of hope. Only in aesthetic contemplation are we able to find some release from the evil will that controls us. For when we appreciate beauty, we can become completely immersed in the object of appreciation and for a few moments lose all sense of our self and its striving. Instead of selfish desires, we know only pure perception of the object (1851: vol. II, 415). We completely forget our own person (1818: vol. I, 185).

Such a release is something we often find in watching sport. Gumbrecht reports something like it when he watches (2006: 55): he feels a focused intensity, composure and euphoria. Many people live a kind of hum-drum life in which their work brings them little satisfaction and in which they may have personal and financial difficulties. But for a few hours in the week, when they attend the sports stadium, all those problems are cast aside. While watching the game, all their worries are forgotten. They become immersed in the sporting event, thinking nothing of themselves but only of who will win, how the contest will unfold and what drama they may find. The collective emotions of which we spoke in Chapter 12 are a further sign of this. It is as if we go to watch sport almost in the hope that our individuality will be subsumed into the whole, such that we are then released from our personal strivings and difficulties and have only a common interest as a plural subject in the outcome of the sporting challenge. Unpaid bills are out of the mind, stress at work can be forgotten, professional grudges temporarily forgiven, and difficult personal problems put on hold. Many sports fans experience it this way. And it is thus often seen as an outlet or stress relief. It gives them something outside their regular lives about which they can elect to care. And as it is a form of observation, they can be become immersed in the experience for a few short hours, finishing refreshed enough to resume their regular routines.

The triviality of sport – a theme to which we have alluded a number of times – thus becomes crucial. If sport was for something instrumentally important, it would not be fit to play the role it does. If we really needed sport for some further end, it would become part of what our will strives towards. It would not give us release from striving. We would be too worried about the outcome if something serious depended on it. We wouldn't be able to enjoy it, in such circumstances.

Instead, we have created a fantasy. We have chosen to care about something that matters little for anything else. Victory has no instrumental value. Yet we have chosen this to be an end in itself, appreciating sport for its own sake. Watching sport thus gives us pleasure directly. It does not give us something else, which in turn gives us pleasure. And this pleasure is one that allows our immersion in contemplation, facilitating deeper and more profound benefits.

Such a benefit, of a Schopenhauerian release, can of course be obtained in other ways. If Schopenhauer is right, then contemplation of the arts achieves the same goal. But not every art does so in the same way. Different arts provide different kinds of experience. We have not focused narrowly on arts but on any kind of aesthetic experience, which may be focused on a natural object, such as a sunset, as much as a work of art. Sport provides aesthetic experience, it has been argued, but it can be argued that it provides a distinctive kind of aesthetic experience. If the account in this chapter is correct, it provides an aesthetic insight into the nature of our embodied existence and the extent of our capabilities. Dance may serve a similar function but not always with the addition of improvisation and testing of capacities, which competition specifically encourages. Sport adds something to the human form that cannot be found even in dance.

We now have a better idea of why we tend to care about watching sport: why it is important to many but not all people. It has a number of features that many of us have chosen to care about and find interesting, even though there is nothing that compels such care. And with this we end our foray into the philosophy of watching sport. It will be helpful to summarise our main findings.

We started with a division between two types of sports enthusiast, the partisan and the purist. We then proceeded to consider the aesthetics of sport, noting that such matters are more the concern of the purist than the partisan. Although sport is a source of aesthetic pleasure for many, we noted that this alone was not sufficient to make it art. What made something art we said was a complex matter involving a relation to certain complex social institutions, which differed from the institutions of sport. We saw, however, that some putative disanalogies between sport and art did not bear scrutiny and thus that our experiences of sport and art were not as widely differing as some might say. We then looked more closely at the difference between the partisan's and purist's experience of sport and defended a claim that there were different ways of seeing. The partisan's way of seeing sport is primarily competitive, always preferring a dull win to a dramatic defeat. The purist's way of seeing sport is one we called aesthetic, thus defending the idea that there is a specifically aesthetic way of seeing. We then bridged the topics of aesthetics and ethics, noting that part of the aesthetic content of sport could be determined by moral matters and, indeed, vice versa.

This led us to the ethical reasons for watching sport, and it was argued that there was enough in common between the ethics of sport and those of life more generally that we could see these two domains as continuous. The ethics of sport can both inform, and be informed by, our wider morality. But how can sport inform that morality? We went on to consider sport as providing a contest of virtues: where we can witness the virtues and vices pitted against each other in a real, as opposed to fictional, contest. Having acquired knowledge of virtue and vice in an artificial sporting contest, we can then exercise those virtues ourselves in other parts of our lives and gain the benefits thereof. It was then argued that virtue and vice are best understood in the abstract. We may learn about them from them being exhibited by individuals, but it is virtue that is important for morality, not the individual who exhibits it, and for this reason we should resist making our sports stars our role models.

Our third theme was issues in the philosophy of emotion. Sport can provide the watcher with a rich and deep emotional experience, and this is often a chief motivation of the partisan, though the purist can also be affected by it. It was argued that the depth of emotion felt in a sporting contest can be explained because it is something experienced collectively and this can provide emotion with a special intensity. We then looked at the objects of our emotional attachments in sport, which tend more to be sports clubs than individuals. An explanation of this is that the sports club is a complex social entity of which the fans themselves are a part. They really do, in that case, belong to the club: they are indeed a part of it. Finally, in the present chapter, we considered the question of why we care about sport. It seems that we really do; many of us in any case. There are reasons for this. It may well be that we have chosen to care, rather than discovered some objective property of sport that is 'careworthy'. But we have chosen something that may provide a profound insight into the nature of human existence. We are embodied creatures, with mental and physical capacities that we are able to test and exercise as free agents. Sport allows us to do this and, in witnessing it, we therefore learn about embodiment. We do so in a relatively safe environment in which no one dies and little of importance is at stake. But this is what allows us to find sport so enjoyable and take in it a kind of release from striving that Schopenhauer had described in aesthetics.

It has been shown that there are many issues worthy of our attention to be found in the watching of sport. Philosophers of sport should find this of interest. But it is also hoped that enough of an interest has been raised for people outside this specialist area to see sport as something that is worthy of our attention; for the watching of sport is not merely pure dumb entertainment. At its best, we can discover something profound when we watch sport. Having considered the issues in this book, it is hoped that we will be in a better position to do so.

References

Aristotle, *Nicomachean Ethics*, J. Thomson and H. Tredennick (trans.), London: Penguin, 1976.

—— *Physics*, R. Waterfield (trans.), Oxford: Oxford University Press, 1996.

Armstrong, D. (1978) *A Theory of Universals*, Cambridge: Cambridge University Press.

—— (1989) *Universals: An Opinionated Introduction*, Boulder: Westview Press.

—— (1997) *A World of States of Affairs*, Cambridge: Cambridge University Press.

Aspin, D. (1974) 'Sport and the Concept of "The Aesthetic"', in H. Whiting and D. Masterson (eds) *Readings in the Aesthetics of Sport*, London: Lepus, 1974, pp. 117–37.

Beardsley, M. (1958) *Aesthetics*, New York: Harcourt Brace.

—— (1976) 'Is Art Essentially Institutional?', in L. Aagaard-Mogensen (ed.) *Culture and Art*, Atlantic Highlands, NJ: Humanities Press, pp. 194–209.

—— (1982) 'Redefining Art', in M. Wreen and D. Callen (eds) *The Aesthetic Point of View*, Madison: University of Wisconsin Press, pp. 298–315.

Bell, C. (1914) *Art*, London: Chatto and Windus.

Berger, J. (1972) *Ways of Seeing*, London: Penguin.

Best, D. (1974) 'The Aesthetic in Sport', *British Journal of Aesthetics*, 14: 197–213.

—— (1978) *Philosophy and Human Movement*, London: George Allen and Unwin.

—— (1985) 'Sport is Not Art', in W. Morgan and K. Meier (eds) *Philosophic Inquiry in Sport*, Champaign, IL: Human Kinetics, 1988, pp. 527–39.

Brentano, F. (1874) *Psychology from an Empirical Standpoint*, L. L. McAlister (ed.), Atlantic Highlands, NJ: Humanities Press, 1973.

Butler, D. (1988) 'Character Traits in Explanation', *Philosophy and Phenomenological Research*, 49: 215–38.

Calhoun, C. and Solomon, R. (1984) *What is an Emotion?*, Oxford: Oxford University Press.

Camus, A. (1942) *L'Étranger (The Outsider)*, J. Laredo (trans.), London: Penguin, 2006.

—— (1960) 'The Wager of Our Generation', in *Resistance, Rebellion, and Death*, J. O'Brien (trans.), New York: Vintage, 1961.

Carr, D. (1998) 'What Moral Educational Significance has Physical Education? A Question in Need of Disambiguation', in M. McNamee and J. Parry (eds) *Ethics and Sport*, London: Routledge, pp. 119–33.

Carroll, N. (1988) 'Art, Practice, and Narrative', *The Monist*, 71: 140–56.

Cohen, T. (1973) 'The Possibility of Art: Remarks on a Proposal by Dickie', *Philosophical Review*, 82: 69–82.

Cooper, W. (1978) 'Do Sports Have an Aesthetic Aspect?', *Journal of the Philosophy of Sport*, 5: 51–5.

Cordner, C. (1984) 'Grace and Functionality', *British Journal of Aesthetics*, 24: 301–13.
—— (2003) 'The Meaning of Graceful Movement', *Journal of the Philosophy of Sport*, 30: 132–43.
Crawford, G. (2004) *Consuming Sport: Fans, Sport and Culture*, London: Routledge.
Croce, B. (1920) *Aesthetics*, D. Ainslie (trans.), London: Macmillan.
Culbertson, L. (2008) 'Does Sport Have Intrinsic Value?', *Sport, Ethics and Philosophy*, 2: 302–20.
Dancy, J. (1993) *Moral Reasons*, Oxford: Blackwell.
—— (2004) *Ethics Without Principles*, Oxford: Oxford University Press.
Danto, A. (1964) 'The Artworld', *Journal of Philosophy*, 61: 571–84.
—— (1973) 'Artworks and Real Things', *Theoria*, 39: 1–17.
Davies, S. (1991) *Definitions of Art*, Ithaca: Cornell University Press.
—— (2005) 'Definitions of Art', in B. Gaut and D. McIver Lopes (eds) *The Routledge Companion to Aesthetics*, 2nd edn, London: Routledge, pp. 227–39.
Davis, P. (2001) 'Issues of Immediacy and Deferral in Cordner's Theory of Grace', *Journal of the Philosophy of Sport*, 28: 89–95.
—— (2006) 'Game Strengths', *Journal of the Philosophy of Sport*, 33: 50–66.
De Coubertin, P. (2000) *Olympism: Selected Writings*, Lausanne: International Olympic Committee.
Dennett, D. (1991) *Consciousness Explained*, London: Penguin.
De Sousa, R. (1987) *The Rationality of Emotion*, Cambridge, MA: MIT Press.
Devereaux, M. (1998) 'Beauty and Evil: The Case of Leni Riefenstahl's *Triumph of the Will*', in J. Levinson (ed.) *Aesthetics and Ethics: Essays at the Intersection*, Cambridge: Cambridge University Press, pp. 227–56.
Dewey, J. (1958) *Art as Experience*, New York: Capricorn.
Dickie, G. (1964) 'The Myth of the Aesthetic Attitude', *American Philosophical Quarterly*, 1: 56–66.
—— (1969) 'Defining Art', *American Philosophical Quarterly*, 6: 253–6.
—— (1974) *Art and the Aesthetic*, Ithaca: Cornell University Press.
—— (1984) *The Art Circle: A Theory of Art*, New York: Haven.
Dixon, N. (2001) 'The Ethics of Supporting Sports Teams', *Journal of Applied Philosophy*, 18: 149–58.
Doris, J. (2002) *Lack of Character: Personality and Moral Behaviour*, Cambridge: Cambridge University Press.
Dougan, A. (2002) *Dynamo: Defending the Honour of Kiev*, London: Fourth Estate.
Durkheim, E. (1895) *The Rules of Sociological Method*, W. D. Halls (trans.), New York: Free Press, 1982.
Dworkin, R. (1986) *Law's Empire*, Cambridge, MA: Harvard University Press.
Eaton, M. (2004) 'Art and the Aesthetic', in P. Kivvy (ed.) *The Blackwell Guide to Aesthetics*, Oxford: Blackwell, pp. 63–77.
Elliott, R. (1974) 'Aesthetics and Sport', in H. Whiting and D. Masterson (eds) *Readings in the Aesthetics of Sport*, London: Lepus, pp. 107–16.
Fisher, A. (2005) 'Watching Sport – But Who is Watching?', *Journal of the Philosophy of Sport*, 32: 184–94.
Gaskin, G. and Masterson, D. (1974) 'The Work of Art in Sport', in H. Whiting and D. Masterson (eds) *Readings in the Aesthetics of Sport*, London: Lepus, pp. 139–60.
Gaut, B. (1998) 'The Ethical Criticism of Art', in J. Levinson (ed.) *Aesthetics and Ethics: Essays at the Intersection*, Cambridge: Cambridge University Press, pp. 182–203.

—— (2007) *Art, Emotion and Ethics*, Oxford: Oxford University Press.

Gilbert, M. (1989) *On Social Facts*, Princeton, NJ: Princeton University Press.

Goldman, A. (2005) 'The Aesthetic', in B. Gaut and D. McIver Lopes (eds) *The Routledge Companion to Aesthetics*, 2nd edn, London: Routledge, pp. 255–66.

Goodman, N. (1978) *Ways of Worldmaking*, Hassocks: Harvester.

Gordon, R. (1987) *The Structure of Emotions*, Cambridge: Cambridge University Press.

Gough, R. (1998) 'Moral Development Research in Sports and Its Quest for Objectivity', in M. McNamee and J. Parry (eds) *Ethics and Sport*, London: Routledge, pp. 134–47.

Gregory, R. (1966) *Eye and Brain: The Psychology of Seeing*, 3rd edn, London: Weidenfeld and Nicolson, 1977.

Gumbrecht, H. (2006) *In Praise of Athletic Beauty*, Cambridge, MA: Belknap Press.

Hanson, N. R. (1958) *Patterns of Discovery: An Inquiry into the Conceptual Foundations of Science*, Cambridge: Cambridge University Press.

Hawley, K. (2001) *How Things Persist*, Oxford: Clarendon Press.

Hegel, G. (1830) *Philosophy of History*, in *The Philosophy of Hegel*, C. Friedrich (ed.), New York: The Modern Library.

Heidegger, M. (1927) *Being and Time*, J. Macquarrie and E. Robinson (trans.), Oxford: Blackwell, 1962.

Hobbes, T. (1651) *Leviathan*, R. Tuck (ed.), Cambridge: Cambridge University Press, 1991.

Hoffman, J. and Rosenkrantz, G. (1997) *Substance: Its Nature and Existence*, London: Routledge.

Hofstadter, D. (1979) *Gödel, Escher, Bach: An Eternal Golden Braid*, Hassocks: Harvester.

Hohler, V. (1974) 'The Beauty of Motion', in H. Whiting and D. Masterson (eds) *Readings in the Aesthetics of Sport*, London: Lepus, pp. 49–56.

Huizinga, J. (1950) *Homo Ludens: A Study of the Play Element in Culture*, Boston: Beacon Press.

Hume, D. (1739–40) *A Treatise of Human Nature*, L. A. Selby-Bigge (ed.), Oxford: Clarendon Press, 1888.

—— (1741–2) *Essays, Moral, Political, and Literary*, E. Miller (ed.), Indianapolis: Liberty Fund, 1987.

Hursthouse, R. (1999) *On Virtue Ethics*, Oxford: Oxford University Press.

James, W. (1884) 'What is an Emotion?', in C. Calhoun and R. Solomon (eds) *What is an Emotion?*, Oxford: Oxford University Press, 1984, pp. 137–41.

Kant, I. (1785) *Grounding for the Metaphysics of Morals*, 3rd edn, Indianapolis: Hackett, 1993.

—— (1790) *Critique of Judgement*, J. Meredith (trans.), Oxford: Oxford University Press, 2007.

Keller, H. (1974) 'Sport and Art – The Concept of Mastery', in H. Whiting and D. Masterson (eds) *Readings in the Aesthetics of Sport*, London: Lepus, pp. 89–98.

Kenny, A. (1963) *Action, Emotion and Will*, London: Routledge and Kegan Paul.

Kretchmar, S. (2005) 'Game Flaws', *Journal of the Philosophy of Sport*, 32: 36–48.

—— (2008) 'Calling the Beautiful Game Ugly: A Response to Davis', *Sport, Ethics and Philosophy*, 2: 321–36.

Kuhn, T. (1962) *The Structure of Scientific Revolutions*, 2nd edn, Chicago: University of Chicago Press, 1970.

Kupfer, J. (1983) 'Sport – The Body Electric', in W. Morgan and K. Meier (eds) *Philosophic Inquiry in Sport*, Champaign, IL: Human Kinetics, 1988, pp. 455–75.

Lacerda, T. and Mumford, S. (2010) 'The Genius in Art and in Sport: A Contribution to the Investigation of Aesthetics of Sport', *Journal of the Philosophy of Sport*, 37: 182–93.

Lewis, H. (1993) 'Conspiracy: The Plan', *Inside Out: Mind and Related Matters*, 8: 1.

Loland, S. (2002) *Fair Play in Sport: A Moral Norm System*, London: Routledge.

Lowe, E. J. (1995) *Locke*, London: Routledge.

—— (2002) *A Survey of Metaphysics*, Oxford: Oxford University Press.

Macpherson, C. B. (1962) *The Political Theory of Possessive Individualism*, Oxford: Oxford University Press.

Martin, C. B. (2008) *The Mind in Nature*, Oxford: Oxford University Press.

McFee, G. (2004) *Sport, Rules and Values: Philosophical Investigations into the Nature of Sport*, London: Routledge.

—— (2009) 'The Intrinsic Value of Sport: A Reply to Culbertson', *Sport, Ethics and Philosophy*, 3: 19–29.

McNamee, M. (2008) *Sports, Virtues and Vices: Morality Plays*, London: Routledge.

Merleau-Ponty, M. (1945) *Phenomenology of Perception*, C. Smith (trans.), London: Routledge, 1962.

Mill, J. S. (1843) *A System of Logic*, London: Longmans.

—— (1861) *Utilitarianism*, in *Collected Works of John Stuart Mill*, vol. X, Indianapolis: Liberty, 2006, pp. 203–59.

Molnar, G. (2003) *Powers: A Study in Metaphysics*, S. Mumford (ed.), Oxford: Oxford University Press.

Morgan, W. (1994) *Leftist Theories of Sport: A Critique and Reconstruction*, Urbana, IL: University of Illinois Press.

—— (2006) *Why Sports Morally Matter*, London: Routledge.

—— (2007) 'Caring, Final Ends and Sports', *Sport, Ethics and Philosophy*, 1: 7–21.

Mulgan, T. (2001) *The Demands of Consequentialism*, Oxford: Oxford University Press.

Mumford, S. (2004) 'Allegiance and Identity', *Journal of the Philosophy of Sport*, 31: 184–95.

—— (2010) 'Breaking It or Faking It? Some Critical Thoughts on the Voluntary Suspension of Play and Six Proposed Revisions', *Sport, Ethics and Philosophy*, 4: 254–68.

Mumford, S. and Anjum, R. (2011) *Getting Causes from Powers*, Oxford: Oxford University Press.

Møller, V. (2009) *The Ethics of Doping and Anti-Doping: Redeeming the Soul of Sport?*, London: Routledge.

Noonan, H. (1989) *Personal Identity*, London: Routledge.

Parfit, D. (1984) *Reasons and Persons*, Oxford: Clarendon Press.

Pawlenka, C. (2005) 'The Idea of Fairness: A General Ethical Concept or One Particular to Sports Ethics?', *Journal of the Philosophy of Sport*, 32: 49–64.

Plato, *Republic*, F. M. Cornford (trans.), Oxford: Oxford University Press, 1941.

Pompa, L. (1967) 'Family Resemblance', *Philosophical Quarterly*, 17: 63–9.

Reid, H. (2010) 'Athletics and Ancient Philosophy in Ancient Greece and Rome: Contests of Virtue', *Sport, Ethics and Philosophy*, 4: 109–234.

Roberts, T. (1986) 'Sport, Art, and Particularity: The Best Equivocation', *Journal of the Philosophy of Sport*, 13: 49–63.

Rousseau, J. J. (1762) *The Social Contract*, G. D. H. Cole (trans.), London: Dent, 1973.

Russell, J. (2007) 'Broad Internalism and the Moral Foundations of Sport', in W. Morgan (ed.) *Ethics in Sport*, Champaign, IL: Human Kinetics, pp. 51–66.

—— (2010) 'The Moral Ambiguity of Coaching Youth Sport', in A. Hardman and C. Jones (eds) *The Ethics of Sports Coaching*, London: Routledge, pp. 87–103.

Schiller, F. (1882) 'Play and Beauty', in W. Morgan and K. Meier (eds) *Philosophic Inquiry in Sport*, Champaign, IL: Human Kinetics, 1988, pp. 451–3.

Schopenhauer, A. (1818) *The World as Will and Representation*, E. F. J. Payne (trans.), 2 vols, New York: Dover, 1966.

—— (1851) *Parerga and Paralipomena*, E. F. J. Payne (trans.), 2 vols, Oxford: Clarendon Press, 1974.

Shiner, L. (2001) *Invention of Art: A Cultural History*, Chicago: Chicago University Press.

Sibley, F. (1959) 'A Contemporary Theory of Aesthetic Qualities: Aesthetic Concepts', *Philosophical Review*, 68: 421–50.

Simon, R. (2001) 'Internalism and the Internal Values in Sport', in W. Morgan (ed.) *Ethics in Sport*, Champaign, IL: Human Kinetics, pp. 35–50 (original version in *Journal of the Philosophy of Sport*, 27: 1–16).

Simons, P. (2000) 'Continuants and Occurrents', *The Aristotelian Society*, supp. vol., 74: 59–75.

Skillen, A. (1998) 'Sport is for Losers', in M. McNamee and S. Parry (eds) *Ethics and Sport*, London: Routledge, pp. 169–81.

Still, K. (2010) *Crowd Dynamics*, http://www.gkstill.com, accessed 6.9.10.

Stolnitz, J. (1960) *Aesthetics and Philosophy of Art Criticism*, New York: Houghton Mifflin.

—— (1961) 'On the Significance of Lord Shaftesbury in Modern Aesthetic Theory', *Philosophical Quarterly*, 11: 97–113.

Suits, B. (2005) *The Grasshopper: Games Life and Utopia*, 2nd edn, Peterborough, Ontario: Broadview Press.

Swanton, C. (2003) *Virtue Ethics: A Pluralistic View*, Oxford: Oxford University Press.

Tolstoy, L. (1896) *What is Art?*, A. Maude (trans.), Oxford: Oxford University Press, 1995.

Torres, C. (unpublished) 'Interpretivism, Ethics, and Aesthetics'.

Tymowski, G. (unpublished) 'Why Athletes Ought to be Role Models'.

Urmson, J. (1958) 'Saints and Heroes', in A. Melden (ed.) *Essays in Moral Philosophy*, Seattle: University of Washington Press, pp. 198–215.

Wann, D., Melnick, M., Russell, G. and Pease, D. (2001) *Sports Fans: The Psychology and Social Impact of Spectators*, New York: Routledge.

Weber, M. (1922) *The Theory of Social and Economic Organization*, T. Parsons and A. M. Henderson (trans.), Glencoe, IL: Free Press, 1964.

Weitz, M. (1956) 'The Role of Theory in Aesthetics', *Journal of Aesthetics and Art Criticism*, 15: 27–35.

Wieand, J. (1994) 'Perceptually Indistinguishable Objects', in R. Yanal (ed.) *Institutions of Art: Reconsiderations of George Dickie's Philosophy*, University Park: Pennsylvania State University Press, 39–49.

Wilson, J. (2006) *Behind the Curtain: Travels in Eastern European Football*, London: Orion.

Wittgenstein, L. (1953) *Philosophical Investigations*, Oxford: Blackwell.

—— (1958) *The Blue and Brown Books: Preliminary Studies for the 'Philosophical Investigations'*, Oxford: Blackwell.

—— (1980) *Remarks on the Philosophy of Psychology*, v. 2, G. von Wright and H. Nyman (eds), Oxford: Blackwell.

Wollheim, R. (1987) *Painting as an Art*, Princeton, NJ : Princeton University Press.

Wright, A. (1991) 'Dispositions, Anti-Realism and Empiricism', *Proceedings of the Aristotelian Society*, 91: 39–59.

Yanal, R. (1998) 'The Institutional Theory of Art', in M. Kelly (ed.) *The Encyclopedia of Aesthetics*, Oxford: Oxford University Press, pp. 508–12.

Young, J. (2001) *Art and Knowledge*, London: Routledge.

Zangwill, N. (1995) 'Groundrules in the Philosophy of Art', *Philosophy*, 70: 533–44.
Zemach, E. (1997) *Real Beauty*, University Park: Pennsylvania State University Press.
Ziff, P. (1974) 'A Fine Forehand', *Journal of the Philosophy of Sport*, 1: 92–109.

Index